DEEP DOWN IN THE JUNGLE . . .

DEEP DOWN IN THE JUNGLE . . .

Negro Narrative Folklore from the Streets of Philadelphia

ROGER D. ABRAHAMS

FOLKLORE ASSOCIATES
Hatboro, Pennsylvania
1964

Portions of this work have previously appeared in *The Golden Log* (Publication XXX of the Texas Folklore Society), *The Texas Studies in Literature and Language, Journal of American Folklore,* and *Folklore In Action: Essays for Discussion in Honor of MacEdward Leach.*

LIBRARY OF CONGRESS CATALOG CARD NUMBER: 64-14132

MANUFACTURED IN THE UNITED STATES OF AMERICA

To those women
who have most affected *my* life:
my wife, Mary
my sister, Marj
and my mother

CONTENTS

1 : ACKNOWLEDGMENTS

3 : INTRODUCTION : ON A METHOD OF FOLKLORE
ANALYSIS

SECTION ONE : THE TELLERS

19 : CHAPTER I | THE NEIGHBORHOOD

41 : CHAPTER II | THE ELEMENT OF VERBAL CONTEST

65 : CHAPTER III | THE HEROES

SECTION TWO : THE TEXTS

89 : INTRODUCTION | STYLE AND PERFORMANCE

99 : CHAPTER IV | THE TOAST

175 : CHAPTER V | THE JOKES

245 : APPENDIX I : TOWARD THE DISCERNMENT OF
OIKOTYPE

259 : APPENDIX II : ON CERTAIN OBSCENITIES

263 : A GLOSSARY OF UNUSUAL TERMS AND EXPRESSIONS

269 : BIBLIOGRAPHY

277 : INDEX OF TALE TYPES AND MOTIFS

281 : INDEX OF SUBJECTS, TITLES AND PERSONS

ACKNOWLEDGMENTS

There have been so many who have helped and given encouragement in this study, that it would not be fitting if I did not point them out at the very beginning. The one person, more than any other, who is responsible for the completion of this work is Gershon Legman. This study arose from some of the work in my dissertation. I sent him a copy of that collection and he answered voluminously and perceptively, and provided me with the kinds of questions and approaches which made me see at least a few of the trees in the forest, the ones I dissect here. Legman's immense contribution to this work will be further testified to in the copious quotations from his letters and works which I have included.

There have been many others who have offered assistance in regard to special sections. Peter Tamony, for instance, helped a great deal with the glossary. Page Stegner shared with me his knowledge of Stackolee, as did Richard Buehler. D. K. Wilgus kindly sent me some toast texts out of his Kentucky Archives. Richard M. Dorson sent me a number of kind letters on various subjects concerning Negro lore. Mack McCormick helped a great deal with discographical materials, and shared his immense experience with Negro musicians with me in a tremendously helpful way. Bruce Jackson sent tape recordings and comments from his collections in Indiana prisons, and also shared many of his more general and exciting ideas. Frank Hoffman, with his growing knowledge of bawdry, has helped on numerous matters.

In a more general way, Professors MacEdward Leach and Tristam Coffin, being responsible with the ease and dispatch with which my dissertation was effected, are in line for my special thanks. Claire Rosenfield and Mary Edrich both helped a great deal by their careful reading and editing of certain chapters. My sister, Marj Slavin, read a nearly complete manuscript and gave many helpful comments. Kenneth S. Goldstein has been of great assistance at every stage in this work, as a friend, commentator, folklorist, editor and publisher. To all of these I tender my thanks.

Most of all, and apart from the rest, my thanks to my good wife, Mary, who has borne the brunt of the whole thing, listened and commented carefully, helped with the annotation and bibliography, and best of all, got excited with me as pieces began to fit together.

Austin, Texas   ROGER D. ABRAHAMS

1

ON A METHOD OF FOLKLORE ANALYSIS

WITH THE GROWTH OF INTEREST IN FOLKLORE, IT BECOMES INCREAS-
ingly evident that the presentation of a collection needs some
rationale more than the fact that traditional materials have been
collected and properly annotated. Too much has been gathered and
become accessible through journals, archives, and finding-lists to
justify publication simply because of collection. If a corpus of lore is
not presented in some way which bears new light on the process of
word-of-mouth transmission, on traditional forms or expressions, or
on the group among whom the lore was encountered, there is little
reason to present it to the public.

This work represents an attempt to present a body of folklore
collected among one small group of Negroes in a neighborhood in
South Philadelphia. My approach toward collection and presentation has been intensive. I have tried to collect "in depth," and to
recreate in my presentation the social background in which the
lore was found, and to relate the lore with the life and the values
of the group.

I believe this work represents in some ways a departure from
past methods of analyzing folklore, and therefore a description of
my point of view and my method will be given first. I must own
that the majority of this work was written before my methodology
was actually formulated. However, I have — throughout the project
— known that my object was to illuminate as fully as possible the
lore of one small group of Negroes from urban Philadelphia. The

methodology which developed did so because of this objective more than anything else. Though the formulation of this theory may seem *ex post facto*, it is included because it clarified much during the rewritings of this book, and more importantly, because I believe it will clarify many matters for the reader. Though it will cover a lot of familiar ground for the professional folklorist, it will also turn over some new, I trust.

Folklore, like any other humanistic discipline, must utilize as many methods as possible to illuminate data under study. It is rightly called an eclectic discipline. Yet as any folklorist will admit, this area has been more prone to special pleading and less to a catholic approach than almost any other. Sociology, literature, psycology, anthropology, history, economics, all have recently used knowledge or method from the others in order to bring new light to their discipline. Folklore, on the other hand, has become the whipping boy for anthropologists and has provided data for a number of insular analytic systems, but little consistent effort has been made either to analyze folklore on its own terms or to develop a methodology which is coherent, comprehensive, empirical, catholic, and thoroughly analytic. Certain pleaders see traditional lore as quaint vestiges of the past (and this is long after the antiquarian movement has otherwise run its course). Others view it as data through which we can anatomize the oral process, but of little intrinsic worth beyond this. Still others see it as a bearer of enigmas, the solving of which will give us clues into the history of the race, or of the individual psyche. One further group regards it as a minor and mishandled aspect of culture.

A potential order exists in this chaos, and salvation lies in eclecticism — the use of as many points of view as possible in order to cast light on folklore and the society within which it exists. As they have been relied upon most heavily in the body of this book, I will discuss the anthropological and comparative approaches, how they have been used on folklore matters in the past and how their use can be expanded. I will then treat some other approaches which complement the traditional ones and which I have used in the course of my analysis of the Philadelphia material. Throughout I will be speaking in terms of analyzing folk narrative, since they make up the substance of this book, but I believe the method which I am attempting to develop in this introduction could be expanded to include any piece, or series of pieces, of folklore.

4

Folklore is, as the anthropologists would have us believe, but one facet of culture. It is material which obeys culture's general laws, those generated by the conflict of innovation and stability, and complicated by the interactions of different groups. The traditional process, oral transmission, which folklorists long have been claiming as their own, is but one argument of an evolutionary theory of history which sees all forms and ideas as mutable.

Too often, because the theoretical ideal of pure oral transmission loomed before his eyes, the folklorist has seen himself as dealing with sacrosanct matters, lore transmitted from the pure "golden age" of the primitive past by word-of-mouth, and thus divorced from contemporary discourse, except as survival. But recent scholarship has slowly erased the concept of a pure process of oral transmission; increasingly we are led to see the influence of the written and the printed, the recorded word, upon pieces of traditional literature. As these preconceptions are being modified, we must realize concurrently that folklore is not only not made up of sacrosanct antiquities, but is in fact a very live cultural phenomenon, subject to the same processes as other things cultural, and therefore available to the same type of analysis as other similar humanistic studies.

Every agency, artifact and entity within a culture is potentially capable of reflecting much of the constructs of that group. But in order to so reflect, it must be presented within the context of the culture from which it emerged, in as full a manner as possible.[1]

Folklore is an important aspect of any culture, and one which yields much illumination through its study. It is a prime example of the variety and incredible breadth to which man is capable of giving form. As with any object or concept, every work of folk creation or transmission is material potentially capable of providing great insight into the totality of its culture, because that work, both in its form and function, reflects the preoccupations and values of the ones who create and transmit it. Folklore represents or reflects the functional unity which man in groups can create for himself. This unity is not delusive, one which speaks for all time of permanence, but rather represents a constantly shifting, but nonetheless

1. "The full significance of any single element in a culture design will be seen only when the element is viewed in the total matrix of its relationship to other elements." Clyde Kluckholm, *Mirror for Man* (New York, 1956) Signet edition, p. 33.

5

effective, dialectic unity — one that relies for its existence on contrarieties, on balanced oppositions:

> The various forms of human culture are not held together by an identity in their nature but by a conformity in their fundamental task. If there is an equipoise in human culture it can only be described as a dynamic, not as a static equilibrium; it is the result of a struggle between opposing forces.[2]

Any study of folklore must be presented so that the "opposing forces" can be isolated and understood; otherwise the lore will not be comprehended except insofar as the dynamic unity it illustrates approximates that of the culture of the reader. This is simply extending the anthropological methodology of presenting material in as full a cultural context as possible, at the same time as insisting, with some anthropologists, that culture produces artifacts or mentifacts which are not only of passing interest as such, but of lasting value as evidences of process. It is those explorers of process to whom we must turn to develop our concepts and methodology. Although it is perhaps less important, it is hardly unnecessary to present a collection of folklore with a full description of its cultural context to the group from whom it was collected. Such data can serve as an index to the preoccupations and problems of that group, the things which provide the oppositions in this dynamic unity of dialectic. These are matters which should be explored in any group, especially one's own.

It is vitally important to present any corpus of lore with some analysis of the conflicts which exist within the culture that produces this dynamic unity, and to attempt to relate the lore, as strategies within this universe of conflict, to the conflict (or unity) itself. To do so is to recognize that dialectic produces not only conflict but synthesis also, and that exploration of such matters is going to explain not only much about the lore itself, but also much about the process of that group. Even if the analyst's presentation is not wholly correct, it can be corrected toward illumination; lack of any analysis precludes even this possibility. Though we recognize the fact that most of us collect because of our acquisitive compulsion, our burden must be greater than a simple presentation of our acquisition.

2. Ernst Cassirer, *Essay on Man* (New York, 1944), p. 279.

This procedure is not inherently difficult nor is it complex. The oppositions present in different cultures, the polarities that create the dynamic unity to be described, are usually ones that fit into general categories. And the enumeration and subsequent consideration of the common areas will at least guarantee a modicum of proper analytic approach.

The study of folklore itself inherently contains one pair of oppositions, the analysis of which can cast much light on the lore itself and its creation and transmission: the conflict between stability (tradition) and change. Any study of a body of collected lore should at least contain some discussion of the place of improvisation and the improvisor within the group from which the material has come. Improvisation can be a traditional mode itself. Because folklore is by its nature traditional, therefore conservative, that does not mean that the influence of conscious change, of innovation, is alien or inimical to any given group. The creative individual within the folk community has been pointed out too often to ignore him any longer.

The opposition of permanence and innovation is by no means the only dynamic polarity that exists universally. There are numerous other pairs which exist to varying degrees of importance in every group. Certainly the biological differences of male and female cause polarities in all groups, delineating the relative position of men and women. A similar opposition exists between generations, which, in one way or another, will affect the constructs of a group. Furthermore, a hierarchic set-up may exist other than those above, based on strength, verbal ability, inheritance, caste system, or any of a number of other "mysteries" which may cause other dialectical oppositions.

If these exist in all groups to some extent, then they must find expression; government, religion, economic system, marriage practice, family pattern will illustrate these forces it is true, but it is often only in the realm of folklore that these oppositions find their expression in words.

Of all forms of folk literature, the narrative is the most interesting from the point of view of such analysis. It is capable of embodying or reflecting more facets of the dialectics of a group than any other form, with the possible exception of the ritual, for the dialectic can be expressed in the dramatic structure of the story. The device of narrative permits free play of hostile actions on a fictitious level; it allows for the construction of a fictive playground in which these important conflicts, which both express and effect the dynamic unity of the group, can be fought. Because the playground is life-like and yet not really life, many otherwise dangerous arguments can be waged, courtships proposed, tests entered into, quests engaged upon, without involving the physical well-being of the principals. The narrative can be looked to for insights into the polarities of a group, and the ways in which some sort of working synthesis is established.

Viewing folklore in this way is to see not only that lore is an index into the dialectical unity of a group, but also that it functions within the dialectic. Though we may not agree with their individual applications, Freud and Marx and their followers have clearly shown that there is no such thing as nondirected actions within the context of culture. This is especially true of any formal grouping of words. Nothing exists because of form alone. If there are forms whose function is outmoded, they will cease to be transmitted if no subsequent function is assumed by them. And the function of words is more than to entertain or communicate. Words exist to persuade, court, control. Viewing society agonistically or dialectically, words in formal arrangement then exist primarily for rhetorical purpose.[3]

Thus narrative is a rhetorical expression of the dialectical unity of the culture, and the oppositions that exist in the group as a group or as individuals are mirrored in the dramatic antagonism of the story. But just as there is a dialectic structure of the narrative, so we must look for its synthesis, or in proper dramatic terms, transformation or regenesis. This transformation, as an approved resolution of the struggle, will be value laden, and therefore something to which we can look for significance. In this immediate way dialectic reflects dramatic and an analysis of one in terms of the other, if only analogically, will be valid. But basically these matters are more literary than anthropological and will be returned to later.

To analyze the strategic effect of any piece of folk-literature is to consider its function. However, by insisting on such considerations I am not espousing any strict functionalist approach. Rather I am concerned with viewing folklore organically, as a living process.

---

3. Kluckhohn, *Mirror*, p. 115: "Mainly language is an instrument of action. The meaning of a word or phase is not its dictionary equivalent but the difference its utterance brings about in a situation." See also Kenneth Burke's *Rhetoric of Motives* (New York, 1953), to which I am indebted throughout this rhetorical discussion, both for terms and concepts.

In fact we can profitably look at each piece of folklore as an organism. It lives and dies or mutates. It has the primary attributes of an organism: it acts both as a receptor and an effector, and the two functions act, not separately, but in equilibrium. It is a receptor because it is sensitive to outside stimulus, both in inherited forms and the dialectics of the group. It is an effector because it reacts to these stimuli so that change occurs affecting the chain of causation.

The mutating "organism" or piece of lore reflects its history in its very constitution. And it also echoes the special preoccupations of the group in which it is found. But the "organism" also acts as a generator, not only embodying but also furthering, through the strength of its culturally accepted position, the values implicit in its construction. Thus lore does not just result from past and present forces upon it, but is also able to affect its own future. This accounts to some extent for the conservatism of folklore phenomena.

As form and function do act jointly, it is often hard to separate them. Certainly when viewing oral literature from its rhetorical base it is not difficult to see how persuasive purpose is going to influence ultimate form. But, as mentioned, cultural necessities are mutable, can and do change. With their function gone, pieces of folklore will naturally fade and disappear. But any piece of lore has both form and function and the form may be able to achieve other cultural function and therefore continue to exist, though in a different place in the life of that group.

> Any given culture trait can be fully understood only if seen as the end point of specific sequences of events reaching back into the remote past. Forms persist; functions change.[4]

It is important to investigate such forms historically in any collection of texts, but in a way that present rather than past function is stressed; for one can ascertain function now, but can only hypothesize what uses might have been in the past. On the surface, this would seem to gainsay the method of the comparative folklorists, but it is not intended as such. The analytic direction of the comparative approach is wholly laudable and quite serviceable. It is the sort of conclusion toward which the comparativist is driving that seems to me to be questionable, not the way in which he arrives there.

4. Kluckhohn, *Mirror*, p. 56.

It is not within the scope of this introduction to point out at any length the ultimate distracting fact of the law of diminishing returns in relation to this method. Much more work goes into amassing the incredible number of versions and variants of a tale than is warranted by the limited conclusions with which the comparativists have emerged. Nor shall we pursue the argument that any collected text is a mistake of history and not therefore necessarily as representative as the comparativists would have us believe. More apposite for our discussion are the misconceptions which such method fosters, and the way in which we can, by pointing them out, further develop our analytic method.

The major misconception that concerns us is, of course, the idea which emerges that tales are reduceable to motif formulae, eliminating the meat and keeping the bones. (The bones won't decay, but the meat may!) Further, the comparative approach fosters the idea that tales by their very nature are international and are able to cross cultural and linguistic frontiers with ease.

But as C. W. Von Sydow and other theoretical comparativists since have pointed out, we should not delude ourselves into thinking that tradition is an easy process. Because we have a large corpus of tales of international currency from numerous regions and in various languages, we should not assume that this dissemination was achieved at any small cost. For a piece of oral literature to transcend the bounds of language and culture, a strong impulse must exist (usually in the form of an emigrating traditional storyteller) and an ability for that bit of lore to adapt itself (or more properly, to be adapted) to the values of the new group. Often enough, this transition has been affected with a modicum of cultural changes. Any study of an international tale-type will indicate this.

On the other hand, for every story that has made this transition, there are certainly many that have not. The problem of culture is one that is far more complicated than simply one of language. In order for a story to make a transition between two cultural groups there must be some element in it that will appeal to the specific sensibility and value-complex of the culture into which it is entering. This element (or elements) may or may not correspond to the "emotional core" of the story as it was told in the area from which it is coming. If it does correspond, the story may enter oral currency in the new area in much the same form in which it was told in the old. If, however, it is different, there is a good chance that the story will mutate because of the inevitable change of emphasis that will occur in the new situation, creating a new and local form of the story. One cannot help but realize that changes which occur in the migration of a story happen as much because of a disparity of cultures as of language.

Though the comparativist has realized the existence of the local variant he has chosen to ignore for the most part its implications in favor of the broader historical-geographical study. However, a full appreciation of these local changes that may occur as a tale crosses a linguistic and/or cultural frontier is perhaps the greatest asset of the comparative approach for the student of the folklore of a specific group. For it is by comparing the forms and style of a story among other groups that we are best able to arrive at a knowledge of the biases, the "cultural imperitives," that operate upon stories in the group from whom the collection was made.

Von Sydow, in his considerations of the problems of transmission within the method of the comparativists, saw this potential weakness and attempted to compensate by a formulation of a theory of "oikotype." He said that, as important as the study of the forms of a story are, in search of its archetype, just as important is the form which this story attains when it reaches a specific area and achieves a distinct manner. This local variation he called the "oikotype." Von Sydow was concerned with the organic nature of the folktale, as most comparativists have not been.

> One of the most serious deficiencies in the study of folk tradition has been that investigators have, to a far too great extent, been content with extracts, instead of seeing their information as part of a natural, living whole. In questions of belief and custom this had led to their concentration over-much on chance similitude, and neglecting to find out if there was any deeper connection.
>
> The same fault has been committed in folk-tale research. To be able to survey your material you have, of course, to use extracts; but if you are content with them without bothering about the original, you will not be able to treat your material critically but will get involved in purely schematic methods which will almost certainly lead you astray. But it is not enough to study folk-tales as tales only. It is also necessary to make oneself familiar with the use of folk-tales, their life in tradition, their transmission and spread.[5]

5. C. W. Von Sydow, *Selected Papers on Folklore* (Copenhagen, 1948), p 44.

Von Sydow here has hit upon a very important principle, and one that the anthropologists have spent much time developing (probably independent of his remarks). He has explicitly recognized the organic quality of folklore, the fact that lore does not live in schemae but in the mouths of individuals existing within groups. But he has been schooled in the comparative method and his schism is only minor (especially in view of the fact that he doesn't seem to have carried his preaching into practice). He sees the local variant, the oikotype, as important, not because it gives us insight into the dynamic unity of the group, but because it allows us to more fully understand patterns of dissemination. His object is not to show the interrelationship of forms of various tales within a specific locale, but rather to show that tales, in their complex travels, tend to assume local forms.

But the oikotype is a notion that has value beyond pointing out the way in which tales change as they travel. If one can isolate an oikotypical form of one tale in one region or among one group, why not similarly note oikotypes of other tales in the same group and then analyze what makes them oikotypical? This should cast light on that group and on their attitude and approach toward life, language and expression.[6] Thus the methods of the anthropologist and comparativist could be made complementary.

Similarly, a literary approach can be made useful too for folkloric analysis, adding distinctions where the comparative and anthropological methods stop. Folk-literature, if properly distinguished from written works, can be illuminated by internal analysis. There are important considerations of genre, style, structure and content, form and feeling, and objective intent and subjective reaction to be utilized in discussing the traditional narrative in its relation to the culture in which it is encountered. It is important to point out the prevalence of specific genres, for instance, and to attempt to investigate what it is about this form that appeals to the audience or so aptly encompasses the thought and style of the teller.

Most of these structural matters can be discussed in regard to individual stories, or stories as told by one informant or those which conform to one type or genre within a group. But just calling

6. Theoretically it would be possible, if enough oikotype studies were made, to look at an individual traditional narrative or other piece of folklore and to tell approximately where it came from just from internal evidence. Thus this procedure could become predictive as well as descriptive.

a folktale a "traditional narrative" is qualifying it in a literary manner. "Traditional" indicates that because of oral change, it has no recognizable author. And "narrative" indicates that the strategies it utilizes will be from the point of view of the embodied story. It is just this consideration of rhetoric which provides us with the greatest benefit from the literary approach.

As Kenneth Burke has so forcefully shown, on the hint from Freud (and many others before him), there are few literary motives which cannot be shown to be strategic in conception and nature. Most consciously conceived sets of words exist for a purpose, and the essence of this purpose is to convince. As outlined in our discussion of cultural dialectic, words exist to produce action. Any convincing is in the interest of future action. It is true that the more reflective and complex the words and word-relationships become, the greater distance is created between the words and the potential actions.

The strategy involved in the traditional story is not so complex, however; it is usually one of attempting to induce action through a portrayal of action. Which is not to say that the story induces immediate performance. Rather, the tale will in most cases direct our emotions toward values of which it approves or disapproves, and thus guide future action. It is not my purpose, however, to outline all of the strategies inherent in the telling of a folktale; I am merely pointing out how a literary approach to narrative lore can yield some results otherwise unattainable.

There are further literary or linguistic considerations that would contribute to the development of this analytic method. Style and content analysis exist somewhere between standard literary and linguistic approaches, for literature looks to the larger elements of word progressions, and linguistics to the smallest. It is as necessary to point out certain words (important to the individual or the group) which are given more persuasive weight in traditional narratives and to point out why and how they achieve this, as it is to analyze key words and concepts in works of *belles lettres*. It is also important to attempt to discover syntactical patterns of individual informants and of groups and to attempt to relate these patterns to technical and aesthetic values. It is obligatory to consider the aesthetics of the group and the individual performers within it.

Perhaps even more important is the consideration of these narratives as contrastive phenomena, a wholly linguistic matter. If it is agreed that construction of the narrative involves a playground much like life but not exactly life-like, then it is necessary to establish how the contrast between the playground and life is conveyed. This should be provided by an analysis of contrastive devices of language: that is, how the method of constructing word groups in narrating differs from conversational speech patterns.

The literary aspect of the method under development is capable of pointing out the materials and coherence of structure. But there still remains the problem of establishing the relationship between the fictive playground and the agonisms of the culture and this is where the methods of the psychologist and the sociologist help us most greatly. Psychology tells us the importance of the fictive experience as a release mechanism in expression of matters otherwise repressed and sociology shows how much an experience can represent not only the individual but also the group. To discuss a story in psychological terms is to recognize that the tale is a physical embodiment of an internal experience of the individual, and through psychological considerations we can firmly establish the relationship of the story and its inherent values to the lives of those telling or listening to it. Further, psychological studies have shown us the importance of two major folkloristic matters, form and repetition, in the creation of pleasure, one of the cornerstones of any value system, especially aesthetic values.

However, psychology, perhaps more than any other discipline, has produced insular theories. Freud, Jung and Adler, among others, all developed systems of thought which cast much light on folkloristic matters, but because of their preoccupations, more than because of their actual formulations. We are indebted to Freud because his theories insist on the facts of rivalry among family members, especially father and son. Similarly Jung has shown the universal nature and pattern involved in the individual's struggle for a unified conception of himself (he calls it the process of individuation). Adler's preoccupation with the individual's search for control or power has been equally illuminating. But as many have pointed out, alliance with any of these theories asks us to accept much more of the system of the individual teacher than we otherwise might want.

Both Freud and Jung asks us to recognize forms as explanations, when we see clearly that forms are mutable and the examination of process is more apposite. To recognize that a story fits into the Oedipal pattern, the Electra pattern, or any of the number of Jungian archetypal patterns does not necessarily explain how that story achieved its form. It simply gives us some notion as to what its psychological function may be, and even then, as Herskovits has pointed out, "It is . . . only one of the causal factors, and not *the* causal factor."[7] This does not destroy the usefulness of even the most insular psychological approach. Recognizing that the method being developed looks for answers in terms of process rather than through categorization by simple recognition of form, it is possible to accept the theories for what they can tell us about the process which the texts illustrate. If a story fits into the "quest archetype" or the "Oedipal pattern" this may point out important relationships between life within the group and that specific fictive experience.

Perhaps a greater indictment of the Freudian and post-Freudian approaches in regard to their use in matters of ethnography and culture has been their primary concern with investigating the abnormal personality. Recently, however, there has emerged a whole school of analysis called "ego psychology" which has used as its point of departure the normal personality. These studies are important because they emphasize the importance not only of the individual psyche but also somatic growth, group experience and the mechanisms which groups have invented, utilized, transmitted, which help in the creation of an integrated personality.[8] They have shown how the use of psychological techniques can help us relate the individual with his group and group-approved mechanisms. It is through such psychological investigation that we have one of our clearest insights into values and biases and their operations in an age group and culture. We are also deeply indebted to the psychological approach for the articulation of the proposition of purposive tendency of all expression. If the idea can be accepted, and indeed it must, that all methods and modes of expression exist for some purpose, conscious or unconscious, perceptive psychological analysis will be able to lay bare the force behind the expression, and more fully expose both the form and the function in which the expression has been embodied. And because everything is viewed as having intention, one can gain some insight into the problem of where value resides within a group by noting at which places the group reacts to the fictive experience, for through

7. Melville and Frances Herskovits, *Dahomean Narrative* (Evanston, 1958), p. 95. They go on to note that both are notoriously unscientific in their inability to refer their theorums to empirical cultural proof, but rather must rely on them as articles of faith.

8. See especially Erik Erickson, *Childhood and Society* (New York, 1953); *Identity and the Life Cycle* (New York, 1960); John H. Rohrer and Munroe Edmondson (eds.), *The Eighth Generation* (New York, 1960).

reaction we can see tendency. And the effectiveness of strategy, of course, relies on the effective manipulation of just such reactions. Where people laugh, cry, howl, or make any other physical manifestation is the place in which some soft spot in their psychic lives has been hit. From such moments we can begin to judge why certain values have been developed, and how these values (and these soft spots) have ultimately affected the form of the piece.

What is being espoused then is an eclectic manner of analyzing folklore. In the corpus of this work I have attempted to put some of these ideas into practice. Primarily, I have attempted to place the lore in its cultural context. I have done this not only by inclusion of relevant ethnological data, but also by expanding the idea of the oikotype to include analysis of lore from both a comparative and an intracultural point of view. Further, formal, psychological, and sociological considerations have been utilized wherever I felt they could illuminate. Internal examination of the pieces of folklore have been engaged upon as a full partner to the historical and cultural approaches. The formal matters considered by the comparativists have been extended so that they include not only motifs but also genre, style, structure in general. The matters of process of the anthropologist have been expanded so that they embrace the same formal preoccupations, but in such a way that structure is understood on its interrelation with function. (Theoretically at least we should be able to compare both form and function in the ideal oikotypical approach.) And finally I have tried to utilize any approach which might cast light on the corpus of folklore being studied, even at the risk of becoming diffuse or weighted down with jargon.

This study then is not for the sole purpose of presenting a group of stories. It is rather an attempt to show how much insight can be attained into the life of a group through the analysis of its folklore. It is also an exercise in the utilization of a number of different ideas and approaches that I would hope would help to develop some consistent method of folkloristic analysis. Though undoubtedly I have not been able to use all of the approaches outlined here as fully as possible, I have tried to do so to the best of my understanding of them, and to suggest further possible uses of them by those more skilled or initiated than I.

THE TELLERS

CHAPTER I

THE NEIGHBORHOOD

THE AREA IN WHICH THE FOLKLORE PRESENTED HERE WAS COLLECTED IS one small four-block marginal neighborhood just south of central Philadelphia, bounded by Pine Street on the north, Juniper on the west, South Street on the south, and Twelfth Street on the east. The headquarter of this neighborhood in respect to the collecting was my home at 421 South Iseminger Street. The neighborhood was christened "Camingerly" by one of its residents — a combination of three of the names of the small streets, Camac, Iseminger, and Waverly — and for reasons of its brevity this name will be used in the study.[1]

The neighborhood, as many others in this section of Philadelphia, is made up of two types of dwellings: four and five-story tenements and small, three-story houses, the latter built between 1790 and 1830 and known affectionately by those who have lived around them as "Father, Son, and Holy Ghost" houses, because their three rooms are one on top of the other. They have a winding stairwell in the corner and a small shed kitchen on the back of the first-floor room.

1. The neighborhood is called Twelfth Street by other neighborhoods because of the gang which used to represent it and which was called "The Twelfth Street Gang." As this was a much wider area than the one in which I was able to collect, I have not used it for the purposes of this study.

These houses were built on the small back-streets for which Philadelphia is so well known, and served as servants' quarters for the large town-houses which were found on the wider streets, Pine, Locust, Spruce, and Broad. Thus many of these houses have always (until recent rehabilitation) served as residences for Negroes. When I moved onto this street in September of 1958, it was still inhabited primarily by Negroes, and it was from my neighbors that I was able to collect the folklore on the following pages.

I began making this collection more by following my nose than through any plan. Early in this period I found that as soon as I went more than two blocks away from the area in which I was known, I ran into a stone wall. To many Negroes in this section of Philadelphia a white man is either a policeman or a bill collector. All of the material here then was collected within Camingerly, and most of it in the living room of my house. Frequently I was able to collect from some who lived outside the boundaries of the neighborhood, but only when they were with people I already knew and had collected from. Because of these others, I am fairly certain that this collection is representative of the lore of all lower-class Negro culture in Philadelphia.

In my original formulation[2] of these cultural matters I had deluded myself into thinking that I had been able to see a complete picture of life in this neighborhood. It will be obvious to the reader, as it is to me in retrospect, that what I *have* been able to do is to explain the life and values of the group from the viewpoint of the men. Looking back, this is all I could have done, as most of my informants were men. I did have many acquaintances among the females of the group, but I learned very little about them except as mothers. The reason for this will probably become self-evident as my description proceeds — basically the problem was that I, a male, was collecting in a group which insists on such social and sexual distinctions more than we do in middleclass white American society. Consequently, in my re-formulation I have restricted myself to a discussion of the lore of the men, calling other pieces into play only to show development or to present a contrast.

2. My dissertation, *Negro Folklore from South Philadelphia, A Collection and Analysis,* Department of English, University of Pennsylvania, 1962. For a fuller, more discursive discussion of my collecting technique, see that work, especially pp. 1-14.

I : *THE WOMEN*

The greatest single distinguishing feature of Negro life in South Philadelphia is the importance of the mother in the family. A majority of the women in the neighborhood are either not married or not living with a man on a regular basis. The women not only assume all of the usual motherly roles of cooking, keeping house, providing the warmth of the family, but also those usually associated with father, i.e., discipline and providing income. Even in homes where a man lives with a woman, the mother seems to assume most of these roles.[3]

This system has existed since early slavery, and because of modern hiring practices, social attitudes, and methods of obtaining relief from the state, will remain. The Negro woman is capable of earning a more regular income than is the man. They can get domestic work any time they wish. If they take commercial training in high school there is no difficulty in getting a secretarial job upon graduation. Even with only a partial high school education, some companies will take Negro girls as clerks. If a girl has a child, custom provides that she can always find someone to care for it, her mother or some other older woman, if she cares to continue to work. If she doesn't the state will pay her a subsistence allowance for herself and each child; that is, if she has no one "living" with her, or providing visible, adequate support for the children. Thus,

3. This is not an unusual situation among Negroes in this country. Similar family units have been noted by every sociological study made of lower-class Negro groups:

> The . . . major differences between Negro family organization and that of the white majority touches on the position of woman when compared to that of the man, in terms of common American convention, that the adjective "matriarchal" has come to be employed in recent years when describing this family type. (Melville J. Herskovits, *The Myth of the Negro Past* [Boston, 1958 (reprint)], p. 173.)

> In the lower socio-economic groups the family is more often dominated by the woman than man. (Charles S. Johnson, *Growing Up in the Black Belt* [Washington, D. C., 1941], p. 58.)

the women of the community can regard themselves as financially independent in one way or another.

It is not surprising then that under such a system a woman hesitates to marry, except where she can be sure, in some way, that the man she marries will be able to provide for her (and himself) better than she herself can. Furthermore, because of a natural bias (perhaps inherited from farm life) that having children is beneficial (to provide in old age is the rationale often given) plus the incentive provided by state relief laws, most of the children in the neighborhood are born out of wedlock.[4]

4. A variety of explanations has been devised for this family system as it exists throughout the United States. Herskovits, in commenting on Africanisms in New World Negro life, makes some interesting observations on the unusual function of the mother in West African societies. In summation he says:

> It cannot be regarded as only coincidence that such specialized features of Negro family life in the United States as the role of women in focusing the sentiment that gives the family unit its psychological coherence, or their place in maintaining the economic stability essential to survival, correspond closely to similar facets of West African social structure. And this becomes more apparent when we investigate the inner aspects of the family structure of Negroes in the New World outside the United States. Though everywhere the father has his place, the tradition of the father as sole or principal provider essential to the European pattern is deviated from.

He qualifies his statements on these matters, however:

> As in the case of most other aspects of Negro life, the problem becomes one of evaluating multiple forces rather than placing reliance on simpler explanations. From the point of view of the search for Africanisms, the status of the Negro family at present is thus to be regarded as the result of the play of various forces in the New World experience of the Negro, projected against a background of aboriginal tradition. Slavery did not cause the "maternal" family; but it tended to continue certain elements in the cultural endowment brought to the New World by the Negroes. The feeling between mother and children was re-inforced when the father was sold away from the rest of the family. . . . (Herskovits, Myth, pp. 180-81.)

Further recent studies of West Indian family life bear this out in great detail. See M. G. Smith, *West Indian Family Structure* (Seattle, 1962).

Many other commentators relate the problem to the social situation under slavery:

> Under the slave system, the Negro woman frequently enjoyed a status superior to that of the man. . . . In the lower class family today a pattern similar to that of the slavery period persists. (Johnson, *Growing Up*, pp. 58-59.)

The standard study of the subject is E. Franklin Frazier's *The Negro Family in the United States* (Chicago, 1939). He, too, speaks of the effects of the

This is not unusual among lower-class Negroes living in urban areas. It is but one facet of the seething drama of the Negro under slavery and since, a depiction of an uprooted dependent people exposed to new social situations without understanding them, a story of their transportation to the United States as slaves, of their subjugation, their freedom and of the subsequent migrations around the country looking for a way to earn a living.

The older members of the Camingerly neighborhood were actors in this great social drama; the younger members were born of it. Many of the younger members, as well as the older, were born on farms in the South. Some, such as Sam Stogie, had seen all of the varieties of experience that were available to him during his long life. He had been born on a farm and worked there on and off for many years. He had worked in lumber camps, turpentine camps, as a stevedore, a railroad line worker, etc. Others tell the same story.

slave system upon the Negro family. Women were more highly valued on a plantation, he tells us, because of their breeding capacities, and their ability to perform most of the same jobs as the men (especially during harvest). The Negro, further, could not marry legally because to do so would have been to give him legal rights. As the production of more slaves was desirable, the slave owners encouraged free sexual habits among their chattels, while denying them the benefit of marriage vows. They were even known to increase the Negro population by the addition of their own seed (though this practice is perhaps overstressed by critics of the "Old Order").

As Frazier brings out, nothing since the liberation of the slaves has militated to change the social system which was formulated under it. As a matter of fact, much of the father-dominated family life that was fostered then was eliminated by social forces after the Civil War. Suddenly at the end of that period, the Negroes found themselves freed, but without any means of livelihood. Many were able to either sharecrop or to buy or rent land. This group, though to some extent mother-oriented, has more of the basic pattern of European family life.

On the other hand, for a large group

> . . . as the old order crumbled, thousands of Negro men and women began to wander aimlessly about the country or in search of adventure and work in army camps and cities. (Frazier, *Family*, p. 209.)

This group grew each time there was any reason, such as drought or depression, that drove the agricultural Negro from his land, especially during the periods after the depressions of 1879 and 1929. With the opening of new factories during the industrial expansion, many Negroes came north in search of employment. This northward movement was intensified during the period of manpower shortage of World War II, when jobs and opportunities opened up for them that had never existed before. During less crucial periods, this migratory group usually went from farm to lumber to turpentine camps or railroad gangs to the towns or cities. There was a large dispossessed class of people who wandered about the country looking for whatever work they could find. As in any similar class, idleness, poverty, and the tensions that surrounded these problems, prevailed. The dispossessed, developing upon the mother-

The women came when the men sent for them; they and their families. Eula came that way from North Carolina, with her first child. Eugenia came with her husband Charlie, a blind street singer, playing the streets from Georgia to Chicago and finally settling in Philadelphia. Gladys came with her father when she was ten. He had been a farmer in Virginia and had come north to find work when he lost the farm. With them came their attitude toward the family, unhappily heightened, decayed by life in the city.

Because the woman has the greatest financial independence among the group, she tends to develop a personality that is positive, forthright, aware of her superior position. She knows that she is, in many ways, in command of the male, and she often expresses it by alternating attitudes of enticement and disdain. As a woman gets older, much of this dominating attitude is transferred to the raising of her children. Before she is ready, however, to resign sexual byplay, she may have many children. As children tend to restrict her activities to some degree, she often will give them to some older person to raise. This person is often her own mother or some other older relative experienced in the job of rearing.[5]

oriented family life (functional in the earlier slave society) formed new attitudes in relations with each other, especially in regard to sex and crime and violence. The anonymity afforded by the migrant nature of their lives gave them an almost complete freedom from social controls within their own ranks.

As Sterling Brown has pointed out in *Folksay* [(Norman, Oklahoma, 1930), ed. Benj. A. Botkin, pp. 324-29], the blues was a natural expression of the values and emotions of these people. Paul Oliver, *The Blues Fell This Morning* (London, 1960), has recently taken blues texts and shown how they documented the life and struggle of this class. Frazier attempts to explain this sudden emotional eruption as

> . . . an awakening of the (romantic) imagination which contrasts sharply with the unromantic attitudes of the peasant Negro toward sex and mating in the isolated rural communities of the South. (Frazier, *Family*, p. 212.)

5. This grandmother figure is in effect the center of the Negro concept of the family.

> The Negro grandmother's importance is due to the fact not only that she has been the "oldest head in a maternal family organization but also her position as 'granny' or midwife among a simple peasant folk." As the repository of folk-wisdom concerning the inscrutable ways of nature, the grandmother has been depended upon by mothers to ease the pains of childbirth and ward off the dangers of ill luck. (Frazier, *Family*, p. 153.)

This is especially true in rural society. It is a situation that once again probably comes from the slavery system, for it was the "granny" who raised not only her own children, but often many of the young of the others. Negroes who were needed in the fields or in the house, and the children of her owners.

Eula had thirteen children of her own, and many of these, after moving to a place of their own, have sent some of their children to be raised by her. She had living with her at the time of this study, not only three of her own children (now grown), but two children of another daughter, plus numerous others who would come for a short stay. Her household was in constant flux. The boys she had raised often came to see her, to bring her presents and to help her keep her house in good repair (something in which she took great pride).[6] Even with those of her children not living with her, she regarded it within her province to teach them manners, good habits, and generally to "keep them in line." She was looked to by many of her female neighbors as a great help in controlling their children and as the person to go to to find out what to do in case of sickness or emergency. In any questionable decision, however, she tried not to "meddle in other people's business."[7]

She is an extremely forthright, positive woman, having channeled her impulses into her dominant relationship with her family and neighbors. Naturally any woman who is in an equally dominant role will react to her negatively, and this was true of many of the women in the neighborhood. Foremost of these was Eugenia, a "granny" herself in many respects.

Eugenia had lived two doors from Eula but had moved further down the street before the time that I moved into the area. She is the mother of a number of children and grandmother of many. She was obviously an extremely strong family woman from the stories she tells and from the letters and support she receives from her children. They are living in different parts of the world (one son in the Army, another in the Navy). She finds full expression of her expansive feelings through her activities in the church, at which she serves sometimes as preacher, sometimes as song leader, and always as spiritual healer. People from all over the East come to consult her on the problems of illness, physical and spiritual. Both were regarded by her as curable by the same method — prayer. Her "family" then was a large one and constantly fluctuating, people coming to her for the wisdom of the ages (or the aged, as it were). Eula seems to have resented her power (and perhaps her income) and called her a "witch woman." Eugenia in turn envied Eula in

6. Once she publicly "broomed" one of her daughters that lived close by for not keeping a clean house.

7. This value, because of crowded housing, etc., is much wished for but seldom obtained. It is only the older women who don't seem to care for gossip so much as maintaining their own privacy.

having her own family around her. She indicated this when she tried to adopt foster children, but she couldn't at that time because she was not married, her husband having died some years earlier. I have seen such rivalries result in violence (though not as often of course as among younger women), but in this case the only expression was slur and disdain.

Eugenia got married to a man who had been boarding with her and who took to sleeping overnight. She said that she would not allow any man to stay with her without getting married. In this she does not echo the attitudes of most of the women in the neighborhood. There are, to be sure, many marriages among its members, but for different reasons. There does not seem to be much relationship between sex or even having a family and the legal sanction. Marriage is generally regarded as an act of love, in which one vows to live with another for life (even though in practice this does not always work out).

Margaret (age eighteen) and Petey (age sixteen) were married after Margaret had already borne him one child and conceived another. At their wedding, Margaret's mother marched down the aisle holding their baby girl and they stood at the altar proudly (if distractingly) watching the ceremony. It seemed to be regarded as an announcement to their friends that they were solemnizing their union, and that they were doing it properly (especially from the "white" point of view). Thus, they had all of the trappings of a traditional wedding, the flowing white dress, the veil, the descent down the church steps, the throwing of the rice, the horn-tooting ride to the reception, the actual reception with the cutting of the wedding cake. The wedding was held in the same building as the reception, so after the ceremony the happy couple exited to the front steps, had rice thrown at them, came down, got into cars, drove around the neighborhood in a wide circle with appropriate sound effects and returned to continue the festivities.

Some of the other young people, as much through envy as conviction, followed suit. Yet in no way can it be considered a movement away from the basically mother-oriented family organization, or the very free attitude toward sexual relations and the conception of children. I don't believe that this will change until the male can become financially dominant. In those families where the man has been able to provide a steady income, such as Woody and Joanna's, their family life more nearly conforms to the European middle-class pattern. Yet even in cases such as this, they don't seem to attach any stigma to others having sexual relations apart from marriage.

Having children, whether in or out of wedlock, is considered the highest good. The more fertile one is, the more pride one has in her capacities. This may represent a further residuum of slavery days when the Negro woman was encouraged to breed as often as possible. Much more plausible is the relation of this to any agricultural society.

> In a system which requires the labor of the entire family to earn a living, children of a certain age are regarded as an economic asset. They come fast, and there is little conscious birth control. The coming of children is the "Lord's will." . . . There is pride in large families. Good breeders are regarded with admiration.[8]

On the other hand, the problem of birth control may exist because of the unwillingness of the performers in the sexual act to use contraceptives. As in the rural society, children in the city are looked upon as possible economic assets to help the mother in old age, if not before. However, this seldom works out as it is difficult enough for each to provide for himself. The state must consequently assume the burden of providing for the aged.

The functional reason for the large family has passed, yet all of its trappings remain. There is still a great stigma attached to birth control (furthered perhaps by the fact that the Catholic Church is strong in the neighborhood), even though various methods seem to be known by the men and women. A woman such as Constance, one of Eula's daughters, who only has one child, is very defensive about it; those with no children at all are almost pariahs. Sissy, Constance's sister, for instance, though she was only eighteen, was quite conscious of not having a child (most of her contemporaries have at least one by this time). For a long period she went about saying that she had been sick and in the hospital and had one breast amputated and that was why she hadn't yet had a baby. She later told everyone that she was pregnant. All of these stories were denied by Eula. My wife and Sissy had many conversations on the subject of children and Sissy could never understand why my wife did not want one yet.

8. Charles S. Johnson, *Shadows of the Plantation* (Chicago, 1934), p. 57.

The dominant position of the women in this group has, of course, a great effect upon the rearing of the children. And consequently the rearing pattern has the effect of furthering the relationship of the sexes in later life. Though outwardly treated the same, the boys seem more emotionally attached to their mothers than the girls. Further, the girls seem considerably easier to train. Just like girls in many other groups, they are more conscious of their grooming, appearance, habits than are the boys. This is undoubtedly caused by the fact that they are both able to act in imitation of their mothers and they sense a greater feeling of security in regard to the permanence of their mother's affections.

The women see men as inconstant and weak, "no good." This naturally has an effect upon rearing attitudes. Up to a point all children are the same, but boys will grow up to be men and must consequently be rejected for that reason alone. Girls, on the other hand, have to be taught about the treacherousness of men. They are the ones who gain the greater part of mother's attention and affection. The boys will have to leave the home eventually, or submit to the emasculating influence of their mothers; girls are potentially permanent and loyal members of the household.[9]

This situation can result in extremes of imitation on the part of the girls. Woodretta, Joanna and Woody's oldest daughter, comes from a close-knit family, perhaps not as strongly matrifocal as some of the others in the neighborhood. She is capable of cooking, ironing and helping with the housework, and has been since she was eight. On the other hand, under a stronger matrifocal influence, Eula's granddaughter Josie emulates older women in attitudes rather than actions; at five she bossed people around, used her

9. See in this regard the excellent recent study of New Orleans Negro individuals, *The Eighth Generation*, referred to in the last chapter, especially pp. 158 ff. They say:

> It does not appear that they [the boys] get markedly different maternal treatment from that accorded to little girls, but it seems clear that vesting all parental authority in a woman would have rather different consequences for boys and girls, and the spirit of rebellion against authority so prominent in the gang is mainly derived from this source. The matriarchs make no bones about their preference for little girls, and while they manifest real affection for their boy children, they are clearly convinced that all little boys must inexorably and deplorably become men, with all the pathologies of that sex.

It is interesting that women in Camingerly, before they achieved full matrifocal status, were not in absolute agreement on this last point.

feminine wiles, learned to smile at the right time, and in general was very conscious of her superior role as a "little mama."[10]

The picture that is presented of the women in the neighborhood is one of close cohesion, except when a clash between matriarchs occurs. The women visit back and forth and there seems to be a depth of affection in their relations with each other that I never perceived in the men. This is perhaps due to the presence of a latent lesbianism found in many similar matrifocal societies.[11] The command of the older women upon the younger ones begins at childhood, remains throughout the life of the mother in many cases, and can be fanatically observed by both mothers and daughters. This close relationship does not include in its ken the world of men. They are the outsiders except as they conform to the demands of subservience by the matriarch, thus producing the passive, masochistic type of subservient Negro so common during slavery days but becoming less predominant now.

Men are regarded by the women as untrustworthy, for the most part. An active division of sexes is thus created that is only brooked by temporary alliances. Even then, the women sense their superior position and seem to enter the situation for the sensual pleasure involved more than to build any sort of relationship. The paradoxical situation arises where the state, guided by its laudably humanitarian aims, has provided laws which encourage the continuation of these sensually oriented, temporary relationships. It has

10. The names "Mama" and "Little Mama" are bestowed on many little girls seemingly almost in order to encourage the proper descent of dynasty. Whenever a girl shows any propensity to act like a woman, she is encouraged, and such nicknames serve firmly as just such impetus.

11. Legman has been of great help in clarifying these matters. As he has reduced his theories to schemae in private correspondence, let me quote directly from him:

> When, as in the Negro family situation here under discussion, the matriarchic structure involves the domination of the family by the mother, the effect on the children is precisely reversed as to the sexes [than in a patrifocal set-up]. The sons become masochistic. . . . The daughters are the ones who are overpowered by the mother's sexual strength (the mother having no male consort is also easily able to take the daughter's boy friends away), and who give up the struggle and become lesbians.

For a fuller discussion of Legman's views, see his *Love and Death* (New York, 1949), especially the chapter "Avatars of the Bitch Heroine." Legman is quick to note that lesbianism has been little investigated among Negroes and that his remarks are based as much on covert as overt manifestations of homosexual impulses.

not only made the women with children financially independent, but it has insisted that in order to get money, a man should not be living with the woman. The law then seems to foster the male-female dichotomy.

II : *THE MEN*

This family structure continues, partially because the Negro man cannot find employment that pays sufficient wages to support his woman and children in the manner in which they can provide for themselves. Even though factory work has opened new areas in which unskilled Negro males can get employment, it is still very difficult for the average man to get a steady job without some kind of special training. Often when skills are developed through vocational schools, they are wasted because of a color line drawn by many factories and some unions. Most of the men in the neighborhood do odd jobs for subsistence. The younger men often are able to get seasonal jobs such as working for four or five months in the spring at a factory in Camden assembling outdoor summer furniture. Both men and women during harvest season take farm buses out into the New Jersey countryside to pick crops, which, though paying poorly, has the advantage of the "kindness" of the farmers who hand out damaged, unmarketable produce to the pickers, and they sell it to their neighbors.

The men, because of these same economic and psychological pressures that they felt since slavery, are still leading a mobile existence. Even the young men and youths have long histories of wandering, sometimes to find work, sometimes just adventure. Bobby and Charley, two of my finest informants, had gone to Florida together. Victor, a member of one of the many quartets that used to come to our house to tape themselves, went down to Richmond, Virginia, on a lark, got into a crap game, killed a man in a fight and is now in jail in that state. Arthur also went to Virginia to go into the tonsorial business, but returned after "having some fun."

It is this ability to be mobile that makes the Negro male so adaptable to army life. Since the armed services have become integrated they offer the men one of the best possibilities for employment. Many of the boys who formerly lived in the neighborhood are in the services as a career. Bobby attempted to enlist on a number of occasions but always failed the examinations. But this mobility, this lack of roots, is just one manifestation of the great problem which the men have in establishing any sense of themselves as individuals.

The Negro man from the lower class is confronted with a number of social and psychological impediments in establishing any sort of healthy identity. He is not only a black man in a white man's world, but he is a male in this matrifocally oriented group. And of these, the latter is his greatest burden. As pointed out, family life is dominated by the mother. Often a boy will grow up in a home which only sporadically has an older male in it; marriage is seldom longstanding, if it occurs at all. Casual alliances are much more the standard. Women, then, are not only the dispensers of love and care but also of discipline and authority. The concommitant of this system is a complex of attitudes which is far-reaching in its importance. Significant in this regard is the absolute and divisive distrust which members of one sex have for the other. Young girls brought up by their mothers are taught early and often about how men are not to be trusted. Men learn later to say the same thing about the women.

Growing up in this matrifocal system, the boys receive little guidance from older males. There are few figures about during childhood through which the boys can achieve any sort of positive ego identity. Thus their ideas of masculinity are slow to appear under the tutelage of their mothers, and sometimes never do emerge — witness the highly masochistic, effete, smiling Negro type, the "white man's nigger." Yet when most reach puberty, they will ultimately be rejected as men by the women in the matriarchy, and enter a period of terrific anxiety and rootlessness around the beginning of adolescence. The result often is a complete reversal of attitudes and an open resorting to the apparent security of gang existence in which masculinity can be overtly and impersonally expressed.

Life for the boy is a mass of oppositions. He is both a part of his mother-oriented family and not a part of it. His emotional attachments are wholly to his mother, but he, as a male, must seek for his masculine identity, and consequently must seek rejection and be rejected from his family. The rejection will occur anyhow, for with puberty comes a distrust from his mother in her role as a female. Male children seem more emotionally dependent upon their mothers than females. The young boy, without the dominant male in the family to emulate, seems to have a more difficult time adjusting to life outside his family. In the boy children from ages three to ten there seems to be a high incidence of bedwetting, sissyism, stammering and other speech defects, etc. Often the boys of this age try to compete with the girls in their games and, of course, are not very good at it. It seems that their only training toward a masculine approach to life is achieved through the influence of older boys in school, or, a little later, through the gangs.

Because there is often no father figure in the home, not only does the mother have to take over the disciplinary role, but the boy loses the whole meaning and conception of fatherhood. It is often humorous to see small boys of the same mother but different fathers arguing about whether the man who came to visit was one's father or another's. But when considering the implications of the problem, it becomes somewhat less of a laughing matter.

For each person to react in some way against authority when he is maturing is natural. This is his way of asserting his selfhood, of reorienting his life so that he can exist as an independent being. In middle-class family life, the authority figure against whom the youth rebels is, of course, the father. This is not possible for the young Negro as his father in most cases has had little to do with his life. He might, and does to some degree, react against his mother as the authority. But he is emotionally attached to his mother as his source of love and security. This attraction-repulsion paradox is further complicated by the fact that the trauma of rejection is persistently re-enacted for him. He sees his mother sharing herself not only with the other children, but also often with numerous men. Finally, rejection comes completely when the boy begins to become the man, and the mother rejects him as a member of that other group.

In other and earlier Negro groups this transition was not always accomplished because the mother's feelings were able to predominate over woman's, and protection prevailed over rejection. The results were the personality type among the men of docility and good humor: the slave type known so well to us as "Uncle Tom." But with greater mobility, and greater economic opportunities, especially for the women, these values changed and produced the more belligerent personality types.[12] Rejection does occur. The result is generally a violent reaction to the world of women which has turned its back on him, a world filled with expressions of virility and manliness. Femininity, weakness, become the core of the despicable. The expression for these reactions is the gang.

Thus an organizational form that springs from the little boy's search for a masculinity he cannot find at home becomes first a protest against femininity and then an assertion of hypervirility. On the way it acquires a structuring in which the aspirations and goals of the matriarchy or the middle class are seen as soft, effeminate, and despicable. The gang ideology of masculine independence is formed

12. This discussion does not attempt to meet head-on the problem of homosexuality among Negro men. It is certainly a problem, as was exhibited by a number of "faggots" in Camingerly. One bit of folklore classifies homosexual types for us (see 13. "The Freak's Ball," plus note the slur of homosexuality leveled at preachers in 30. "The Preacher and the Sinners"). Homosexuality seems to exist in many highly male situations, such as in the army, among sailors, and prisons, where females are denied them. Inevitably in such situations there will be some attracted to other men simply as the only available target for their sexual impulses. Just as often, however, will be those who, though not overtly homosexually oriented in regular society, are attracted to the male's world because they are retreating from women and their world, and the company (and love) of men is safer. One could see a possibility of this kind of situation in the fantastically strong dichotomy between the man's and woman's world in lower-class Negro society, even though they aren't geographically separated. The homosexual gang acts reported by Rohrer and Edmondson, *Generation*, p. 167, certainly seem to exist as part of the absolute rejection of women.

The love-hate ambivalence, on the other hand, is undoubtedly responsible for many of the apparent effeminate traits of this otherwise masculine group. "Don Juanism," the method of hair grooming reminiscent of the handkerchief tying of Southern "Mammies," the importance of falsetto voices in quartet singing, the high prevalence of lisping, the whole "dandy" feeling of dress and walk — all are explicable because of this ambivalence. The "ego ideal" of these men is a confused one; though rejecting women, they have accepted unconsciously certain symbols and actions of females. Only when the mother is fully accepted as the ego ideal does overt and habitual homosexuality of the "faggot" occur. Legman says of this:

The hatred of women and flight from them . . . are not necessarily homosexual — which is more clearly indicated by motions toward men, if present — but simply represents ambivalent love-hatred of persons by whom one feels one has been badly treated, but to whom one is uncontrollably attracted by biological determinants and secretions.

See also Oliver, *Blues*, pp. 112-114; 191-197.

from these perceptions, and the gang then sees its common enemy not as a class, nor even perhaps as a sex, but as the "feminine principle" in society.[13]

However, before any such metamorphosis can occur, the transition must be made by the boy from his mother-oriented to the gang-oriented values. This means a complete reversal of values, after all, and in order to achieve this anxious change-over, a violent and wildly permissive atmosphere must be established through which the boy can express the subsequent emotions involved. "Playing the dozens" and other such activities seem to have evolved exactly to fit this need.

Having been denied a natural development of his sense of manness, he must constantly prove to himself that he is a man. Throughout most of the rest of his life this will be his major preoccupation, his "fixation." His group provides him, as a youth, with the kind of organization within which he can attempt to prove his manliness, the gang. This establishes an institution, a symbolic structure on which he is able to attach all of his need for security, denied him by his mother's rejection, plus one which represents all of the values which the youth needs because he has had no effective male ego ideal and because he has been rejected by the female world.

Within the gang, the boy gets a chance to test out and exhibit the new values thrust upon him by his situation. He is capable of finding constant expression for his virile impulses because he is doing brave deeds in the teeth of authority. This authority is impersonal, depersonalized, part of the white man's world, not his own. Just as in "playing the dozens" (to be described in detail later), where mothers are attacked impersonally by projecting the image of the fallen woman into terms of the other person's mother, so in the gang activity war is waged against the impersonalized effemination of restrictive law. The gang is used to sublimate their individual problems, not really to solve them.

Here is where the paradox of gang values exists. The gangs are created to encounter and solve a specific problem of identity, but they solve nothing. They only serve to fixate. This is because a further paradox exists; what women reject in men is exactly what they most highly value, physical strength. It is almost as if the women enjoy saying "Go out and prove you're a man" and "I hate men" at the same time. Men can prove their virility temporarily,

13. Rohrer and Edmondson, *Generation*, p. 163.

but they have little chance to do more than that because of the conflict in the desires of their women. Thus gang values (and other fixated or regressive features) continue to hold sway among this group long after the usual period of adolescent reaction against authority would normally last. Men who think they are reacting against woman's values are really falling prey to them without realizing it.

Naturally the heroes of the group are going to be the bad men, Stackolee and Jesse James, or the trickster like "The Signifying Monkey," flaunting the rule of established order to prove their abilities and exercise their egos. They have the values of the rebel and the devil, those reactors against authority and a constantly rejecting society. We cannot doubt that such criteria rule in the minds of these young men when we hear them talk about the pleasures and hazards of gang activity.

Gangs offer a kind of organization for their values, and thus a structure for otherwise highly chaotic motivations and impulses. By not acquiescing in the manliness of the individual male for any great period of time, the women establish a situation not only where the men have to prove their masculinity to them constantly, but they have to do it through contest. Contest, after all, is the easiest kind of demonstration of such matters. In gang activity (and later in other unlawful acts) the Negro is striking out against an almost impersonal foe, and thus is able to come off fairly undamaged in the eyes of his group even if he loses. Being put in jail or getting "sliced up" by a group you don't know personally is just as manly as winning. Physical violence is preferred to cowardice. But all of this would not be worth it if the individual boy did not have the concept of the gang organization's protection in the neighborhood. This kind of contest is exhibited in all phases of the folkloristic activity of the men as well, and we will devote the next chapter to a consideration of this.

Proving virility in their own eyes and those of their women provides the impetus for most of the activities of the Camingerly men. They seem to recognize that the only way that they are going to master a potential mate is to present an appearance of great strength, especially of great physical power. Most of the time this recognition is expressed by "big talk," boasting (and this is done in front of other men for the most part — not the women). The women, mistrusting the men as they do, and implicitly sensing their superior strategic position, look only for a "love" through sexual satisfaction. The most valued kind of strength then is sexual ability.

35

Perhaps for this reason so many of the stories, jokes, and toasts are concerned with the sexual feats of the men. One informant, "Kid," who has had his share of really bad experiences with women's fickleness and demands, says only half-kiddingly:

> Yeah, I'm fast. I'm so fast, a girl told me one time, she said, "Kid, now if you can get some cock 'fore my mother get back home, and she's coming 'round the corner right now, you can have it." So I said, "Lay down." She laid down, I pushed the light switch, got undressed, jumped in bed, busted two nuts, got dressed and got outside the room before that room got dark.

Though this kind of boasting is rarely done in front of the women, an equally overt, but not quite as raw, verbal byplay has developed. The male makes some kind of "smart" overture which is either ignored or answered in equally "smart" but negative terms. Cleverness and strength of language become ends in themselves because the woman is asking the man to prove his masculinity and he can do so by words as well as subsequent actions.

Bobby, from time to time, concerned with my apparent ineptness with the opposite sex, would give me long lectures on how one had to "deal rough" with women. He would say, "You go over to a who's house (any woman is a 'who') and say, 'lookahere, bitch, when I say jump you jump, 'cause I didn't come here to fool around. I come for business.' If she gives you lip, just smack her one and she'll mind you." Although in the case of Bobby, the "smacking" never occurred because his words were almost always much bigger than his deeds, in many other cases actual physical violence is the only way that the man can finally subdue the woman, "put her in her place." The bruises, even scars, that result are worn proudly.

This attitude toward virility is shown clearly by the fact that the men are so proud when they impregnate a girl. Even in cases where they cannot be sure that they are the father (how could they be when they argue that you can't trust any woman in matters of this sort), they will claim to be so and be proud of it.

Similarly, choices of professions and heroes of real life are dictated by the manliness of the activity. It is true that there are a few fields open to Negro men, but the ones they have chosen and excelled in are the ones in which strength (physical or verbal) is openly exhibited. The heroes of the Negro are the ones who pioneer and excel in these areas and who exhibit their control in the "classiest" way. Athletics is the most obvious of these activities, and the greatest heroes of the neighborhood are Willy Mays and Hank Aaron and the numerous other baseball players that have made a name for themselves. Boxing was one of the sports in which Negroes were able to excel earliest, and "Sugar Ray" Robinson still excites great admiration, both because of his athletic ability and his style of life. One could give numerous further examples in other sports.

The profession in which the Negroes made their earliest gains is entertainment.[14] Many fixed conceptions about the Negro concern their entertainment abilities, their musical sense, their ability to "hold a tune," their rhythmic sense, etc. Naturally, these are just as false as fixed conceptions about any group, but the fact that the white world has this view of the Negro has instilled in him a worship of those Negroes who have made successes in the entertainment field and has created a desire on the part of an unnaturally large number of Negroes to make a success on the stage. Nearly every boy that can sing belongs to a quartet, and every quartet dreams of professional success, which many of them are getting through rock-and-roll recordings. Kid features himself a professional comedian. Because of their ability to perform such rhythmic folklore items as "Hambone," many young Negroes dream of rising to stardom playing the bongo drums. Singers, song writers, dancers are to be found everywhere in the area. The fact that Charley had been in a group (The Turbans) that made a record made him the object of much respect in the neighborhood.

This kind of exhibitionism for purposes of attraction is manifested in many aspects of Camingerly life from gang activity to the style of playing cards, pool, baseball, or any contest activity. Style of living is more important than life itself. They say in their boasts and toasts "I'm a mean motherfucker and I don't mind dying," and

14. It is interesting to note the importance of entertainment here, and the interplay between white and colored forms. Just as the white-written minstrel songs were picked up by the Negroes and became at least semi-traditional, perhaps the most emulated of modern performers are "Amos n' Andy," radio characters created by whites.

Recently Hollywood has seen the potential of the Negro audience and has been casting Negroes in major roles in many movies. The rise of such performers as Harry Belafonte, Sammy Davis, Jr., and Sidney Poitier has undoubtedly been stimulated by attendance of their movies in Negro neighborhoods.

It is difficult to ascertain whether this opportunity in the entertainment field makes the young Negro (especially the men) any more aware of popular forms of entertainment than any other group. At any rate, the lore shows great influence of radio, television, and movies in its form and subject matter.

one cannot doubt that there is a good deal of truth to their words. It *is* more important for many of them to feel "mean" or "tough" (anything good is "tough," as "that was a tough movie") than for them to go on living.

Most noticeable in this regard to outsiders is the individual's manner of dress and way of walking. His cock-of-the-walk attitude is echoed in his clothes; he reflects the trends in men's fashions, but uses them with brighter colors in more daring combinations. As is clear from the toasts, he is very conscious of the sharp dresser. The "Signifying Monkey's" clothes are described in detail for instance:

> Now a few stalks shook and a few leaves fell.
> Up popped the monkey one day, 'bout sharp as hell.
> He had on a one-button roll, two-button satch.
> You know, one of them boolhipper coats with a belt in the back.

The baboon, too, gets a once-over:

> The baboon stood with a crazy rim.
> Charcoal grey vine with a stingy brim.
> Handful of dimes, pocket full of herbs.
> El Dorado Cadillac parked at the curb.[15]

This consciousness of dress is further expressed in emphasis on hair style. Negro women for some time have attempted in one way or another to have their hair straightened so that they can wear the same styles as white women. This is still true, but recently (purportedly due to the influence of boxer "Sugar Ray" Robinson) the men have taken to having their hair straightened in a pompadour style, called a "process."

The spirit of contest then is exhibited in nearly every visible facet of the life of the Negro, from gang play to interplay among the sexes to clothes and choice of employment. And through it all the contests are self-defeating because they are never able to give the men a secure sense of their own identity. They remain throughout most of their lives men *manqué.*

These remarks about the Camingerly Negro's attitudes and problems are made in an effort to clarify some of the corresponding facets of their folklore. They can only be considered as a gloss on the material found in the later chapters. There are many other

15. Text 3A. "The Signifying Monkey."

facets to these attitudes and problems which will be brought forth in the future chapters on the life histories, on contest and verbal dexterity, on heroes and oikotypes, and in special applications in the introductions and headnotes to the lore itself.

CHAPTER II

THE ELEMENT OF VERBAL CONTEST

FORM, ORDER, STRUCTURE — THESE ARE IMPORTANT IN CREATING THE psychological situation where instincts otherwise repressed can be represented within the confines of the unreal, yet lifelike, playground of folklore. By creating or utilizing previously created formal unities (the rules of play), the individual (or ego) is able to dupe society (or the super-ego) into allowing the expression of certain aggressive attitudes which otherwise would remain unuttered or unacted. No group will allow unchanneled aggression. In one way or another, methods will be developed which will allow a free play of the agonistic impulses of the individual. A balance will be struck between the needs of the community and the needs of the individual, though in many cases that balance will be a precarious one.

This aggression is usually allowable in a play (or contest) situation. Folklore is play in its broadest sense. All folklore involves us either in the play world of the game or in the play world of the fictive experience. It then offers us two ways of "playing out" our aggressions: through the symbolic movements of games and players, or through the vicarious dramatic expression of the narrative world. Either play world has restrictive conventions (rules and boundaries) and both involve symbolic role playing (mimesis). Both are intimately related to the real world and are yet substantially removed from it by the psychic distance provided by these conventions. The elements of society in our psyches (and in our group existence) both allow this kind of aggressive expression as long as it does not exceed the bounds of the rules. When it does, as in such play-like contest situations as stone-throwing among children and gangsterism in adult life, society must step in and end it.

As we grow older, our competitive instincts become more complicated and sublimated. Our playgrounds change from the child's play world to the athletic field, to the law courts and the stock market. Our intentions remain the same, our strategies and expressions become more diffuse and our motivations more complex as we begin to realize the existence of the intentions. Our symbolic actions become more and more removed from their immediate objective; we use to an increasing extent the more vicarious expressions, viewing the battle and identifying with the contestants rather than engaging in it ourselves. It is only the very remarkable individual who is able to divorce himself from participating in contest.

This growth in strategy and complexity is important for our psychic development. Contest does not exist for itself; it is a mechanism for the dramatic dialectic expression of specific psychic problems, ones generally brought about by the inherent conflict of the individual living (or trying to live) with society. This conflict has many facets, and the individual's psychic and somatic growth causes these facets to be progressively (rather than simultaneously) developed. Erikson sees personality development as a series of these basic conflicts. His schema for psycho-social growth, paralleled and influenced by somatic development, is:

    I.   Trust vs. Distrust
    II. Autonomy vs. Shame, Doubt
  III. Initiative vs. Guilt
  IV. Industry vs. Inferiority
    V. Identity and Repudiation vs. Identity Diffusion
  VI. Intimacy and Solidarity vs. Isolation
 VII. Generativity vs. Self-Absorption
VIII. Integrity vs. Despair[1]

Our lives are not just psychologically fixed for us, but are also somatically determined; our problems change as we grow older. These challenges confront us at every stage in life. If we are unable to find an effective synthesis to the conflict we are forced to play out the problem over and over. We are, as the psychoanalysts

1. Erickson, *Identity and the Life Cycle*, pp. 50-100. He has a chart on p. 166 that reduces the entire schema for quick perusal.

would say, "fixated." Furthermore, "All . . . developmental periods are intimately interrelated and defective development of one phase will serve to make the successful negotiation of a subsequent phase more difficult."[2]

Perhaps it would be clearer to express this in dialectic terms. We encounter at a specific period a problem of psychic growth, paralleling a somatic development. This involves a struggle between opposing forces, analogous to a thesis and antithesis. We must expect an effective synthesis to come from this struggle. In a fixated state none emerges, and if the synthesis is only partially successful, the next conflict will be harder to fight, and the less chance remains that further syntheses will be effective. We encounter, in situations of this sort, non-committal syntheses, resolutions that are at best temporary.

Of all of these conflicts, the ones brought on by adolescence are the most crucial and the most difficult. This is due to the tremendous somatic change which is occurring, a change which insists on an equally radical psychic re-orientation. It is during this period that we attempt to develop our sense of ego identity. Without this sense in full development, we are unable to become adults with any completeness.

> When childhood and youth come to an end, life, so the saying goes, begins: by which we mean work or study for a specified career, sociability with the other sex, and in time, marriage and a family of ones own. But it is only after a reasonable sense of identity has been established that real *intimacy* with the other sex (or for that matter, with any other person or even with oneself) is possible.[3]

This is precisely the situation which we began to explore in the last chapter. The Camingerly men are only temporarily able to fully express their masculinity — that is, achieve a sense of ego identity. At every stage in their personality development, because of the lack of an effective male ego ideal in their lives, these individuals are placed in a position in which they never gain any firm acceptance of themselves as men. This situation is further aggravated because they are excluded from family life, for the most part, once they reach manhood. This family situation causes them to be fixated by their adolescent problems; their lives and values are

2. Rohrer and Edmondson, *Generation*, p. 87.
3. Erickson, *Identity*, p. 95.

permanently retarded. Contest, ubiquitous in any group, is confined for the part of these men's lives to its adolescent type of expression, and their heroes are the ones who reflect these values.

In the last chapter we discussed these values in terms of their expression in gang life. In this chapter we will be concerned with the major folkloristic representation of this fixation, the word-battle. In the next chapter we will explore the relation of these values to the heroes of the narratives of this group, and show how these heroes differ from those of past Negro groups. Finally we will look into how this situation and these values have resulted in producing lore directly related to that of other groups, yet different in important ways, ways which may establish a specific type of urban Negro narrative. However, before we can do this we must determine how, and from where, the Camingerly men develop their vocabulary and what it means to them.

One of the first and most anxious situations with which any child finds himself confronted is the inability to control his motor responses. Folklore, especially in the form of rhymes and songs, provides him a controlled context within which he can practice safely with words (one of his major motor problems) to gain some feeling of mastery, of control. The formal unity of pieces of folklore presents an atmosphere potentially free of anxiety. When control of the limited word units is achieved, a great deal of pleasure ensues, due to the release from the previous anxious situation. The formal unit has been an active agent in the attainment of this control, as it has provided oral cues which have helped the child remember (rhyme, repetition, meter, etc.). Furthermore, the pleasure which the control initially gives is relived constantly (by future recitals of the same piece). We all play over our conquests, children perhaps more than others because their anxieties are greater.

The child's tacit recognition of the importance of words as controlling agents remains a subconscious resource the rest of his life. Words are power, the child learns. The capacity to name and describe allows us the secure feeling of control, even before we learn the further power of words in their strategic uses. Our physical growth is paralleled closely by our growing power with words; both are sources of control.

When we subsequently run into other situations productive of anxiety, we tend to use those devices to conquer them which have been successful in the past. One of these early victories that we keep returning to is our first efforts at power through word control. We constantly use rhymes and other forms of childish wit to express, and therefore combat, our otherwise most guarded anxieties. The subjects of the witticisms are different, but the technique is the same. This is why we seem to be able to tell jokes and make quips about things we otherwise can't talk about.

Especially when we reach adolescence, we revert to childhood formalities of expression in order to attempt to control the new social situation brought about by the emergence of interest in the opposite sex. We use folklore then as a familiar weapon for fighting a new battle. Songs, rhymes, taunts, etc., change subject matter, but return to the forms and formulas of childhood expression. To return to these devices is, in a large sense, regressive.

The Camingerly Negro not only goes through this regressive process when he reaches adolescence; because of the difficulty of winning a permanent decision in the adolescent contest, he must continue to fight this kind of battle for the greater part of his life. This is amply illustrated in the large place rhyming plays in the life of the man of words. He not only uses traditional rhymes as part of his entertainment repertoire, but uses his abilities to insert rhymes into any social situation which may entertain. Such devices as "See you later, alligator" and "after 'while, crocodile" (which I feel certain are Negro in origin) are to be found in much of the public discourse of these men. One day, for instance, while "Kid" and others were sitting around telling jokes, he said:

> We can sit here and shuck and shive.
> We can sit here and do the split.
> We can sit here and do this.
> We can sit here and shit.

Almost any cliche is stated in rhyme form. Here is a common dialogue routine illustrating this:

> What you mean, jelly bean?
> What I said, cabbage head.

Similar rhyming situations emerge with other expressions:

> Me and you, Fu Manchu.
> Tell the truth, Snag-a-tooth.
> 'Nough said, Ted.

This propensity to rhyme found wide use in the days of be-bop (late 1940's, and on into the 1950's) by disc-jockeys. Even today, Negro disc-jockeys use rhyme to introduce their records, but the technique is not nearly as wide-spread as it used to be. "Jocko" was a favorite be-bop disc-jockey and the rhymed introduction which he used for his show remains a part of the lore of Camingerly in a hand-clapping version of "Who Stole the Cardinal's Hat?" ("Who, sir? Me, sir?")

> Be, be-bop
> This is your Jock
> Back on the scene
> With a record machine.
> Saying "hoo-poppsie-doo,
> How do you do?"
> When you up, you up,
> And when you down, you down
> And when you mess with Jock
> You upside down.

The conscious manipulation of words in rhyme for exhibition of (sexual) strength is nowhere more clear than here. Jock (the man who owns, controls the jock-strap and its contents) is not a man to be "messed with" because he will turn you upside down (put you into the female position.) Because of a constant need for such expression, the man of words, the "good talker" has an important place in the social structure of the group, not only in adolescence but throughout most of his life.

Words are power to him in a very real way. And they function powerfully, not as in childhood, but as elements in the sexual battle which is typical of adolescent life. The sexual power of words is, of course, patent. To recognize this, one need only see a popular singer or an effective speaker at work and watch the effect of such language upon women.[4] The men of Camingerly not only sense this inherent power, they use it in their most important battles, their verbal contests. They use words for the purposes of establishing a much needed, but unfortunately only too transitory, feeling of masculine control.

4. Newbell Niles Puckett, *Folk Beliefs of the Southern Negro* (Chapel Hill, 1926), p. 30, has pointed out that the Negroes of the South went to school to an older man who was

> . . . experienced in the words and ways of courtship, [who could teach] young gallants . . . the way in which they should go in the delicate matter of winning the girl of their choice.

This tacit acceptance of the relationship of words and sexual attraction is found

Verbal contest accounts for a large portion of the talk between members of this group. This oral butting of heads is a constant part of their lives. Proverbs, turns of phrase, jokes, almost any manner of discourse is used, not for purposes of communication, but as weapons in verbal battle. Any gathering of the men customarily turns into some kind of teasing or boasting session. Here for instance is a description by "Kid" of the kind of talk to be heard in pool halls:

Just like mounting on the wrong guys down at the pool room. Cats be coming in there, gambling. Suddenly one them says, "Suck my ass." He say, "You suck my ass and the box, that way you can't miss my asshole." Cat says, "Sucking ass is out of style, button your lipper, suck my dick awhile." He said, "Sucking dicks ain't no trick. Button your motherfucking mouth up my asshole, nuts and dick." Anything. Just one's trying to get above another one, each time they say something you know.

"Now you suck my ass." "Ain't nobody fucking with you." "You fuck with me and I'll bust your motherfucking mouth." You might say to him, "Well, you'd be better locked up in a phonebooth sandpapering a lion's ass (and that's close contact) than fucking with me." "You'd do better jump in a fire with gasoline suit on than be jumping on my chest." They say like, "You'd be better in a lion's den with a motherfucking side of beef on your shoulder, than do any fucking with me." Might tell a guy something like, "Don't you know I ain't worrying about you 'cause I'll run up your motherfucking throat, jump down your motherfucking lungs, tap dance on your kidneys, remove your motherfucking appendicides, move out your god damn intestines, kill your dick and die, your heart stop beating." It's just passing speech. Guys don't mean no harm; they just saying it. If people walked past and didn't know you,

in many parts of the world. The whole idea of love letters is anchored here, as is the strategy of the love poem and song. As Legman says:

It is very well known in the theater and in particular among singers, lecturers, ministers, and so forth, *that women are affected by the male voice,* and collapse into a sort of helpless sexual availability before a particularly fine (not necessarily bass, or other "virile") male voice, whether in speaking or singing. This is a phenomenon observable not only among other mammals, but throughout animal nature (with the exception of fish, which are mute). . . .

they'd swear there'd be blows coming. You get used to it. And when somebody say something, just say something back. People that don't know you would figure you're just getting ready to fight. Just passing speech.

"I'ma put something on your ass." You know, just passing speech. Words that just comes naturally, you heard, and heard, and you repeat 'em and repeat 'em. After a guy gets to hanging around so long, he learns them. You find a guy coming in who never cursed in his life, after a month or two, same thing. He come in, say, "What doing man?" "Fuck my ass." You know, before he came in never cursed in his life. Now every third word he's going to curse. Rabbit's cattin' pool, every second word is "motherfucker." Just passing speech.

And this kind of talk is by no means limited to the pool hall. With some modifications it is found in practically every area of social intercourse, both in male groups and between males and females. The terms in which the arguments are waged indicate that the word-battles derive their impetus from sexual matters. A verbal attack is called "mounting," or "getting above," that is placing the other in the female position. Getting the best of someone is called "putting him down," a similar sexual slur. Winning such a battle not only proves the masculinity of the victor; it conclusively effeminates the other.

The verbal contest exists, of course, among the Camingerly children. Taunts, jokes, riddles, catches all exist as an opportunity for the child to indicate his individual capacity through the triumph of the control of words. Their catches (tricker, by means of questions or leading statements or by establishing patterns, leads the answerer into an indefensible position which is rewarded by a penalty) illustrate this element most clearly:

> Look up. (other does)
> Look down. (other does)
> See my thumb? (holds his thumb up)
> Gee, you're dumb.

> Could you read?
> Yes.
> Could you write?
> Yes.
> Could you smoke your daddy's pipe?

Say "washing machine."

"Washing machine."

I'll bet you five dollars your drawers ain't clean.

It is just this impulse, to verbally best someone, when coupled with a growing awareness of sex and the complex of emotions that surround it, that results among youths in the practice of "playing the dozens" in rhyme. As this verbal game is an important aspect of Camingerly agonistic expression, and an integral part in the growth and verbal dexterity, it will be described in some detail. A discussion seems even more important since the "dozens" has excited critical attention, some of which has been either uninformed or misguided. Variously called "playing the dozens," "playing," "sounding,"[5] and "woofing," this phenomenon stands as a mechanism

5. This is the more common way of referring to the game today. "Dozens" is not even understood by some Negroes now. There has been some speculation as to the origin and history of the game under the name "playing the dozens." John Dollard in "The Dozens: The Dialect of Insult," *American Imago*, I (1939), pp. 3-24 (referred to as Dollard henceforth) feels that the name may have come from one of the rhymes which went from one to twelve describing the obscenities "mother" engaged in. C. S. Johnson, *Growing*, pp. 184-85, suggests that the name owes its origins to the unluckiness of throwing a twelve in "craps." Newman Ivey White, *American Negro Folk Songs* (Cambridge, 1928), p. 364, seems to agree implicitly with this, as he gives a "dozens" reference ("I don't play the dozen/And don't you ease me in.") among songs about gambling. Paul Oliver in *Blues*, p. 128, says of its history,

"Putting in the Dozens" developed as a folk game in the late nineteenth century, . . .

but he gives no documentation for this.

William Griffin has suggested, in recent correspondence, that the name may come from one of the formulas, "At least my mother *doesn't* . . ." dozens being an easy mutation.

Peter Tamony, in a letter, suggests the derivation of the name may come from "DOZEN," v., to stun, stupefy, daze, which can be used both transitively and intransitively (OED). If this were true, its etymology would concur with many other Negro words which come eminently from English parlance of the eighteenth century. This would attach an English name to a phenomenon possibly brought from Africa. Newbell Niles Puckett, *Folk Beliefs*, p. 23, quoting Kingsley, says,

The dominant affection in the home is the intense devotion of the African for his mother, more fights being occasioned among boys by hearing something said in disparagement of their mothers than by all other causes put together.

This would place the game, or something like it, quite far back historically. The first mention I have found of the game with this name is from the popular magazine, *Current Opinion* (September, 1919) in an article on Gilda Gray, a white blues singer. The chorus of a song is printed called "The Dirty

which helps the young male Negro to adapt to his changing world
and trains him for the similar and more complex verbal endeavors
in the years of manhood. The nature of the terms indicates the kind
of procedure involved; "playing" illustrates that a game or contest
is being waged, "sounding" shows that the game is vocal, and
"wolfing" or "woofing" points out the similarity of the procedure
with a dog's bark.

"Sounding" occurs only in crowds of boys.[6] One insults a member
of another's family; others in the group make disapproving sounds
to spur on the coming exchange. The one who has been insulted
feels at this point that he must reply with a slur on the protagonist's
family which is clever enough to defend his honor (and therefore
that of his family). This, of course, leads the other (once again, due
more to pressure from the crowd than actual insult) to make
further jabs. This can proceed until everyone is bored with the
whole affair, until one hits the other (fairly rare), or until some
other subject comes up that interrupts the proceedings (the usual
state of affairs).

When the combatants are quite young (just entering puberty),
they are obviously trying out some of the words and concepts they
have overheard and are just beginning to understand. Thus, their
contest is liable to be short and uncomplicated, but the pattern is
established:

"I hear your mother plays third base for the Phillies."

"Your mother is a bricklayer, and stronger than your father."

Dozens." This song is different from the one sung by "Speckled Red" (Rufus
Perryman) as quoted in Oliver, *Blues,* p. 128. The white reference above could
be considered an even earlier one.

The songs concerning the dozens creates a problem quite separate from that
considered here. Briefly, the record referred to above seems to have achieved
sufficient popularity that a number of others were subsequently issued. Paul
Oliver has kindly sent me a list of the following: "The Dirty Dozens," Lonnie
Johnson, OK 8775; "Double Dozens," Sweet Peas Spivey, Decca 7204;
"Twelve," Kokomo Arnold, Decca 7083; "Dirty Dozen," Leroy Carr, Vocalion
1454; "The Dozing Blues," George Noble, Melotone 70605; "Dirty Mother
for You," Shuffling Sam, Vocalion 03329; "Mother Fuyer," Dirty Red, Aladdin
194. All of these have some relationship to the earlier record.

6. One will occasionally find girls making dozens-type remarks, but for the
most part not in the organized fashion of the boys. The boys do not generally
play in front of girls, except where one boy is trying to put another down.
In this case the game can lead to a physical fight. Dollard seems to have encountered more girl "players" than I have. It certainly could not perform any
similar psychosocial function among females, but the mechanism does exist as
an expression of hostility by either sex.

"Your mother eats shit."

"Your mother eats shit and mustard."

Here the emphasis is on reversal of roles, with the mother playing the male role, a realization of a basic fact of lower-class Negro family life.

As sexual awareness grows, the vilification of the mother is changed to sexual matters, the contests become more heated and the insults more noteworthy. Many of them take the form of rhymes or puns, signaling the beginning of the bloom of verbal dexterity which comes to fruition later in the long narrative poem called the "toast," and indicating the necessity of applying strict formal structure to highly volatile matters. A sample of a fracas involving two fourteen- or fifteen-year-olds might run as follows: Someone mentions the name of someone else's mother in the course of a joking conversation — "Constance," for instance. At this point someone in the crowd says, "Yeah, Constance was real good to me last Thursday." Then Constance's son has to reply in kind, "I heard Virginia (the other's mother) lost her titty in a poker game." "Least my mother ain't no cake; everybody get a piece." The other might reply:

> I hate to talk about your mother,
> She's a good old soul.
> She's got a ten-ton pussy
> And a rubber asshole.
> She got hair on her pussy
> That sweep the floor.
> She got knobs on her titties
> That open the door.

And this in turn elicits any of the numerous retorts which are listed in the following pages. Eventually the boys' verbal dexterity increases to the point at which they can achieve more through subtlety and innuendo than through rhymes and obvious puns.

Somewhere between the ages of sixteen and twenty-six, "playing" begins to lose its effect and passes out of frequent use as an institution. When someone indicates that he wants to start, the one who is supposed to be insulted may reply, "Oh man, don't play with me." If he needs a more clever retort, he may rely on the proverb, "I laugh, joke, and smoke, but I don't play." Yet the game is never really forgotten. Any time within the period in which the boys are still running in groups of their own sex, an argument which arises can be complicated and enlivened by some fleeting derogatory reference to a member of the other's family. It has been reported to me many times that the "dozens" is often invoked by Negroes in the army, under those very tense and restrictive conditions of regimentation. When it is used under such circumstances, it almost invariably leads to a fight. Similarly, when used by older males in a verbal battle, in such places as a bar or a poolroom, it also ends in blows. As such, the institution functions quite differently among men than with adolescents.

Among the older males the references to the family of the other are fleeting, and not necessarily directed against anything specific. Among adolescents, especially the younger ones, the insults are much more rigidly constructed and are directed toward or against certain things. Most prominently, they are concerned with sexual matters. Usually both the rhymes and the taunts are directed against the other's mother, alleging sexual wantonness:

> I fucked your mother on an electric wire.
> I made her pussy rise higher and higher.

> I fucked your mother between two cans.
> Up jumped a baby and hollered, "Superman."

At least my mother ain't no doorknob, everybody gets a turn.

Sometimes the rhymes just place the other's mother in an embarrassing position:

> I say your mother flying through the air.
> I hit her on the ass with a rotten pear.

Another common subject is the effeminacy or homosexuality of father or brother:

Least my father ain't pregnant in the stomach.

Least my brother ain't no store; he takes meat in the back.

Whether the game involves rhymes or not, the language which is used is different from the everyday language of the contestants. Such linguistic (or paralinguistic) elements as changes in pitch, stress, and sometimes syntax, provide the signals of contest. Just as counting-out introduces us to the world of the children's game, with its resultant suspension of reality, or the phrase "Have you heard the one about . . . ?" leads us into the permissive world of the joke, so when someone of this group makes a "dozens-type" preliminary

remark, it can be predicted that he is about to construct a hypothetical playfield on which a verbal contest is to be played.

These contrastive linguistic features outline the rules of the game,
a verbal battle. Within specific forms, the rules seem to say, "You
can insult my family, but don't exceed the rules because we are
dealing with something perilously close to real life." The most
prominent linguistic features are (1) the reliance upon formulaic
patterns, (2) the use of rhyme within these patterns, and (3) the
change of speech rhythms from natural ones to ones that conform
to the demands of the formula. These are the strictest boundaries
imposed by this game. As the youths learn to use words more
securely, any contrived witticism will supply the needed formulaic
requirement. Until such an age, it is psychologically safer to be
clever within the confines of the appointed rhyme form.

This point is made convincingly by Martha Wolfenstein in considering the strategy of children's rhyming habits, specifically in
regard to the ancestor of the dozens rhyme, the taunt:

> What is the function of rhymes in these joking attacks?
> I would suggest that the first rhyming word has the effect
> of compelling the utterance of the second, thus reducing
> the speaker's responsibility. . . . There is a further reduc-
> tion of responsibility in the use of a rhymed formula: the
> words are not my own. Moreover the rhyme is apt to in-
> duce other children to take it up; the attacker will cease to
> be alone. It should be added that rhymes are often in
> themselves funny to young children. Children of three,
> for instance, may laugh simply at finding two words that
> rhyme or a word that rhymes with a name. Thus the
> rhyme affords a facade of harmless joking to facilitate the
> expression of hostility in the rhymed insult.[7]

The relationship between the taunt and the dozens is an important one, for it points out the important fact that the dozens utilizes
many of the devices of the controlled aggression of children. The
technique, length, rhyme, meter, and restriction of form are a
regression to children's forms; in subject they are wholly adolescent
and look toward the more complex verbal contests:

7. Martha Wolfenstein, *Children's Humor* (Glencoe, 1954), p. 182.

> Roses are red,
> Violets are blue.
> I fucked your mama,
> And now it's for you

The rhyme

> I fucked your mother between two tracks.
> It stung so hard, the train fell back.

is very similar to these lines from one of their children's rhymes:

> Just before your mother died
> She called you to her side.
> She gave you a pair of drawers.
> Before your father died.
> She put 'em in the sink.
> The sink begin to stink.
> *She put 'em on the track.*
> *The train backed back.*
> She put 'em on the fence.
> Ain't seen 'em since.

A device which links the "dozens" to childhood behavior is that of "signifying."[8] This is a technique of indirect argument or persuasion that underlies many of the strategies of children and is utilized more subtly in the "dozens." The unity of approach of both "signifying" and the "dozens" is illustrated in a toast from an older age group, called "The Signifying Monkey and the Lion." In this verse narrative we have a dialogue between a malicious, childlike monkey and a headstrong lion, in which the monkey is trying to get the lion involved in a flight with the elephant. The monkey is a "signifier," and one of the methods he uses for inflaming the lion is to indicate that the elephant has been "sounding" on the lion.

8. The term "signifying" seems to be characteristically Negro in use if not in origin. It can mean any of a number of things; in the case of the toast, it certainly refers to the monkey's ability to talk with great innuendo, to carp, cajole, needle and lie. It can mean in other instances the propensity to talk around a subject, never quite coming to the point. It can mean "making fun" of a person or situation. Also it can denote speaking with the hands and eyes, and in this respect encompasses a whole complex of expressions and gestures. Thus it is "signifying" to stir up a fight between neighbors by telling stories; it is signifying to make fun of the police by parodying his motions behind his back; it is signifying to ask for a piece of cake by saying, "My brother needs a piece of that cake." It is, in other words, many facets of the smart-alecky attitude. See Glossary for further discussion.

54

Now the lion came through the jungle one peaceful day,
When the signifying monkey stopped him, and that is
    what he started to say:
He said, "Mr. Lion," he said, "A bad-assed motherfucker
    down your way,"
He said, "Yeah! The way he talks about your folks is a
    certain shame.
"I even heard him curse when he mentioned your grand-
    mother's name."
The lion's tail shot back like a forty-four
When he went down that jungle in all uproar.

It is significant that the monkey is childlike, and for his "signifying" he gets killed in many endings to this toast. "Signifying" is
a children's device, and is severely "put down" by adults. They say,
"Signifying is worse than dying," at the same time recognizing that
they themselves easily fall into the same pattern, by saying "Sig-
nification is the nigger's occupation." Thus the "dozens" uses many
of the techniques of childhood discourse, but places them in a
context that leads directly to adult modes of expression. Both the
reliance on rhyme and wit and the use of "signifying" remain as
major parts of adult male expression, but in considerably mutated
form. The "dozens" signals this mutation.

Many have commented upon the institution of playing the "dozens," but few have discussed the function which it performs in the
life of the young Negro.[9] John Dollard's article, "The Dozens: The
Dialect of Insult," perceptively points out that the game acts as a
release mechanism for the anxieties of Negro youths; his article

9. R. F. Berdie, *Journal of Abnormal and Social Psychology*, XLII (1947),
pp. 120-21, describes the game accurately in a note. William Elton in two
notes, *American Speech*, XXV (1950), pp. 148-49, 230-33, indicates a number
of places in which the term is to be encountered in contexts literary and
scholarly. He ties the practice up with the "joking relationship," especially
among the Dahomeans and the Ashanti, an attribution which is both strange
and unsound, the two phenomena being similar only in the socially permissive
and initiatory functions. But "joking relationships" develop their permissiveness out of a familistic structure, and the "dozens" do not.

Samuel J. Sperling discusses the procedure quite cogently in relation to
teasing in general, in "On the Psychodynamics of Teasing," *Journal of the
American Psychoanalytic Association*, I (1953), p. 470. C. L. Golightly and I.
Sheffler have a once-over at the literature on the subject in a note, bringing
Berdie up to date, in *Journal of Abnormal and Social Psychology*, XLIII
(1948), pp. 104-105. They conclude:

These youths are blocked off from most of the avenues of approved
self-expression. They live in a limited cultural world with patterns for

stands as a unique document in the field. But his uncertainty as to the manner of release, and a misunderstanding of the exact nature of its psychosocial importance, leads me to make further remarks on the way in which the "dozens" function. Specifically, Dollard does not seem to differentiate between the "dozens" as played by youths and by adults. Further, he sees the game as a displaced aggression against the Negro's own group instead of against the real enemy, the whites, a reading which I find untenable not because it is wholly wrong, but because it is too easy.[10]

Certainly these rhymes serve as a clever expression of the growing awareness of the adolescent performers, especially of matters of sex. But "growing awareness" signals the fact that "dozens" are an expression of boys in transition to manhood. In fact, "sounding" is one of the major ways in which boys are enabled to become men

> emulation and stimulation. In their play groups they frequently use sex experience and prowess as a means of attaining status.

See also A. Davis and John Dollard, *Children of Bondage* (Washington, D. C., 1960), pp. 82-83; *American Notes and Queries,* I (December, 1941), p. 133; Robert C. Elliott, *The Power of Satire* (Princeton, 1960), pp. 73-74; Dollard, "Dialect"; Johnson, *Growing Up*. For all of the texts which I collected in Philadelphia, see the *Journal of American Folklore,* LXXV (1962), pp. 216-19.

10. Dollard's arguments are tenable from an outside view, because almost any aggression committed by the underprivileged group within a society can be seen as a "substitute aggression," a principle similar to sublimation. But looking at the problem generically, the psychosocial problem of a healthy ego development exists before any sociological situation incurs itself upon the individuals, and the dislocation of the ego through the mother-dominated system will create an anxiety situation that is only aggravated by the fact that the values which grow out of such a system often produce illegal or immoral acts in the white man's eyes. The result, as many have pointed out, is a double standard of law, with acts of violence being tolerated within the Negro group to a great extent, especially in the South.

Sperling, "Psychodynamics," seems to be driving at somewhat the same point as Dollard.

> This teasing game promotes the toughening of emotional sensitivity, and the inhibiting of impulses toward physical aggression. Frustrated outgroup aggression is safely channeled into the ingroup. In this way the formalized game of "The Dozens" has social value to a group subjected to suppression, discrimination and humiliation.

The social values do exist, I would argue, but not just because this is a group suppressed and discriminated against.

For a discussion of such problems in a vein similar to these arguments, see Hortense Powdermaker, "The Channeling of Negro Aggression by the Cultural Process," *American Journal of Sociology,* XLVIII (1943), pp. 750-58. For a corroboration of my thesis, see Rohrer and Edmondson, *Generation,* pp. 158 ff., an excellent recent study of gang values.

in the limited sense in which Negro males from the lower class ever attain a sense of masculinity.

In the first chapter, the family situation of the Camingerly youth was described in some detail. In short, the boy finds himself in a love-hate position at adolescence, being emotionally attached to his mother as a source of love and comfort, but rejecting her because she is also his source of authority. This is further complicated by the fact that his mother also has a similar ambivalent attitude toward him, because he is a male, as well as her child, and therefore a member of that "no good" group, the other sex.

At the beginning of this stage, the boy cannot openly attack his own mother (and her values) either to himself or to his peers. His emotional stability will not allow him to do this, for his oedipal attractions fasten his affections on his mother. But his impulses are not unified, for his mother (or some other woman) has been the source of authority from which he must react in order to achieve manhood. And the fact that it has been a woman who has thus threatened his potential virility with her values and her authority makes the reversal of his attitudes that much more potentially explosive. Yet reverse them he must, for not to do so would be to place oneself in a vulnerable position with his peers and with the older males. So he must in some way exorcize her influence. He therefore creates a playground which enables him to attack some other person's mother, in full knowledge that that person must come back and insult his own. Thus someone else is doing the job for him, and between them they are castigating all that is feminine, frail, unmanly. (This is why the implications of homosexuality are also invoked.) By such a ritualizing of the exorcism procedure, the combatants are also beginning to build their own image of sexual superiority, for these rhymes and taunts not only free otherwise repressed aggressions against feminine values, but they also affirm their own masculine abilities. To say "I fucked your mother" is not only to say that womanly weakness is ridiculous, but that the teller's virility has been exercised. At the same time he has prepared a defense for himself against incest, homosexuality, or any other forbidden sexual motive. In this way the youths prepare themselves for the hypermasculine world of the gang.

But the "dozens" functions as more than simply a mutual exorcism society. It also serves to develop one of the devices by which the nascent man will have to defend himself — the verbal contest.[11] It is not gratuitous that this *agon* should first arise at the period of emerging sexual awareness. Through the "dozens" the youth has his first real chance of declaring the differences between male and female and of taking sides in the struggle. The feminine world that has gripped and yet rejected him has been rejected in kind and by a complete negation. (It is not unusual for such complete rejection to occur toward something that has so nearly seduced us to its values.) Significantly, this first "manly" step is done with a traditional manly tool, the power of words. Thus this declaration of sexual awakening and independence also provides the youth with a weapon of sexual power, one which he will have to cultivate and use often.

The importance of these contests is heightened when one realizes that they are indulged in by the very ones who are most conscious of their appearance of virility to the outside. Being bested in a verbal battle in a group of this sort has immense potential repercussions because of the terror of disapproval, of being proved ineffectual and therefore effeminate, in the eyes of peers. This leads to the apparent paradox that those who are most afraid of public humiliation have institutionalized a procedure of humiliation for the purpose of releasing aggressions and repressed instincts, while at the same time learning verbal skills.

11. Johann Huizinga in Homo Ludens, *A Study of the Play Element in Culture* (Boston, 1950), p. 65, in discussing the widespread nature of this type of insult contest, says:

> The nobleman demonstrates his virtue by feats of strength, skill, courage, wit, wisdom, wealth, or liberality. For want of these he may yet excel in a contest of words, that is to say, he may either himself praise the virtues in which he wishes to excel his rivals, or have them praised for him by a poet or a herald. This boosting of one's own virtue as a form of contest slips over quite naturally into contumely of one's adversary, and this in its turn becomes a contest in its own right. It is remarkable how large a place these bragging and scoffing matches occupy in the most diverse civilizations.

Earlier he has equated virtue and virility, so that the sexual nature of these contests is within his plan. Elliott, *Power of Satire*, devotes a major part of his book showing how satire derives from just such contests. He adds the factor of the magic quality of words and how they can have power over an adversary. Oliver, *Blues*, p. 128, sees the "dozens" as also coming from the idea of casting spells with words. He indicates that the game developed out of a contest of real enmities, with an offended man "putting his foot up" (jamming the door of his cabin with his foot) and singing a blues that "put the Dozens" at the expense of his enemy, "calling out his name." This would agree in many respects with Tamony's derivation of the word (cf. n. 5).

It is astonishing to find that the same people for whom ridicule's destructive power holds such terror institution-alize it for therapeutic purposes; they turn its primary function inside out as it were, and ridicule properly conducted becomes a thing to be enjoyed for the health of society.[12]

This is only a seeming paradox, however, for the "dozens" situation calls for extreme permissiveness, which must apply as much to the audience as to the contestants. Beyond this, one would not play the "dozens" with just anyone, but someone with whom it was safe to play. The boys then are developing the tools of battle on their own home field.

Mechanisms like this verbal game exist in many groups of adolescents, passing out of use as the problems of that age are solved. But playing remains a part of the Camingerly man's life for a long time, though as mentioned, not in the same ritualized form. The fact that later uses are more inflammatory indicates strongly that the problems have not only not been solved but have, in fact, gotten worse.

Such verbal contests remain extremely important in their lives, but their expression mutates, becomes more complex both in vocabulary and in strategy. The youths become more assured in their use of words, but not in their masculinity. Other men continue to represent challenges to the youths' maleness, and as a result, most conversations turn into word battles, albeit comic and friendly ones. In other words, the release of aggression through ritual word-battles still has group sanction and provides a release from anxiety while remaining a masculine expression. Here, for example, is a comic routine given by "Kid." This uses many of the conversational devices observable in the group's discourse, but because it is a routine, it brings them to a higher pitch.

"Man, why you want to look at me like that?"

" 'Cause you ugly."

"I'm ugly? You got the nerve to call me ugly?"

"Yeah, you ugly."

"No, I ain't."

"Look, boy, you so ugly that the stork that brought you here should be locked up by the F.B.I."

12. Elliott, *Power of Satire*, p. 78.

"Look here, man, you was so ugly when you was a baby that your mother had to put a sheet on your face so sleep could creep up on you."

"And your girl, your wife ain't no cuter."

"Wait a minute. Don't you talk about my wife."

"Your wife is ugly. Me and your wife went out to get a drink and have a good time and she was so ugly she had to put on sneaks to sneak up on the drinks. Now you know there ain't no sense to that. She look like something I used to feed peanuts to in the zoo."

"You calling my wife ugly?"

"No, I ain't saying she's ugly. I just said she was ruined. Now I don't know where she was but when they was giving out looks she must have been hiding down in the cellar somewhere. And you. When they was giving out looks you must have been playing craps. You look like you been slapped in the face with a stick of dynamite and knocked down with a sack of razor blades. You ought to be 'shamed of yourself."

But the "good talker" is not just the good arguer. He is also the story teller, and the stories he tells represent a further ability of his to convince and thus illustrate his masculine power. The routine above shows some of the boastful and deprecatory techniques with which Negro parlance abounds. It indicates that the verbal strategy so important in Negro life involves an attempt to parade strength through boasting and through "putting the other down." But a further strength is offered in this dialogue, for the narrator has become both sides in this contest, and therefore cannot lose. His assumed *persona* can only be enhanced by the dazzling verbal display. He, as a performer, is assuming all of the strengths of the combatant, without having to be afraid of any of the consequences.

But this is a routine, not a story. Tales, jokes, anecdotes, any fictive expression, involve a strategy one step more complex. In narratives, the performer is utilizing the most subtle of word possibilities of which he is capable with his range of experience. He is defeating his peers through his use of words (by comparison rather than by actual besting), but at the same time he is creating a world wholly his own. He is master of the situation he is narrating; he is the director of the lives of the heroes of the pieces and of the structure in which they are appearing. He is able to achieve this kind of control, not only through the force of his vocal powers, but through the creation of a narrative *persona* called, for want of a better term, the "intrusive 'I'."

Throughout the narratives we are conscious of a close relationship between the hero of the tale and the person doing the narration. In most cases, especially in the toasts, the point of view is strictly first person, allowing the complete identification of narrator and hero. In others, this identification is put at a slight remove by placing the narration in the third person, but allowing the hero some attribute by which one can identify him with the narrator (a colored man competing with members of other races, a man of words in a dupable group, etc.).

This "intrusive 'I'" is a convenient gambit in the narrative game. It allows the narrator two *personae* at the same time, his own as narrator or commentator and that of the hero. He can unite the two at will if he is artful in his narration; he can also dissociate the two if he wishes. It is important in certain stories that he be able to vary his position, as there will be actions which he (the narrator) will not approve, or situations in which he would not want to be found. As opposed to the classic English and Scottish ballads, there is nothing removed, long ago, impersonal about these narratives. Even when the narrator's *persona* retreats from that of the hero or main character, the narrator remains, intruding as a commentator. The "I" never disappears completely, though it may occasionally recede temporarily.[13] Thus, any of the battles won, physical or verbal, are won by both the hero and the narrator. Yet he is in so much control of this small universe that he can be both protagonist and antagonist in this contest. He directs this battle as well as winning it. The glory is all his and the triumph is more than just a verbal one.

13. Odum and Johnson, *The Negro and His Songs* (Chapel Hill, 1925), pp. 279 ff., use the term "the Dominant Self" in a similar sense, but in reference to Negro songs:

> The self feeling is important in the Negro pictures. The individual plays the most important part and the singer is most generally the subject of the object of the action concerning which he sings. "I" and "my" are the keynotes to the great majority of situations. Next to the first person, "you" follows prominently; but it will be seen that the second person is ordinarily only the object-relation of the first person. "You" must do something, but it is either something that "I" have done, think you ought to do, or something that you must do in order to understand what "I" now understand. . . . For the Negro there is largely himself and the other person.

But the victory is Pyrrhic, for the gains are shortlived and must be played and replayed to continue to have any effect. Word ability has grown and strategy has become more complex but the weapons of the struggle remain the same. The culmination of verbal growth occurs in the "toast," the long narrative poems constructed with the highest wit and performed only by the the best talkers. But the toast utilizes the same devices of rhyme, rhythm, word-play and repetition which we find in the earliest of verbal triumphs, the children's rhymes. Remarkably enough, even the metrical structure of the toast (four-stress lines) is but a complication of that used in nursery rhymes. The toast-teller is returning to safe ground to fight his recurring battle. He is further strengthening his arsenal by placing the battle, fought in the fictive battlefield, wholly under his control.

The man of words is an important member of the Camingerly male group. His ability with words is as highly valued as physical strength. There are two possible outlets for his ability: (1) as a bard or singer, on the street corner with the gang, or at parties, dances and other heterosexual occasions, and (2) as a preacher. It may seem strange that preaching asks for the same type of word control and has the same emotional basis in sexually oriented contest as the bard, but such is the case. Not only does the similarity exist on the basis of ability to persuade, and to construct effective fictive playgrounds (in the use of Bible stories), but also on the level of the overt contest of words. One of the most important recent phenomena in regard to the Negro preacher is the preaching contest where two or three or more preachers appear on the same platform, and see who can create the greatest emotional appeal, and who can convert the most sinners.

What is *not* surprising is that the two groups of "good talkers" violently hate each other. The preacher of course regards the street-corner bard as a corrupt sinner. The other goes even farther. He gets back by telling stories about the hypocrisy of the preacher, of his effeminacy, homosexuality, and inefficacy with words.

The difference between the two "talkers" is that the preacher directs his words to women as well as men. He is able to use the sexual capacity of words for overt sexual purpose, and in the world of the streets he is consequently renowned for his sexual duplicity. The bard usually does not have the same opportunity. Most of his word-creations are for the entertainment of other men. He is of, and entertains for, a group still acutely suffering from the problems of rejection from home and the consequent love-hate situation engendered. These men only make alliances with the opposite sex when their biological (and social) drives force them to. It is no wonder that fear will overcome these drives in due time; most of the women play on the fear to get as much from the temporary cohabitation as possible. The homosexual, anti-feminine world of the early adolescent remains the safe one for this group, and the bard remains its spokesman.

The man of words is immensely important as a representative of the dispossessed men of Camingerly. By exhibiting his witty abilities, by creating new and vital folkloric expression, he is able to effect a temporary release from anxiety for both himself and his audience. By creating these playgrounds for the playing out of aggressions, he is able to achieve a kind of precarious masculine identity for himself and his group in a basically hostile environment.

CHAPTER III

THE HEROES

THE DISCUSSION, HERETOFORE, HAS BEEN DIRECTED TOWARD DIFFERENT aspects of the Camingerly man's struggle for ego identity and his frustrations in this endeavor. In this chapter the problem will be discussed from another point of view. In order to examine the correlations between the gang values, word contests, and the heroes of the narratives (and their actions), the most forceful and significant of the narratives of these men will be anatomized.

In the last chapter it was mentioned that the heroes and the narrators are even more closely related than in most fictive expressions of other groups because of the importance of the narrators' word control in the psychic release afforded by the pieces. One technical aspect of this close identification is the device called the "intrusive 'I' " — whereby the narrator, either through narration in the first person or through insertion of his own commentary, insists upon the recognition of his presence in the total world of the piece. Psychologists Freud and Rank, Jung and his followers Campbell and Neumann, among others,[1] have effectively shown that there is an important further relationship which the narrative can have with the narrator-actor and the audience. Their remarks make evident the integral relation which exists between the significant

1. See specifically C. G. Jung, *Symbols of Transformation* (New York, 1956); Joseph Campbell, *The Hero With a Thousand Faces* (New York, 1949); Erich Neumann, *The Origins and History of Consciousness* (New York, 1954); Otto Rank, *The Myth of the Birth of the Hero* (New York, 1959).

action of the hero and the values and attempts toward psychic re-orientation of the talker and his audience.

The values a story proposes through its action, if transmitted and appreciated by the group, will represent those of the group. But values are hardly static; they are mutable, and they mutate as the situations and conflicts of the group change. The conflict of the hero must in some way echo the conflict of the narrator and his audience in order for the story to get the approbation of being heard, applauded and remembered. The fictive expression of the narrative is more complex strategically than other "play" expressions (because of its submerged, sublimated, vicarious nature) but it still reflects the same kinds of problems as the lore involving the simpler strategies. Just as our simpler "play" offers an opportunity to symbolically act out a conflict in contest terms, the fictive experience allows us to identify with those who are also doing a similar acting-out. As a psychic experience the fictive expression offers examples of approved desired action (the active expression of which is, in most cases, denied us because of various inhibitory factors). But it can go much farther, because it can offer an end to the conflict, a resolution. In dialectic terms, a synthesis can emerge: in psychic terms, a transformation or re-integration. Thus one must look not only to the hero's position in the conflict, but also to the results (victory, reconciliation, marriage, retribution, etc.) in an analysis of values in narratives.

The question which immediately emerges when considering the Camingerly narratives is with what sort of heroes one finds these men identifying and expressing themselves. The heroes of this group fit into two major categories, the trickster (or "clever hero") and the badman (or a special type of "contest hero").

The trickster figure has been the most identified hero in Negro lore throughout this country and the West Indies. This is perhaps due to a real prevalence of this type character in Negro story. On the other hand, it may be because Joel Chandler Harris noticed the similarities between European animal trickster tales and those found among the Southern Negroes, and collected and printed many of these stories in his Uncle Remus books. His success with these works may have influenced future collections of the same type.[2]

2. Richard M. Dorson seems to agree with this point of view:

"Influenced by Harris . . . subsequent collections emphasized animal tales." (*American Folklore* [Chicago, 1959], p. 176.)

At any rate, we can no longer claim that the trickster figure is the only, or even the dominating, hero type encountered in Negro tales. But he is still to be encountered among the Negroes in the guise of the "Signifying Monkey," the "colored man," "John," and (sometimes) the preacher.[3]

The trickster or "clever hero" is one who triumphs or functions by means of his wits. Or as Orrin Klapp has noted:

> He either vanquishes or escapes from a formidable opponent by a ruse. The clever hero is usually smaller and weaker than those with whom he is matched, frequently being a diminutive animal. The victory of the clever hero is the perennial triumph of brains over brawn, *la sagesse des petits.*[4]

Perhaps the *petit* quality to which Clapp refers has implications beyond matters of size. The trickster figure functions in society not at all like a small animal; he acts like a small human being, a child. His delight in tricking is reminiscent of the similar pleasure children derive from tricking their peers. Indeed, in almost every sense the trickster *is* a child. He has no perceptible set of values except those dictated by the demands of his id. One could not say that he is immoral; he is, rather, amoral, because he exists in the stage before morality has had a chance to inculcate itself upon his being. He is "the spirit of disorder, the enemy of boundaries."[5] "Although he is not really evil," says C. G. Jung (evil = conscious reaction to established order), "he does the most atrocious things from sheer unconsciousness and unrelatedness."[6] He is an individual just beginning on the quest for ego identity; "A minatory

---

3. Dorson's published collections offer the best cross section of recent Negro tales, including important stories of the type listed here.

4. Orrin E. Klapp, "The Folk Hero," *Journal of American Folklore,* LXII (1949), p. 20.

5. Karl Kerenyi, "The Trickster in Relation to Greek Mythology," in Paul Radin's *The Trickster* (New York, 1956), p. 185. Kerenyi goes on, commenting on the release mechanism of the trickster story:

> Disorder belongs to the totality of life, and the spirit of this disorder is the trickster . . . the function of his mythology, of the tales told about him, is to add disorder to order and so make a whole, to render possible, within the fixed bounds of what is permitted, an experience of what is not permitted.

6. C. G. Jung, "On the Psychology of the Trickster Figure," in Radin, *Trickster,* p. 203.

and ridiculous figure, he stands at the very beginning of the way of individuation."[7]

The existence of this amoral, this childlike hero[8] creates important questions. If the narrative functions both as an expression of otherwise repressed anxieties and as a "tutor, the shaper of identities," why has the Negro chosen to represent himself and his values as childlike? Why has he chosen to appear to regress to an early stage of psychological development? There are a number of possible answers. In the guise of the small (childlike) animal, the Negro is perhaps fulfilling the role in which he has been cast by his white "masters" (the childish "Uncle Tom" who is convinced of his simple state and thus needs the protection of his masters). At the same time, in this role he is able to show a superiority over those larger or more important than himself through his tricks, thus partially salving his wounded ego. This is apparent in the "Marster-John" cycles where he is tricking the white man, or in the Br'er Rabbit stories where he is getting the better of larger animals. This might be the function of the trickster on the sociological level: a veiled reaction against overdomination while preserving the role in which he has been cast.

The psychological satisfaction of the trickster story is similar. As Melville Herskovits says of this figure in general: "Psychologically the role of the trickster seems to be that of projecting the insufficiencies of man in his universe onto a smaller creature, who in besting his larger adversaries, permits the satisfaction of an obvious identification to those who recount or listen to these stories."[9] The trickster, then, may represent to the Negro, through identification, the small, often assailed hero in control of his world through guile (the only defense available to the Negro under the slave and the post-slave system).

But it is not the trickster's smallness or his guile which really provides the Negro with his greatest source of anxiety-release. It is his amorality. Reaction against authority, in his deprived situation, is forbidden. But this revolt is vitally important to the psychic growth of the individual. The only rebellion available then is

7. Jung, "Trickster Figure," p. 211.

8. This identity of child and trickster seems to have been recognized early, as a trickster festival mocking the church or government in the Middle Ages, was called among other things *festum puerorum*. (Jung, "Trickster Figure," p. 198.)

9. "Trickster" in *The Standard Dictionary of Folklore, Mythology and Legend* (New York, 1949), p. 1123.

through the actions of a figure who has undergone an (apparent) regression to the childlike (or animal) state where he is not responsible for his actions because he has not yet learned the difference between right and wrong. His acts are unconscious, therefore they preclude his ability to make choices. "He is both subhuman and superhuman, a bestial and divine being, whose chief and most alarming characteristic is his unconsciousness."[10] The controlling factor of his being is apparently the rampant id, that element of our psyche outside the confines of the prison of society. He lives, then, in the permissive world accorded to other childish individuals. The trickster provides a full escape for those Negroes who have been offered no opportunity to feel a control over their own lives, no method for developing their egos through a specific action. As such, the trickster may reflect the real childlike state of a severely stunted ego, or a veiled revolt against authority in the only terms available. At the same time the performer and audience are enabled to express some of their aggressive impulses in this acceptable form.

But the badman, not the trickster, is the most popular hero among these Negroes. The badman represents a conception quite different from the trickster. He is, in many ways, a "contest hero": ". . . the [contest] hero is placed in the position of publicly defeating all rivals. The winner is acclaimed hero or champion. The rivalry may be in skill, fortitude, virtue, or in main strength but such proof of the hero by contest with other humans is almost universal."[11]

The badmen of this group, "Stackolee," "The Great MacDaddy," Jesse and Frank James, are like the classic conception of the "contest hero" in that they are powerful, do overcome all rivals, and are (secretly) acclaimed as heroes because of their strength and will. This is almost the point where the resemblance ceases, for the badman does not seem to work for the benefit of society.

Where the trickster is a perpetual child, the badman is a perpetual adolescent. His is a world of overt rebellion. He commits acts against taboos and mores in full knowledge of what he is doing. In fact, he glories in this knowledge of revolt. He is consciously and sincerely immoral. As a social entity he is rebelling against white man's laws. As a male he is revolting against woman's

10. Jung, "Trickster Figure," p. 203.
11. Klapp, "Folk Hero," p. 19.

attempt to emasculate him. As a poor man he is reacting against his perpetual poverty.

But his expression is not unbridled like the trickster's; rather, it is directed, though not in positive terms as in the usual contest hero, but rather against anything which attempts to constrain him. His expression of his ego is in his physical prowess. He is the "hard man," who, because of his strength, accepts the challenges of the world. He is ruler through his powers and anything which threatens his domain threatens his ego and must be removed. Where guile and banter are the weapons of the trickster, arrogance and disdain serve the badman. He does not aim to be a god, but rather to be the eternal man in revolt, the devil. He is the epitome of virility, of manliness on display.

The rebellion against authority exemplified in the badman is much more overt than that in the trickster. Here we have the open defiance which we are able to see exhibited in real life among the Negroes in the activities of their gangs and the establishment of their gang leaders, and, with some of them, later in their lives as criminals. The values of this group in revolt are implied in the conduct of their badman heroes. Life, as well as lore, admits a more open expression of revolt than in the past, and this is echoed in the nature of the heroes worshiped by these Negroes.

Perhaps it would be more instructive to apply some of these generalizations to specific narratives. Let us first look at a tale of a trickster, "The Signifying Monkey and the Lion." The opening makes it clear what sort of creature the monkey is:

> Deep down in the jungle, so they say,
> There's a signifying motherfucker down the way.
> There hadn't been no disturbing in the jungle for quite
>   a bit,
> For up jumped the monkey in the tree one day and
>   laughed, "I guess I'll start some shit."

The name "Signifying Monkey" shows him to be a trickster, "signifying" being the language of trickery, that set of words or gestures which arrives at "direction through indirection" and which is used often to humiliate an adversary, especially among the young. As discussed in the last chapter, "signifying" is a common device used by Negro children.

The monkey, using this device of the child, is shown to be invoking his powers in an attempt to stir up trouble. And the dialogue that ensues shows how the process of "signifying" finds expression.

The monkey is a master of the technique. Without any known provocation, he involves the lion in a fight with the elephant:

> Now the lion come through the jungle one peaceful day,
> When the signifying monkey stopped him and this is what
>   he started to say.
> He said, "Mr. Lion," he said, "A bad old motherfucker
>   (i.e., elephant) down your way,"
> He said, "Yeah, the way he talks about your folks is a
>   certain shame.
> I even heard him curse when he mentioned your grand-
>   mother's name."
> The lion's tail shot back like a forty-four
> When he went down that jungle in all uproar.

The fight that ensues between the lion and the elephant is almost epic. The lion gets badly beaten, as could be expected. The monkey, "signifying," proceeds to rub salt in the lion's wounds from the safety of his tree.

> When they was fussing and fighting, lion come back
>   through the jungle more dead than alive,
> When the monkey started more of that signifying jive.
> He said, "Damn, Mr. Lion, you went through here yester-
>   day, the jungle rung.
> Now you come back today, damn near hung."
> He said, "Now you come by here when me and my wife
>   trying to get a little bit,
> Tell me that 'I rule' shit. It just tried it out. You ain't
>   shit."
> He said, "Shut up, motherfucker, you better not roar,
> 'Cause I'll come down there and kick your ass some more."

But the monkey's "signifying" leads him to get excited and he falls and is captured by the lion. He must use all of his guile to get out of this situation, first calling on the sympathy of the lion, and then on his pride:

> The monkey looked up with a tear in his eyes.
> He said, "Please, Mr. Lion, I apologize."
> He said, "You lemme get my head out the sand,
> Ass out the grass, I'll fight you like a natural man."
> The lion jumped back and squared for a fight.
> The motherfucking monkey jumped clear out of sight.

71

In many versions, the story ends here. In some others, however, the monkey once again, while "signifying" from his tree-retreat, loses his footing and this time the lion puts an end to the monkey's ways:

> Again he started getting panicked and jumping up and
>   down.
> His feet slipped and his ass hit the ground.
> Like a bolt of lightning, a stripe of white heat,
> Once more the lion was on the monkey with all four feet.
> Monkey looked up again with tears in his eyes.
> He said, "Please, Mr. Lion, I apologize."
> Lion said, "Ain't gonna be no apologizing.
> I'ma put an end to his motherfucking signifying."
> Now when you go through the jungle, there's a tomb-
>   stone so they say,
> "Here the Signifying Monkey lay."

So in some versions the unusual situation occurs where the hero dies. This fact seems significant. The trickster, as we have noted, is the eternal child. The Negro trickster story had a real place in the ante-bellum and post-bellum South where this was the sort of pose which the Negro was forced to assume, the masochistic, subservient, childlike creature, the "Uncle Tom" who was allowed his few tricks as his idiosyncracies. But the attitudes, the values inherent in this approach to revolt have changed considerably. Because of recent developments in the lot of the Negro, especially in the Northern cities such as Philadelphia, he has been able to express his aggressions more overtly, and thus to escape his image as a perpetual child. With the break-up of the land-oriented matrifocal family of the slave, the men have escaped from the actively masochistic role[12] (the smiling, fawning, "white man's nigger") they were driven to by the plantation sponsored, mother-dominated home in which they were obliged to live. The heroes of this earlier group

12. Wilhelm Reich agreed that behind the masochist's behavior lay a desire to provoke authority figures, but he disagreed that this was in order to bribe the superego or to execute a dreaded punishment. Rather, he maintained, this grandiose provocation represented a defense against punishment and anxiety by substituting a milder punishment and by placing the provoked authority figure in such a light as to justify the masochist's reproach. "See how badly you treat me." Behind such a provocation is a deep disappointment of the masochist's excessive demand for love based on the fear of being left alone. (Leland E. Hinsie and Robert Jean Campbell, *Psychoanalytic Dictionary*, p. 443.)

reflected the values of those existing in this system. Their trickster protagonists existed in a permissive, childlike, neuter world, divorced from sexual conflict completely. To regress was the only way in which these men could express aggressions at all, and thus their fictive expressions had these aggressively infantile heroes.

In light of these remarks, it should come as little surprise that the trickster finds so small a place in the folklore of this group of Negro city dwellers, and when he does persist, his maneuvers lead him not to triumph but to death. Neuterism and childism are as non-masculine as femininity. Lack of "guts" ("balls" would be more precise) in any form is lack of manliness. The trickster and his mechanisms of defence must be eschewed by those espousing gang existence.

The trickster, when he does emerge in Camingerly narratives, is usually quite different from his form in the Old South, though there are some stories that have persisted from that area and era. The things which the monkey says are obviously motivated by sadistic impulses. He wants to see the lion hurt. Br'er Rabbit can be equally sadistic in strategy, but he must mask his aggressions completely if his kind of tricks is to work. But then, two tricksters are working with different dupes. Rabbit is contesting for his life against those not only much bigger than he, but those who desire to eat him. His reasons for tricking in most of the stories about him are defensive in the broadest sense of the term. He must preserve himself from those who want to consume him, a projection of the same emasculation fears which our city dwellers exhibit in their stories. Being in a thoroughly dominated position, both within the family and in ante-bellum type society, his only protection for his masculinity is a retreat to a seemingly pre-sexual stage. He must in a sense play the "clown," be the impotent man.[13]

The monkey, on the other hand, has no apparent reason for his trickery beyond purely sadistic purpose, wanting to see another

13. As Martin Grotjahn points out in his popular study of the subject, *Beyond Laughter* (New York, 1957), the comic is a father figure with the sexuality of the child. Most of the comic's symbols (baggy pants, always falling down, floppy hats, stooped-over walk, drunken state, etc.) emphasize the comic's impotence, are symbols of the "ridiculed penis." Children laugh at clowns, Grotjahn avers, because they represent father-figures without the threatening aspects of their superior strength and virility, thus are on equal ground as the child in his struggle for his mother's affections. The clown operates much more complexly, it seems to me, however. The child sees in the clown a representation of himself, using (apparently) asexual tricks for aggressive purposes.

(and bigger) get beaten. He is the epitome of the little man talking
big. His brag talk is more adolescent than childish. His problems
are cloaked in terms of the ego, not the id. His tricks rely more on
banter than on real guile.

Illustrative of the rejection of the older trickster expression is
the change which occurs to Brother Rabbit in the imaginations of
these city dwellers. The little animal becomes the "hard man." Here
is a comparison of two tellings of the same story. The first comes
from Joel Chandler Harris and is thus a semi-artistic rehandling of
a Negro folktale of the Old South. The second I collected from
"Kid." We cannot rule out the possible influence of the Walt
Disney comic strip on the transmission process here, but as "Kid"
tells it, it is quite changed from any telling, Harris, Disney, or
otherwise.

> "One time," said Uncle Remus, "Brer Fox, he tuck'n ax
> some er de yuther creeturs ter he house. He ax Brer B'ar,
> en Brer Wolf, en Brer 'Coon, but he ain't ax Brer Rabbit.
> All de same, Brer Rabbit got win' un it, en he 'low dat ef
> he don't go, he 'speck he have much fun ez de nex' man.
> "De creeturs w'at git de invite, dey tuck'n 'semble at
> Brer Fox house, en Brer Fox, he ax um in en got um
> cheers, en dey sot dar en laugh en talk, twel, bimeby,
> Brer Fox, he fotch out a bottle er dram en lay 'er out on
> de side-bode, en den he sorter step back en say, sezee:
> " 'Des step up, gentermens, en he'p you'se'f,' en you
> better b'lieve dey he'p derse'f.
> "W'iles dey wuz drinkin' en drammin' en gwine on,
> w'at you 'speck Brer Rabbit doin'? You des well make up
> yo' min' dat Brer Rabbit monst'us busy, kase he 'uz sailin'
> 'roun' fixin' up his tricks. Long time 'fo' dat, Brer Rabbit
> had been at a borbycue whar dey was a muster, en w'iles
> all de folks 'uz down at de spring eatin' dinner, Brer
> Rabbit he crope up en run off wid one er de drums. Dey
> wuz a big drum en a little drum, en Brer Rabbit he snatch
> up de littles' one en run home.
> "Now, den, w'en he year 'bout de yuther creeturs gwine
> ter Brer Fox house, w'at do Brer Rabbit do but git out
> dis rattlin' drum en make de way down de road todes whar
> dey is. He tuk dat drum," continued Uncle Remus, with
> great elation of voice and manner, "en he went down de

road todes Brer Fox house, en he make 'er talk like thunner mix up wid hail. Hit talk lak dis:

"'Diddybum, diddybum, diddybum-bum-bum-diddybum!'

"De creeturs, dey 'uz a-drinkin', en a-drammin', en a-gwine on at a terrible rate, en dey ain't year de racket, but all de same, yer come Brer Rabbit:

"'Diddybum, diddybum, diddybum-bum-bum — diddybum!'

"Bimeby Brer 'Coon, w'ich he allers got one year hung out fer de news, he up'n ax Brer Fox w'at dat, en by dat time all de creeturs stop en lissen; but all de same, yer come Brer Rabbit:

"'Diddybum, diddybum, diddybum-bum-bum — diddybum!'

"De creeturs dey keep on lis'nin', en Brer Rabbit keep on gittin' nigher, twel bimeby Brer 'Coon retch und' de cheer fer he hat, en say, sezee:

"'Well, gents, I 'speck I better be gwine. I tole my ole 'oman dat I don't be gone a minnit, en yer 't is 'way 'long in de day.'

"Wid dat Brer 'Coon he skip out, but he ain't git much furder dan de back gate, 'fo' yer come all de yuther creeturs like dey 'uz runnin' a foot-race, en ole Brer Fox wuz wukkin' in de lead."

"Dar, now!" exclaimed 'Tildy, with great fervor.

"Yasser! dar dey wuz, en dar dey went," continued Uncle Remus. "Dey tuck nigh cuts, en dey scramble over one er 'n'er, en dey ain't res' twel dey git in de bushes.

"Ole Brer Rabbit, he came on down de road — diddybum, diddybum, diddybum-bum-bum — en bless gracious! w'en he git ter Brer Fox house dey ain't nobody dar. Brer Rabbit is dat owdacious, dat he hunt all 'roun' twel he fine de a'r-hole er de drum, en he put his mouf ter dat en sing out, sezee:

"'Is dey anybody home?' en den he answer hisse'f, sezee, 'Law, no, honey — folks all gone.'

"Wid dat, ole Brer Rabbit break loose en laugh, he did, fit ter kill hisse'f, en den he slam Brer Fox front gate wide open, en march up ter de house. W'en he git dar, he kick de do' open en hail Brer Fox, but nobody ain't dar, en Brer

Rabbit he walk in en take a cheer, en make hisse'f at home
wid puttin' his foots on de sofy en spittin' on de flo'.

"Brer Rabbit ain't sot dar long 'fo' he ketch a whiff er de
dram —"

"You year dat?" exclaimed 'Tildy, with convulsive admiration.

" — 'Fo' he ketch a whiff er de dram, en den he see it on
de side-bode, en he step up en drap 'bout a tumbeler full
some 'ers down in de neighborhoods er de goozle. Brer
Rabbit mighty lak some folks I knows. He tuck one tumbeler full, en 't wa'nt long 'fo' he tuck 'n'er'n, en w'en a man
do dis a-way," continued Uncle Remus, somewhat apolo-
getically, "he bleedz ter git drammy."

(The rest of the story is concerned with Br'er Rabbit getting caught
because of his inebriated state and then how he escapes by a ruse
similar to the usual one found in the tar-baby story.)[14]

Here is the text from "Kid":

Brother Fox had been trying to get Brother Rabbit for
a long time. So he told Brother Bear one day, he said,
"Brother Bear, now I know how we can trick that old rabbit into giving himself up." Brother Bear said, "How will
we do it?" He said, "Now we'll invite all the animals in the
forest to a party, all except Brother Rabbit. He'll be so
embarrassed and hurt that he won't want to live and he'll
give himself up. And we'll have rabbit stew before the
week is up."

So all the invitations were around. So that Saturday
evening, you know, all the animals were going down to
the party. Even the skunk washed up and put the perfume
on, went into the party. Brother Rabbit was sitting on the
post and all. Said, "Where you all going?" "Down to
Brother Buzzard's house." "Brother Buzzard?" "Yeah.
Brother Fox is giving a party over there." Rabbit ran to
the house and got dressed, and ran down to the house.
Brother Buzzard said, "Sorry, Brother Fox and Brother
Bear say they don't want you in it. I'm sorry, that's what
they told me."

14. Joel Chandler Harris, *Nights With Uncle Remus* (Boston and New York,
1883), pp. 62-65.

So the Rabbit turned away with his head turned down. He feeling sad, downhearted, tears in his eyes. Felt like he was alone in the world. But then he got mad. He said, "I know what I'll do." He went home and shined his shoes, and got his shotgun and went back and kicked the door open. "Don't a motherfucker move." He walked over the table, got all he wanted to eat. Walked over to the bar and got himself all he wanted to drink. He reached over and he grabbed the lion's wife and he dance with her. Grabbed the ape's wife and did it to her. Then he shit in the middle of the floor and he walked out.

So after he left, you know, the giraffe jumped up. He said, "Who was that little long-eared, fuzzy-tailed motherfucker just walked in here with all that loud noise?" The bear looked at him and said, "Now look, no use getting loud. You was here when he was here, why didn't you ask then?" (Like guys, they like that. You always get bad after the other person is gone, but you never say nothing while they is there.)

The trickster has indeed become the "hard man."

In this retreat from trickster values, agility is an attribute much more acceptably male than guile because it contributes to "style." In his role as the great pool and card player, the monkey finds greater success, as is seen in the toast of "The Monkey and the Baboon." Here, the monkey is adept at games and his agility pays off; he acquires status symbols in his "smart" manner and his sharp clothes.

Now a few stalks shook and a few leaves fell,
And up jumped the monkey, sharp as hell.
Had a one-button roll, two-button satch.
You know, one of them boolhipper coats with a belt in
the back.

The monkey still has power with his words, but he uses it simply to add a brilliant finish to the veneer of his actions. For instance, he is not satisfied to win at a game of cooncan; he must cap the game by laying down his cards in the following flourish of victory:

So hop Mr. Rabbit and skip Mr. Bear.
It's gonna look mighty shady but there's 'leven of them
there.
(*A lay of eleven cards wins the game.*)

But agility is not the ultimate in values to these men; more highly considered are meanness, strength, and the ability to revolt in the face of authority and possible death. Death does not matter, just style of living. If dying results from this style, that is all right. In this realm, the badman reigns. He will often say, "I'm a bad mother-fucker and I don't mind dying." He is highly conscious of his role. The most characteristic and exciting of the badmen is "Stackolee."

Stack is a mean man, a purveyor of violence. He does not hesi-tate to hurt, taunt, kill if someone offers him the slightest insult or challenge. All acts are executed with the greatest show of strength and arrogance, and with the smartest kind of flourish. Down on his luck when we first meet him, Stack doesn't let that affect his pride; it seems to make him even meaner and more deadly.

> I walked through water and I waded through mud.
> I came to a little-old hole in the wall called "The Bucket
>   of Blood."
> I walked in, asked the man for something to eat.
> Do you know that bastard gave me a stale glass of water
>   and a fucked-up piece of meat.
> I said, "Raise motherfucker, do you know who I am?"
> He said, "Frankly, I don't give a damn."
> I knowed right then that sucker was dead.
> I throwed a thirty-eight shell through that motherfucker's
>   head.

A girl comes over and offers herself in an obvious attempt to keep him there until the murdered man's brother Benny Long (or Billy Lyons) gets there. He accepts both challenges and wins them in the grandest of styles. He is as magnificent in sex as he is in battle.

> "Hi there, baby, where's the bartender, if you please?"
> I said, "Look behind the bar, he's with his mind at ease."
> So she peeped at her watch, it was seven of eight.
> She said, "Come upstairs, baby, let me set you straight."
> Now, we went upstairs, the springs gave a twistle,
> I throwed nine inches of dick into that bitch before she
>   could move her gristle.
> Now we come downstairs big and bold.
> They was fucking on the bar, sucking on the floor.
> Then you could hear a pin drop. Benny Long come in.
> He walked over where his brother lay dead, and he calmly
>   said,

"Who had a nerve to put a hole in my brother's head?"
I said, "Me, motherfucker, to put your mind at ease.
I'm that bad-ass so-and-so they call 'Stackolee'."
He said, "I heard of you, Stack, from tales of old.
But you know you tore your ass when you fucked my hole.
But I'ma give you a chance my brother never got. I'ma
     give you a chance to run,
'Fore I reach in my cashmere and pull out my bad-ass
     gun."
Just then some old sucker over in the corner said, "Some-
     body call the law."
He stretched out and put a forty-five shell through that
     motherfucker's jaw.
A cute little broad came and said, "Benny, please."
He blowed that bitch down to her knees.
And out went the lights.
And Benny Long was in both of my 38 sights.
Now the lights came on and all the best.
I sent that sucker to eternal rest,
With thirteen 38 bullet holes 'cross his motherfucking
     chest.

Benny is just as mean and strong as Stack, so that Stack's triumph is a fitting one. An appropriate end to a story of this sort is Stack's violent boast:

I was raised in the backwoods, where my pa raised a bear.
And I got three sets of jawbone teeth and an extra layer
     of hair.
When I was three I sat in a barrel of knives.
Then a rattlesnake bit me, crawled off and died.
So when I come in here, I'm no stranger.
'Cause when I leave, my asshole print leaves "danger."

Because Stack is the prototype of the hero of this group it seems pertinent to examine his actions and values further. It is interesting to notice the relation of his values to those of the heroic age. Stack's actions exhibit the importance of bravery, honor (perhaps "face" would be better here) and ability with words, in his life. But Stack seems to be acting, at all times, for himself, unlike the epic heroes whose deeds represent their group. It is true that Stack's immediate ancestors were "bullies" and as such repre- sented the honor of a town or neighborhood, but Stack seems to have lost this motivation. His acts are an extension of his disturbed ego.

As representative of the group, the epic hero acts in order to protect his land, his home, his *women*. Odysseus's reunion with Penelope is not fortuitous action in that drama; it is the proper and full resolution of it. Through his protection of her and his home, his final actions are the epitome of heroic values. Stackolee acts for nothing but himself, and in direct rejection of women. Stack, the "hard man," doesn't owe any part of his existence to home or woman. He springs into the story full grown, independent, unattached to anything or anyone.[15] He is his own man. All the actions in the story are not only done in order to exercise his virility, but in direct rejection of the women or the feminine (wit-

15. John Henry is a much better illustration of this. He is the prototype of the "hard man" without any immorality. He channels his aggressions toward the machine which is attempting to emasculate him. His leaping into the world full grown (or nearly) is stressed in the songs about him, usually in the first few stanzas, and there is often a stanza following which promotes further the mystery of his birth ("Some say he was born in Texas," etc.) and stresses the aspect of him as being his own man. Commentators have long played down his obvious sexual prowess, indicated by the number of girl friends he had that remained true to him. Among the Camingerly men, he is remembered specifically for his sexual feats.

> When John Henry was a baby,
> You could hold him in the palm of your hand.
> But when he got nineteen years old,
> He could stand that pussy like a man.

> John Henry told his father,
> A man ain't nothing but a man.
> But before he'd let a piece of pussy go by,
> He'd die with his dick in his hand,
> Yeh, he'd die with his dick in his hand.

> Now John Henry took his girl friend
> He layed her 'pon the rock.
> When he got through he looked at her,
> "Umm, such good cock,
> Umm, such good cock."

> Now when John Henry died
> They say he died from shock.
> But if you want to know the truth
> He died from too much cock.
> Yes, the boy died from too much cock.

> Now they took John Henry's body,
> And they layed it in the sand.
> People come from far and near
> To see that good fucking man,
> Yeh, to see that good fucking man.

ness the confrontation with Billy's mother and girl friend). Billy is, as far as the dramatic action is concerned, but an extension of his mother's threat of retribution. Stack's feats, sexual and otherwise, are all motivated by women's challenges. He must prove himself, even if it means dying for it.

This brings up the two major problems in Stack's character and actions: (1) what is the reason for his sadistic action and (2) what is the relationship of this sadism to his self-destructive tendencies. In the broadest sense, sadism is an outlet for repressed male sexuality.

> Viewed as a perversion, sadism is a defense against castration fears. . . . What might happen to the subject passively is done actively to others — 'identification with the aggressor' . . . The discharge of aggression in itself may be pleasurable, but sadism further implies pleasure in the destruction of others.[16]

Not even active proof of virility, such as in the first shooting or the bedroom scene, is enough to assuage this man's severely dislocated ego. He indulges sexually because the girl offering herself does so as a challenge, aggravating his problems rather than soothing them. Because of the family orientation of the society which he represents, Stack's masculine instincts have been so severely restricted in their expression that he must reach deep into his physical resources to find any sort of satisfactory release:

> Sadism installed as the substitute outlet for a forbidden sexuality, it reaches back and absorbs the deeper personality urges out of which sex should emerge in the fullest and final flowering. Sadism is the only shoot left standing, harks back for its nourishment to the personality taproots of sex, and appropriates to its own perverse augmentation all their flow: the sense of individuality, the desire for importance, attention, power; the pleasure in controlling objects, the impulse toward violent activity, the urge toward fulfillment to the farthest reaches of the individual's biological possibilities.[17]

This leads us directly to the second part of our question, Stack's self-destructive tendencies. Stack's activities are not only sadistic,

16. Hinsie and Campbell, *Psychoanalytic Dictionary*, p. 653.
17. Legman, *Love and Death*, p. 62.

but they are consciously self-destructive (in a sense, masochistic). When he says, "Got a tombstone disposition and a graveyard mind, I'm a mean motherfucker and I don't mind dying" he is voicing the interrelationship of the two. Meanness and dying are part of the same style of life. He not only doesn't mind dying, he wants to!

In our discussion of the rejection of women and family, we have noticed that in many ways the men do not emerge unscathed. They are fixed in a permanent love-hate situation, one that causes a vacillation between violent attraction and equally violent rejection of women. This duality can be fully expressed in the sadistic act because both the attraction and the repulsion remain under the control of the actor. But the sadistic action itself must leave its mark, because ultimately it is anti-social and ends with a complete rejection. This must be atoned for, and Stack attempts to do this by dying, or at least coming so close that he attains part of the release of death. What he himself cannot do because of overt masochism, he has others do for him, by placing himself in a position where he may be hurt or killed. This way he has his cake and is able to eat it as well. The guilt accrued for his actions (activated by the attraction part of his ambivalent feelings, and expressed through the agency of society or the superego) is assuaged by the punishment accompanying his actions, and he is able to be punished in a style which fits the dominant image of himself.

But this punishment of living dangerously under the threat of death functions on another level. The love-hate situation which Stack, as representative hero, finds himself in, creates almost unbearable anxieties. His main expression of this tension is, of course, in his overtly aggressive actions. But death would provide a much fuller release. And the audience which is identifying with him might find in his death the kind of regenerative or transforming experience which lead them out of their emotional crevasse. Stack would then be functioning as a "scapegoat." But even in those versions where Stack dies (none collected in Camingerly, but many have been in other similar communities), he goes to hell and begins his evil, hypervirile ways all over. The lack of a transforming experience in the lives of the Camingerly men, then, is mirrored in the circular emotional state of their hero.

With Stackolee, and other characters of his sort, we have the embodiment of the values of the community, especially of the men. Such values, when fictively created and vicariously apprehended, underline the viciously masculine approach of these men. The Negro male must find some manner in which he can achieve self-respect, and this seems to be the easiest way to express it within the confines of this lower-class, semiliterate community.

In one story, the toast of the Negro stoker, Shine, aboard the *Titanic* at the time of its sinking, we can begin to glimpse motivations somewhat different from those of the "badman." Briefly, the story is that Shine is the one who informs the captain of the ship about the holes in the hull after the crash of the ship with the iceberg. The captain keeps sending him down to pump, and he keeps re-emerging, giving the captain further information on the size of the hole. Finally, Shine jumps in the water and begins swimming, and he does so very well. He is then offered three temptations from those still on board — money from the captain, and sex from the captain's wife and his daughter. All of these he turns down in favor of practicality. He is then challenged by the shark and the whale but is able to outperform them. He swims safely to the shore.

In Shine we have a hero who has guile and a trickster's command of the language, but he is no trickster. We have a hero who has amazing physical powers, but he is not mean like a badman. He is able to perform acts which qualify him as a much more complete hero than any of the others we have encountered. First of all, he performs feats, is a "legendary hero." Shine's amazing action of swimming away from the sinking, even in outswimming the creatures whose natural habitat he has entered, qualifies him firmly as a performer of feats. His declining of the temptations of money and sex add other attributes to his status as hero; he is a passer of trials, of tests. Further, Shine undergoes a real transformation, is "reborn." His act of jumping overboard is a conscious rejection of white commands, followed by a rejection of status symbols. He undergoes a symbolic slaying of himself to be reborn in the ocean (not a surprising place to be reborn).

Shine exhibits in his actions a sense of task which is conspicuously absent in those of any of the other heroes. Stackolee, presented with a similar situation, would certainly have accepted the offer of sex and stolen the money. But Shine seems to perceive a direction to his actions. His abilities not only indicate an amazing physical and verbal talent but also show a capacity to turn his back on just those status symbols for which the other heroes have been fighting. After all, Stack and the Monkey are reacting against the insecurity caused by their poor financial state and their inability to firmly express their masculinity (psychologically speaking, two aspects of the same lack of power, of control, equally productive of anxiety). But those very insecurities are represented, and appar-

ently mastered, in the things which Shine rejects in his replies to
the captain, his wife, and his daughter. He has an opportunity to
exhibit his superior abilities in a much grander manner.

Shine makes it very clear that he is turning his back on white
people. He answers one of the offers of the captain's wife:

> You know my color and you guessed my race.
> You better jump in the water and give these sharks a chase.

It is also clear throughout that his triumph is achieved in the name
of his race. He is pointed out as a Negro on a ship that was renowned for not allowing that race aboard as passengers. He was
thus isolated, away from his people, being tested. Do we not then
have in this toast a message of some sociological and psychological
significance? For here is a Negro story which overtly pictures his
enemies as white. And the white man has been one of the authority
figures against whom he has been rebelling. But here he achieves
that greater act of rebellion, the turning of his back. This is then
something of a declaration of independence.

However, we must resist trying to make too much out of this
one story. It is, in the first place, atypical. Secondly, the tone of
the story is pronouncedly defiant; the note on which it ends is a
derisive joke:

> When news got to Washington that the
> great Titanic had sunk
> Shine was standing on the corner
> already one-half drunk.

The thrust of the emotions of the piece is still sadistic. The pleasure
involved is the irony that Shine made it to shore and the white
people, the oppressive yet less strong, didn't. The "others" have
been defeated, but there is still no indication that the mantle of
power will be worn with any sense of security, and that the fruits
of power will be exhibited in any constructive way.

Along with this toast of overt rebellion have come a number of
other stories that are also openly reacting against the white's dom-
inance. Competition between Negro and white on the narrative
level has emerged from the trickster and tricked level to one in
which the terms and ideas are much less veiled. Through the narratives we can begin to see shift of emphasis which if broadened
could have significant implications for the Negro. The emergence
of overt fictive aggression is certainly healthier than the sly, under-
cover aggression of the trickster.

In light of the ambiguous feelings of the men of this group, it is not surprising that most of these stories are comic in tone. Even "Stackolee" is full of laughs, morbid as they may be, and Stack's actions are seen to be both significant and funny. The laugh allows one to accept and reject at the same time. It permits an identification with simultaneous reservation, and thus is utilizing the fullest capacity of the fictive strategy. These are protest heroes that people these stories and comedy is a fine expression for protest. As Wylie Sypher points out, "The Comic rites are necessarily impious, for comedy is sacrilege as well as release."[18]

However, Sypher here is talking primarily of such pieces as satyr plays and other pieces with a saturnalian impulse. All of that which we call comic is certainly not impious, directed against the excesses of society and its restrictions. Much of the derision of the comic may be, in fact, directed against the self or against the image of the powerful parent who is rendered inept. Comic pieces can easily vaccilate between these modes of aggression. This is especially evident in these toasts and stories which have been described. Motivation and direction of humor varies from the exhibitionistic actions of the monkey to the impious, yet self-destructive acts of Stack. In this group aggressive behavior cannot be uniformly institutionalized into protest through lampoon. The ambivalent love-hate situation causes a constant shift to occur in the direction of attack. Aggression is unified only through the persistence of the comic purpose and humorous tone.

In view of this ambivalence, however, it may seem strange that in the narratives described here there is such a predominance of rejection (both through symbolic action and through laughter). A nearly complete reversal seems to have been affected from the masochistic antebellum values in the stories of this group. But this is not true of all Camingerly fictive expression. The narratives it is true are sadist-rejective, but the songs, the lyric expression are still highly masochistic. The "see-how-much-you-have-hurt-me-baby" feeling which has been pointed out so often in reference to Negro song (especially the "blues") still predominates.[19] But then the

18. Wylie Sypher, "The Meanings of Comedy," in *Comedy*, Essays by George Meredith and Henri Bergson (New York, 1956), p. 223.

19. For many reasons, most of them related to my own musical limitations and the differences of song and story traditions, I find it impossible to treat the songs of the group in this work. There is very little musical expression which could be called traditional among these men, most of their songs coming from commercial recordings. It is these popular songs to which I refer here.

narratives are told only in the company of men (for the most part) and seem to state "Look at me, I am a superman." The songs are directed toward the women, and seem to say to them, "I'll come you, baby, and on your own terms, too." Both are lies.

THE TEXTS

STYLE AND PERFORMANCE

IN THE FIRST SECTION OF THIS WORK THE SOCIAL MILIEU OF A GROUP OF young Negro story-tellers was examined along with certain elements of the narratives in order to place these pieces and their performers in as full a light as possible and to explore the process by which their traditional literature interacts with other aspects of their lives. Specifically, the object there was to show how the family life of the group created a situation of emotional deprivation which had great effect on the traditional modes of expression, especially in the oral literature. There, some aspects of the texts were outlined or underlined, not so much to render the stories themselves comprehensible but rather to show more fully the relationship between text and teller.

This section will be devoted to a presentation of the stories themselves, and all discussion therefore will be centering upon them. All of the narratives collected in Camingerly, except for a few reserved for a discussion in an appendix, will be given here in as faithful a transcription as one who is untrained in linguistics can offer. Through discursive headnotes to individual pieces an attempt will be made to trace their history and to reveal any meanings which might otherwise be lost. Any words or expressions of esoteric meaning will be marked with an asterisk and discussed briefly in the glossary. As G. Legman has been so abundantly helpful in matters of annotation, I have elected to present any of his comments, where relevant, in his own words. The reader must therefore continually bear in mind that Legman's remarks are given in something of an alien context as they were originally conveyed in personal letters. They will simply be prefaced by his name and a dash.

The stories will be divided into two categories, the toast and the joke. This division is dictated by stylistic generic considerations, and for purposes of clarification as well as an attempt to tie in matters from the first section, the stylistic patterns and conventions will be described in the introductions to each genre.

The problem of style in literature, oral or written, is one which has been especially clouded by romantic and impressionistic attempts at definition. Ultimately style is *not* definable as the form of expression which a writer will fall into when he finds his "true voice." It is also not something which is revealed in its fullest sense through some adjectival or metaphorical approach. It is rather the recurrence of linguistic entities which provide an objectively describable pattern in terms of sounds, words, rhythms, syntactical constructions, and even perhaps units of meanings. "Style is nothing if it is not an overtly conscious striving for design on the part of the artist."[1] It will be the purpose of the introductions of the genres to attempt to point out the stylistic elements which recur most often in them, and if possible to indicate those which always occur, thus defining the genre.

Any consideration of style, however, creates theoretical problems. Because style has been seen as the dressing of the artist, the literary analyst has been driven to stylistic perceptions in regard to the production of the individual artist. To do so is to emphasize what the linguist would call the *ideolect*. If one is to unite a writer's method with his themes and central vision, his "world," one must, I suppose, do just such an analysis. However to do so is to ignore, or at least take for granted, the existence of a certain number of patterns which a specific language and culture exhibits. These patterns are as truly stylistic as any individual adaptive configurations of them are. For the folklorist at least, these cultural-linguistic patterns are more important than those refinements utilized by the artist, because these embody the forms accepted by the past and utilized in the present; they are the structures of tradition. It is by

1. Charles T. Scott, *A Linguistic Study of Persian and Arabic Riddles: A Language-Centered Approach to Genre Definition.* University of Texas unpublished dissertation (June, 1963), p. 12. I am indebted to Dr. Scott for his fine study as well as for many valuable conversations on this subject.

means of these patterns that the simplest levels of communication are preserved and the forms of the past transmitted to the present.

This point needs clarification. Linguists are fond of making a distinction between casual and noncasual utterances,[2] between "common usage and uses of language for more restricted purposes and often enough, perhaps characteristically, more elevated purposes."[3] The distinction is one which echoes the linguists' preoccupation with common usage (at least as the point of departure for their descriptive grammars). Language has structure and it is best describable in utterances which are part of general discourse. But linguists have long realized that there are certain preset exceptions of usage in every language, where what appear to be the rules for conversational languages are abrogated. These they call "noncasual" utterances, and they look to them for the established and accepted deviations in the language structure. Thus, in a sense, every language has two structures closely related to each other, one called "casual" and the other "noncasual."

The usual method for defining the noncasual aspects of a language are through syntactic constructions and certain elements of diction which are permissible under the special circumstances in which such utterances are invoked. Much more reliable, however, would be to see noncasual language as that exhibiting style, for these diction and syntactical changes are just two areas of change which are used in order to create the kind of recurrent patterns which denominate noncasual utterance. There are linguistic elements found in both casual and noncasual utterance, but when they are encountered in the latter they serve to define it, while when they crop up in the former they do so to no purpose or plan. As Scott says of style, "the mere fact of recurrence of identical linguistic entities does not demonstrate a conscious deployment of stylistic devices throughout a text. It is only when these recurrences are systematic, when they exhibit a tendency towards symmetry, when they occur in sufficiently close proximity to each other that it can be said that they form part of an apparently deliberate design, and, hence, can be regarded as stylistic devices."[4] It is only

2. For a discussion of these problems and further bibliography, see C. F. Voegelin, "Casual and Noncasual Utterances Within a Unified Structure," in *Style in Language*, ed. Thomas Sebeok (Boston and New York, 1960), pp. 57-68.

3. Voegelin, "Utterances," p. 57.

4. Scott, *Linguistic Study*, p. 12.

then too that they denominate noncasual utterance. Rhyme, for instance, may occur in normal discourse, but if it does so with any regularity it will come as a surprise to the speakers and will involve either a humorous response or a further conscious attempt to use the device, which, of course would change it into noncasual expression.

Those utterances which folklorists call folklore are noncasual. They are prepatterned pieces which, because of their traditional and ceremonial nature, are able to utilize the language of "more restricted" or "elevated" purpose. This linguistic distinction becomes an important one for folklorists to consider, because one of the best indications of cultural imperatives is through the linguistic patterns of style, and style is perceivable only in noncasual utterance. There are so many language elements which can be repeated and patterned that an enumeration of such stylistic elements can go a long way in pointing out tropism and oikotype.

Within the total realm of noncasual utterance a wide variance of freedom or fixity of formal patterning can occur. Both a folktale and a ballad are noncasual, therefore utilizing accepted formal patterns, but it is easily perceivable that the folktale is freer in expression (i.e., closer to casual language) than the ballad. The ballad being wed to a tune and all the formal restraints that go with it, is more severely limited in the way in which it may express and develop its story. Thus both are delimited by the stylistic elements involved, but the ballad, being more fixed, will have potentially more recurrent patterns, and thus is liable to be described stylistically in a much more complex manner. In the present study, just such a contrast is observable between the highly fixed and formal toast and the freer joke.

There is a further dimension to the problem of style which must be considered, at least in passing. This is the problem of the existence and importance of the style of the individual performer-creator. If a language has a range of stylistic possibilities, then the individual can, by choosing certain stylistic elements and eschewing others, find something of his own voice. Yet it is only the artist in a very sophisticated and eclectic society who really has this wide range of choice; the folk performer is really working within a tradition which severely delimits the number of different stylistic configurations permissible by the group. This point was well examined in an exchange between Richard M. Dorson and Roman Jakobson. The former pointed out, in reference to folk performers:

In the past we have supposed that most people in a group, in a subculture, told about the same tales in the same way and that the style was uniform for all members of the group. But when we look into it a little more closely and begin to consider individual performers, we see that there is a good deal of difference, variation and individual style. So it seems to me that we can make such a distinction *once the group repertoire has been established.* (italics mine)

To which the latter replied:

In any popular tradition there are several stereotyped styles of performance and corresponding selections of epic or lyric genres, and from these "stock types" *(emplois)* the individual chooses the one particularly suited to him. Likewise the observers of language are often prone to exaggerate the imprint of personality. . . . The strong tendency of the individual to adopt his language to the milieu, and in any dialogue to approach his interlocutor, considerably reduces the notion of the so-called "idiolect."[5]

There were certain elements of style which were exhibited by all of the men and boys whom I heard perform in Camingerly. All seemed to be carried away by the impetus of words into a near-state of euphoria. Word sounds seemed to exist for themselves apart from sense, and all noncasual discourse seemed to gravitate toward rhyme or clever turn of phrase. Performing was performing and there was no attempt by the teller to confuse the reader by introducing pieces which seemed to involve casual speech. Voice pitch and other elements of vocal production were, for each performer, different in a very important way from his usual manner of speaking, whether it was through utilization of a wider range of pitch levels and loudness, by great emphasis on story-line or its embroidery, or simply by sheer rapidity of narration. Sentence units, for the most part, are very short. When they are lengthened, they are done by conjunctions, not by any method of subordination. The emphasis is on action, description being used only to heighten the effect. Because of a peculiarity in Negro speech which utilizes the same verb forms for both past and present, a feeling of things

5. *Style in Language*, pp. 52-53.

happening now pervades these stories.[6] This emphasis on action and "now-ness" has a great effect on the diction. Active verbs dominate. Modifiers are generally intensifiers. There are frequent injected sounds and exclamations used also to give furtherance to the feeling of the intensity of the action. Many of these matters will be given fuller treatment in the introductions to the genres.

However, each informant did show some peculiarities in style, as well as in subject, and thus this seems to be a good place to discuss the individual performers from whom I collected. These stories come from a limited number of informants, many of whom have been discussed in passing in former chapters. Bobby[7] was responsible for the narration of few of the stories himself, but was immensely valuable in helping me gather the material. He was the one with whom I had the closest relationship in Camingerly, and he learned what kind of material I was interested in and how to work the tape recorder. Consequently, he brought many informants directly to me, and on occasion, recorded them himself. At the time of this study he was seventeen and eighteen years old. He had at one time (around age fourteen) taken a trip to Florida with Charley, working his way down and back. Though little and young, he regarded himself as very much a man, especially a lady's man. Bobby, as all of these men, had been a member of the Twelfth Street Gang and had fought for them often, but that was an activity that seems to have been eliminated a few years before I arrived. Bobby explained this as being the result of the departure of too many of the boys for the service or for parts unknown.

As far as his abilities as a story teller were concerned, Bobby was not recognized by his peers as outstanding. His main trouble seemed to be that he tried too hard and yet could not remember stories, and especially the toasts, very well. Thus his sense of the story's direction was often impaired and this was reflected in his faltering method of delivery. When he did perform, which was not often (and I imagine it was more often to me than to his peers), he was definitely attempting to emulate "Kid's" style and method.

6. It was often impossible to transcribe texts faithfully in this regard, as these verbs were often heard by me one way one time and another way another time. I fear that I often heard them in such a way that they would more nearly agree in tense with what came before.

7. I am not using full names here in order to protect, at least in part, my informants. Those who, through scholarly interest, wish to find their full names, may consult my dissertation cited earlier.

"Kid" was by far the most prolific and effective of the informants from whom I collected. This, in all probability, stemmed from his acceptance by the group as an outstanding "talker" and led him to see himself as a professional entertainer. As a result, he was nearly always performing, his roles varying from the bumptious clown to the scathing satirist putting the other down to the boastful bad-man. He knew some of the routines of the Negro nightclub per-former Redd Foxx, as he had heard them on records.

"Kid" was born and raised in Philadelphia, and has always lived somewhere near Camingerly. At the time of this study he was twenty-seven and twenty-eight. He was on the short side, a muscu-lar, stocky type, who, when he didn't see himself as a professional entertainer, pictured himself as a professional softball player. He had been married a few years before, but was at present living with his mother. His wife had taken him to court a number of times for nonsupport and on a few recent occasions had had him thrown into jail. He claimed that she was living with another man and just doing this for spite. At one time during our stay in Camingerly he disappeared for quite a while, returning to say that he had been in a hospital with tuberculosis.

"Kid's" style of rendition was very theatrical. He used as many dramatic devices as possible, changing voices for different char-acters or for varying situations, utilizing the full range of his voice both in regard to pitch and intensity, and he would speed up and slow down at will. He was a masterful rhymster and quipper, but he was also capable of almost endlessly embroidering a story if he wanted to. He was the only one in the neighborhood I ever heard who felt he constantly needed to fill in character motivation in his jokes.

An interesting pattern in his personal repertoire was that he seems to have been drawn to stories in which the young man has relations with an older woman ("Granny" usually) and to those in which the female is the active of the pair and the male more passive. This would suggest the possibility of a wish to resign his male role except in relation to maternal figures, and seems espe-cially significant in light of his marital history and his return to his mother's household.

Charley is an open contrast to "Kid" both in attitudes, style, and delivery. On the short side, light-skinned, when we first met him he was missing most of his front teeth. (Later he got a beautiful set of false ones.) Charley was a brilliant musician, and had per-formed in a quartet that had made a few records by the name of

"The Turbans." He could take any group of boys and give them different singing parts out of his head, and the result was a fine arrangement. His voice was a very flexible one and he was able to sing anything from bass to falsetto melody. When he was not singing, however, Charley was very shy and expressed himself more through a short breathy giggle than any other way. Yet he had a wide and varied repertoire of stories. Whereas "Kid" used all of the theatrical tricks to put across his story, Charley relied almost completely on effects of lesser intensity. His voice was soft and he drawled extensively. Though he had just as great a control on his material, he would often punctuate his narration with a nervous "eruh."

Charley had travelled South with Bobby, though he was four or five years older. He was the most mobile of the regulars of the neighborhood, moving to many different places during our two-year residence, most of them some distance from Camingerly. Yet he had been raised around there and returned regularly, if only to visit his friends. He was not much of a hand with the girls, with all of his talents. He seemed definitely afraid of them on the few occasions in which I saw him in mixed company. He lived, for the most part, with sisters in one or another neighborhood in Philadelphia.

His taste in jokes tended toward the most childish, with a strong emphasis on the clownish doings of drunks and the sexual activities of prepubescent children. He told numerous stories involving drunk talk or baby talk. This could be interpreted as indicative of some kind of wish-fulfillment in fictive terms of regression to the pre-sexual stage, or a resignation to the nonsexuality of drunkedness.

Arthur was the third of the outstanding tale tellers I encountered. Whereas Charley's delivery was deliberately slow, Arthur's was absolute staccato madness, a veritable machine-gun delivery. He spoke so fast that it was tremendously difficult to understand his words. Of the three, we knew Arthur the least well. He was around only for a short time during our stay. He was short and very much the "dandy," and had learned to do "processing," the way in which hair was straightened. Consequently, he went on a crusade to Virginia to teach the boys down there how their hair should be worn, and only returned during the last couple of months we lived in Camingerly. Consequently he was not always available for recording sessions and the only things which were collected were toasts.

The rest of the texts included here came from a number of other less important sources. Javester, a friend of Bobby's, brought me a manuscript which he had from a man at work which had a number of items which I have included here, *punctatim et literarum.* "Boots" and Victor were younger members of the community, singers in a quartet that met at our house. Harry was an elderly man who regularly sat across from our residence in a portable chair. He gave me a couple of items which he had in a manuscript which he carried in his wallet. Petey I have discussed earlier, in the first chapter. He was a young fellow who got married during our sojourn. He brought Freddie around for a couple of recording sessions. Freddie was a school chum of his who knew many stories, but did not tell them very well, as will be noticed in the texts assigned to him.

CHAPTER IV

THE TOAST

THE TOAST MAY BE THE MOST NEGLECTED FORM OF TRADITIONAL NAR-
rative; it has been almost totally ignored by folklore scholarship.
Indeed, beyond my own preliminary report, and an article by
Debra Galoob,[1] one of my students, the only publication that I have
located that prints any texts of these verses is *The Book of Negro
Folklore*[2] by Langston Hughes and Arna Bontemps. Richard M.
Dorson, in his article "Negro Tales,"[3] mentions that one of the tales
printed was "also given . . . in the form of a rhymed story or
'toast' . . ." and he prints some tale texts close to toasts. This situation
probably exists because the toast, by its very nature (and quite often
its subject), calls for the use of "improper" words.

The toast is a narrative poem which is recited, often in a theatrical manner, and represents the greatest flowering of Negro verbal
talent. Quite often they are long, lasting anywhere from two to
ten minutes. They conform to a general, but by no means binding,
framing pattern. This consists of (1) some sort of picturesque or
exciting introduction, (2) action alternating with dialogue (because
the action is usually a struggle between two people or animals), and

1. "The Toast," in *Folklore in Action* (Philadelphia, 1962), pp. 1 ff; Debra
Galoob, "Back in '32 When the Times Was Hard," *Riata* (June, 1963), pp.
24-33.

2. *The Book of Negro Folklore*, ed. Langston Hughes and Arna Bontemps
(New York, 1958).

3. *Western Folklore*, XIII (1954), p. 87.

(3) a twist ending of some sort, either a quip, an ironic comment or a brag. There is generally a unity, or consecutiveness of action; there is no "leaping and lingering" as in sung traditional narratives. They are not sung, and it is perhaps the lack of reliance on the structure of a tune that allows for the freedom of form in the toasts.

But they do have a method of structure. Like so many other forms of oral narrative they are organized by certain conventions, ones which Albert Lord would consider "epic."[4] And these conventions allow for a feeling of much freedom within what proves on examination to constitute a fairly restricted form.

At first glance it seems that there is no conception of length or duration of the individual line. A fairly typical couplet such as the following has a line of five stresses followed by one of three:

> Shine went up on deck, said "Captain, I was downstairs
> eating my peas
> Till the water come up to my knees."

On further analysis, however, the dominant line pattern is seen to be one of four stresses:

> Down in the jungle near a dried-up creek
> The signifying monkey hadn't slept for a week.

This line provides a flexible pattern; lines involving greater or fewer stresses are countenanced. The importance of the stress system is not that it provides an unvarying mold, but that it establishes an expectation pattern. This kind of verse is called *isochronic*.

The pattern is a useful one, as a four-stress line will divide and balance easily, and the balanced line is the core of the wit of these pieces. Very often lines are divided in the middle with a stop (comma, semi-colon, period) or a conjunction.

> Now a few stalks shook, and a few leaves fell,
> Up popped the monkey one day, 'bout sharp as hell.

Balance and caesura are used for a number of effects. Often we have balanced actions, paralleled by a balance in subject-verb-object positions. "The monkey grabbed a stick, and the baboon

4. Albert Lord, *The Singer of Tales* (Cambridge, Mass., 1960). Much of the analysis in the next few pages is obviously indebted to this perceptive work.

snatched the chalk." Or simple syntactic (paratactic or oppositional) balance occurs: "Hand full of chives, pocket full of herbs."

But the major structural unit is not the line but the couplet and the principle of balance extends to it. Rhyme, uniting the two lines of the couplet, creates an initial balance. Further balance can be developed within these bounds by using the first line of a couplet to introduce a character (or an action) and the second to describe him (it). I use here lines from "Jesse James" to illustrate.

> There was the Dalton Brothers, four of a kind.
> They shot a motherfucker for a raggedy dime.

And here the principle of balance is carried farther, for the next couplet parallels the first in both subject, modifiers, and syntax:

> There was John Dillinger in the corner, counting his gold.
> He shot his motherfucker when he was ten years old.

The couplet that follows the above two shows how balance can be preserved, yet varied, for here the name comes after the modifying line, and the first line breaks, with its violent irregularity, the metrical pattern which otherwise might get boring:

> There was a bad motherfucker in the corner we all
> should know
> His name was Geronimo.

The balanced, four-stress line so easily falls into dog-trot rhythm, but the freedom by which the lines are expanded and contracted and the almost endless variety of patterns and durations of non-stressed syllables eliminate the possibility of aural fatigue. Further, because the caesura in a four-stress line falls most often in the center, the toast-teller will seldom provide many consecutive lines with a strong caesura. The most common device he uses is to take a balanced line with a strong caesura and play it off against a line with little or no break in it, at the same time preserving balance between the two lines in sound and syntax:

> He said, "I'ma hold my jacks, spread my queens.
> I'ma do switching in this old fucked-up deck the
> world's never seen.
> I'ma hold my deuces, lay down my treys,
> Get down on your motherfucking ass in a thous-
> and ways."

As noted, the couplet provides the basic structural unit of the toast, in most cases. Even in cases where there is no strong line or couplet balance, the thought, action or description is encompassed within the confines of the couplet. Thus, most lines or couplets begin with the subject of the sentence followed immediately by the active verb, with the modifiers generally following to complete the unit. Personal pronouns are the most frequent first words of the lines in any toast.

These verses are improvisational in character.[5] They are the sort of narrative that is not learned by rote or even by plot line. The primary purpose of the toast-teller, it is true, is to tell the story as quickly, fluidly and dramatically as possible. But they don't remember the toast, having "learned them by heart." Rather they have learned the conventions, the formulas and the themes (or commonplaces) and by means of these have reconstructed or retold the narrative.

The improvisational nature of the toast makes any one text simply a chance recording of a story highly transitional by nature. That rendering is the way it is captured at the specific moment it is given, but will probably never be reproduced exactly by even the same informant. He hasn't learned it by rote, and therefore variation is the essence of the toast's character. This variation[6] would be especially great if the social situation of the telling were changed (for instance, talking on the street corner as opposed to sitting around a room speaking into a tape recorder). The improvisational[7] skills of the narrators vary immensely. The performer's skills in this begin with extending or contracting the line. As mentioned, the four-stress line predominates, but is not the absolute rule. And

5. These toasts may be popular among the Negro because of his predilection, otherwise evinced in calypso, toward improvised pieces of a contest nature. This sort of cross-cultural approach would probably be very revealing, but obviously is not within the confines of the study here.

6. Lord validly objects to use of the term "variation" in references to extemporized narratives of this sort, as the world implies the existence of a fixed form which can be varied from. I use it because the alternatives don't seem any more helpful, and because the concept of variation is still useful, even without the acceptance of the fixed text.

7. Often what I heard in poolhalls or on the street corner by the same informant was extremely different both in method of delivery and in finish of language. I have included a number of texts of some toasts because every one of them represents some capacity of the individual informant to improvise. Some unimaginative texts are included as comparison for the texts of the experienced and master performers.

within that line he can add all sorts of intensives and other modifiers which are unstressed and therefore do not affect the stress pattern.

His ability to recount and recreate is further aided by the structure of the line and couplet discussed above. The balance which is often achieved within these units conforms to certain types which provide the framework for the formulas exhibited in these verses. A line or couplet which is balanced conjunctionally, paratactically or appositionally is easier to remember than one without such definite construction; it also establishes that construction as a pattern for other future expressions and situations. These constructions are the formulas of the toasts.

The themes are another way in which the narrator will recount his story successfully. These are larger units, in which similar situations in different toasts are treated in a similar manner. When such situations are repeated in one toast, incremental repetition occurs. "Squad Twenty-two" for instance begins:

> I ran over to Lombard Street to get my gat,
> I ran back to South Street to get my hat.

and later says:

> Now I run back to South Street to put down
>   my gat
> And back over to Lombard Street to put
>   down my hat.

More often, such similarities exist in different toasts. A common situation is some strong man trying to shut somebody up. When this occurs in a barroom, as in "Stackolee," it ends in violence:

> Just then some old sucker over in the corner said, "somebody call the law."
> He stretched out and put a forty-five shell through that motherfucking jaw.
> A cute little whore came over and said, "Benny, please."
> He blowed that bitch down to her knees.

In a courtroom scene, the structure is similar, the results different:

> Just then my sister-in-law jumped up, started to cry
> I throwed her a dirty old rag to wipe her eye.
> My mother-in-law jumped up, started to shout.
> "Sit down bitch, you don't even know what the trial's about."

Such commonplace situations result in the use of many such themes. The courtroom is a locale returned to again and again in the toasts. The judge's sentencing is invariably announced with a retort from the convicted.

> "Fifty-five ain't no time.
> I got a brother in Sing-Sing doing 99."[8]

As a theme is an improvised form, the same situation is recounted with variation:

> "Judge, 99 years ain't no god-damn time.
> My father's in Alcatraz doing 299."

Occasionally entire scenes are thematic, being found in similar forms in two or more toasts; the hero's descent to Hell and his defeat of the devil, the fight with the bartender, the courtroom and jail scenes are some that occur repeatedly.

A further device by which the toast is remembered by informants is by the use of cliché. The pattern of the four-stress rhymed line, often divided in two, elicits many descriptive images which are used repeatedly for both rhyme and stress purposes. A gun is never a gun; it is a "forty-four" or "forty-five" or "thirty-eight" depending upon which rhyme is needed. A man is never shot; gunplay is rather described as putting a "rocket through his motherfucking head."

Often the clichés called for are proverbial. Such phrases abound as "like a rat eats cheese," "king of the sea," "off like a PT boat," "faster than a streak of lightning," "more dead than alive," "like a ten-ton truck," and the self-consciously Negro proverbs "spend money just like I was white," and "stay in your class."

Yet, as is readily observable, not all images used are clichés. The language used in these poems is, as in many public utterances, highly self-conscious and artful. The well-turned phrase is constantly sought, and he who calls forth the best of phrases is the best of the toast-tellers. Often, the balanced line is created simply for poetic effect, such as the line from "Stackolee" and one version of "Jesse James":

> I walked through water and I waded through mud.

8. This comes from a commonplace blues verse. See Oliver, *Blues,* p. 176. The whole courtroom scene may be a commonplace from early Negro song; see for instance Mary Wheeler, *Steamboatin' Days* (Baton Rouge, 1944), p. 111.

Often the sense of a line is obscured in order to enhance its sound. Once again, our example comes from "Stackolee."

> The bed gave a twist, the springs gave a twistle.
> I throwed nine inches of joint to the whore before
>   she could move a gristle.

In the toast of "The Titanic," fact is sacrificed for a more euphonious opening. This tragedy, which actually occurred on the 14th and 15th of April, begins:

> The eighth of May was a hell of a day.
> When the Titanic was sinking away.

or:

> It was a hell of a day in the merry month of May
> When the great Titanic was sailing away.

This is by no means great poetry, but the interrelationships of the "a" sounds and the "m" sounds in the second are consciously and artistically conceived. Sometimes, these artful effects are used to emphasize a comic point, as in the couplet from Charley's "Titanic":

> Shine said, "You may be king of the ocean, king
>   of the sea,
> But you got to be a swimming motherfucker to
>   outswim me."

Consistent with this attitude toward sound and sense in words is the emotional content of the poems as a whole. The poems are created to play on one's emotions, by their sound, by their diction, by their breath-taking, and by their subject matter. The emotions which are primarily called forth are amusement and amazement. The subject treated is freedom of the body through superhuman feats, and of the spirit through acts which are free of restrictive social mores (or in direct violation of them), especially in respect to crime and violence. The heroes of most of these stories are "hard-men," criminals, men capable of prodigious sexual feats, "bad men," and very clever men (or animals) who have the amorality of the trickster. The diction of the toasts does everything to heighten the effect of these characters. The values of iconoclasm are strongly echoed in the abundance of forceful and obscene words. Such words show the performer to be the kind of strong man that the hero of the tale is. Furthermore, they are lively words that blend well with the abundance of active verbs and expressions found here; "swinging," "running," "stomp," "kill," "knock," "jumped" are the verbs that predominate in these highly active pieces. In the same way, the proverbs and clichés are usually utilized for the purposes of either furthering the action or the iconoclasm, or both. "Like a bat out of hell," "pick on someone your own size," "clean out of sight," "fight like a natural man," "like a bolt of lightning," "a stripe of white heat," "like a ten-ton truck" all behave in this violent way. We have here, then, the concreteness common to much folk-speech, used for desired effect.

Because of the confines of the form, the images and diction of these pieces seem even more vivid, more precise, more imaginative than those found even in the tales and anecdotes. More is borrowed from the economy of the Negro ballad than from the narrative method of the tale. There is much in common in technique between the standard Negro ballad stanza:

> Send for the yellow-tired buggy, send for the yellow-seated hack.
> Gonna carry her to the graveyard. Ain't never coming back.
> (Found in "Delia Holmes," "Frankie and Johnnie,"
> and many others.)

and such a couplet as

> I was standing on the corner, wasn't even shooting crap.
> When a policeman came by, picked me up on a lame rap.
> (From "The Great MacDaddy")

especially in regard to economy and artistic embellishment.

There is much about the toast as an entertainment form that is strongly paralleled in the professional medium of the blackface minstrel stage. It is impossible to say with our present knowledge of early Negro lore whether such narrative recitations existed among the Negro before the beginning of the minstrel shows and were borrowed by white performers for the minstrel stage, or whether they were an invention of the whites, later borrowed by the Negro and recast. At any rate, we know that in the later history of the "blackface" show, recitations, often comic ones, became a part of the show. As Carl Wittke, the historian of the minstrel stage says:

> Another favorite device of the endmen was to entertain their audiences with the recital of a poem. . . . Frequently

the interlocutor would recite a popular favorite correctly,
in order to give the endmen the opportunity to improve
on his rendition by . . . new versions.[9]

Such verse not only found its way into the interplay between the
interlocutor and the endman but also the monologist during the
olio part of the program was known to break into verse.[10] With
what we otherwise know of the effect of minstrel-show materials on
Negro lore, it seems possible that such recitations may have provided an impetus for the toast tradition as we have it today.

A further possible influence of the blackface show may be seen
in the common characteristics of some of the dialogue. In such
toasts as "Stackolee" and "The Titanic," there is much dialogue
between two characters. Often this approaches the form of the
"straightman" and "gagman" jokes, or in more appropriate terms,
"Mr. Interlocutor" and "Mr. Endman." This is most evident in "The
Titanic" where the captain, his wife and daughter, the shark, and
sometimes the whale, serve "feeder" or "set-up" lines for "Shine."

> Shark said, "Shine, Shine, can't you see,
> When you jump in these waters you belongs to me."
> Shine said, "I know you outswim the barracuda, outsmart
>   every fish in the sea,
> But you gotta be a stroking motherfucker to outswim me."

This same element can be seen, with a lesser comic effect, in
"Stackolee," which in general is more concerned with action than
dialogue. After "Stack" has shot the waiter:

> Little lady came in and said, "Where's the waiter, please?"
> I said, "He laying behind the counter with his mind at
>   ease."

It is not being argued that the minstrel show is the point of origin
of the toast, but rather that it exhibits, in some of its facets, similar
tendencies and may have affected the early history of the toast.
On the other hand, somehow the present form derived in some
way from the custom of the dedicatory speech or verse "toast"
recited and pledged with a drink, some of which were quite long

9. Carl Wittke, *Tambo and Bones* (Durham, N. C., 1930), p. 164.
10. Wittke, *Tambo*, p. 171.

and flamboyant.[11] We know that this custom was taken over by the Negro at least as early as the beginning of this century.

> Toasts are given at drinking parties; but all through the South they are given at all kinds of gatherings, even at school "jus' fo' pastime."[12]

The sense of the word here indicates that the custom of "toasting" begun at the drinking parties had already expanded. Perhaps it grew further to include any verse recitation, and from there became particularized into the form as we know it. There did, and does exist among the Negro the custom of creating occasional poems

11. Legman has been very perceptive on this point and has modified my opinion greatly. He relates these toasts to the toast tradition in general, even though they have lost their salutory function. He says,

> In the first place they are clearly related to the quatrain saws of the late 16th and early 17th century almanac type, beginning "When a man grows old," and so on — as these folk-witty apothegmatic statements are just what "goes" when giving a toast at drinking. Also, *toasts* in just this sense continued in all convivial company until the end of World War I in the U. S., when they were killed by prohibition, and the surreptitious drinking thereafter. Even the British, who did not have prohibition, will hardly venture more, nowadays, than a tight-lipped "Cheers," and I understand that the Upper-and-Lower "U" snobbery school has definite strictures on any more flamboyant toasts being given.
>
> However, throughout the 17th and 18th centuries, and well into the 19th — until the period of the British moral reform of the 1830's, which was intended to stave off the threatened working-class revolution (aborted into the labor-union movement then and since) — heavy drinking was *de rigueur* among all classes, and most song and jest books included pages and pages of these ornate "toasts." As late as the 1870's, in the usual anglicized reprints of Burns' *Merry Muses of Caledonia*, a page of such toasts will be found. Scotland was, in fact, a particular center of these toasts, especially among the secret societies, of drinking, singing, and sexual conviviality, such as the stupefying "Beggar's Benison" society, of Anstruther, Scotland, in the early 18th century, whose *Records* were printed at the dissolution of the society in the 1890's, precisely with a few pages of these long and ornate toasts. In America the college fraternities kept the tradition alive, and still does, especially in the Southern colleges, such as Virginia, with such fancy items as "High-riding horses and porcupine saddles fo' ouah enemies!" At the present time in Scotland there is still a secret, or semi-secret society, the "Horseman's Word," of which the Scottish folklorist, Hamish Henderson, has actually tape-recorded a session; and it is a point of honor with the members to "propose" long and ornate erotic toasts, which go on for a paragraph of brag of mythical sexual autobiography.

12. Portia Smiley, "Folklore from Virginia, etc.," *Journal of American Folklore*, XXXII (1919), p. 375.

and other long verse forms. Fauset[13] quotes one from Nova Scotia Negroes and Dorson from Michigan.[14] Perhaps the name "toast" became associated with these longer rhymes.

On the other hand, the name may have been derived from the numerous books containing "After-Dinner Speeches, Jokes and Toasts," which include such recitations as "The Shooting of Dan McGrew" or "The Face on the Bar-room Floor." These books can still be bought at most bookstores. Whenever I asked any older members of the neighborhood if they knew any toasts, they would say that they used to know those toasts about "Stackolee" or "The Face on the Bar-room Floor," and, indeed, I did find one fellow who remembered most of "The Drunkard." Many of them claimed to have books of toasts in their homes (which at first I took to mean their own individual collections), but on investigation they proved to be either bad jokebooks, or books of these recitations.

The relationship of these rather theatrical narrative poems to the toast can be seen in another way. It is certain that "Paul Revere's Ride" is a parody of the famous Longfellow poem; in the same way some of the fornication contest toasts can be seen to be parodies of the type of verse such as "The Shooting of Dan Mc-Grew" or "The Face on the Bar-room Floor." Such origins are a good deal clearer in collected texts from white informants. A good example is found in *Count Vicarion's Book of Bawdy Ballads* (Paris, 1956) XIV, "Eskimo Nell."[15] Closer analysis might show a similar relationship between all of the toasts and the works of popular verse.

The toast is today, as its ancestors have been, an entertainment. It is a social entity, not to be performed alone in the fields or while washing dishes but on the street corners with the gang on long summer evenings, in the poolhall after everyone has run out of money, and occasionally at parties. Though for the most part toasts are male entertainment, the female members of the neighborhood like to hear them performed, and it is only the matriarchs and the sternly religious who look down upon them. There is a tendency not to offend the female sensibility by performing them

13. A. H. Fauset, *Folklore from Nova Scotia*, MAFLS, XXIV (New York, 1931), p. 100.

14. Richard M. Dorson, *Negro Folktales in Michigan* (Cambridge, Mass., 1956), p. 13.

15. Legman says of such recitations and parodies, ". . . there are plenty of 19th century white recitations. . . . There are also certainly plenty of white recitations of a highly erotic kind, and not all of these are parodies."

before women, but the women often tr to goad the men into giving them a show. It is a favorite pastime of some young girls to sneak to a place where, unobserved, they can hear the boys performing these pieces.

Because the object of the toast teller is primarily to entertain, he will narrate with such emphases that it will be just a little funnier (by the addition of incongruous or picturesque expressions) or a little more superhuman or explosive. And there is no doubt that the audience is being entertained when one hears a toast performed well. All sorts of vocal appreciation is expressed at any of the high points of the narrative. A real question is whether the audience is believing that such events actually happened. Most will reply, if asked, that the stories are fictions, but perhaps because they don't want to be suspected of not being in tune with the beliefs of the investigator. However, some whom I asked thought that probably there were men named "Stackolee" and "Billy Lyons," who lived and did the things described in the toasts. All who were asked regarded the toasts about animals as humorous ways of describing people, but none would go so far as to say that the jungle really represented city life.

The element of belief is intricately bound up with the vicarious enjoyment which the members of the audience obviously are exhibiting while hearing these stories. The desire to be sexually superpotent or above the restrictions of (an imposed) society is obviously manifested in the reactions of both the performer and the audience.

The whole question of the belief or vicarious participation is important because of its effect on structure. The ballad form has not been congenial to the Negro, it would seem. Few are the ballads of Negro origin, and those that exist lack much of the direction of those from the European tradition. We do have such Negro ballads as "Betty and Dupree" and "Delia Holmes," but even here where exciting stories are being documented, the lyrical element encroaches, a phenomenon which I have earlier referred to as the "intrusive 'I'." We hear about the doings of these men and women, but insistently we find the singer entering the song to make an emotional point:

Some say he was born in Texas
Some say he was born in Maine.
But I don't give a damn where that poor boy was born.
He was a steel driving man.

Or the chorus from the song, "Stackolee," which warns that "He was a bad man that mean old Stackolee," or "When you lose your money, learn to lose." Somehow we never get that third person objectivity of the European ballad to a great extent in Negro narrative.

An occasional word will have an asterisk (°) after it. For information on that word, see the glossary.

1. *THE TITANIC*

All of the versions of "The Titanic" fit into the same general pattern: a prologue about the terrible day on which the ship sank; the introduction of "Shine," the mythical Negro stoker on board the ship; a description of his argument with the captain about whether the ship was sinking; the jumping into the water and his amazing swimming ability described;[16] the captain's offer of money to save him which he refuses (missing in the E text); the offer of the captain's wife and/or daughter of sexual relations with him if he will save them, which he likewise refuses; a conversation with the shark and/or whale where he claims to be able to outswim them (which he apparently does); and a final ironic twist in which it is mentioned that "Shine" swam so fast that by the time that news arrived of the sea tragedy, "Shine" was already inebriated in some specific location.

There is, as far as I have been able to ascertain, only one complete text of this toast which has previously been printed: in the *Book of Negro Folklore*[17] in a text collected by Langston Hughes on Eighth Avenue in Harlem in 1945. As in the "D" text of this collection, a millionaire (in Hughes' case, he is specified as Jay Gould) is added to the *dramatis personae*. It is he who offers monetary

16. Legman: The speedy-swimmer joke is not original with this text. It exists in France, concerning a man who falls off a boat and is waiting for it when it docks, printed in a number of 1920's French joke collections. There is also a similar French joke called "The Mast of Marseille," which was long ago printed in the *Intermediaire des Chercheurs* (the French *Notes & Queries*), about the man who falls off the boat, thinks of his girl-friend, uses his handkerchief as a sail on his resulting erection, and his thumb up his rectum for a rudder, and sails home to Marseille. I don't know if he also arrives ahead of the boat, but it wouldn't be out of keeping with the Munchausen tone.

17. Hughes and Bontemps, *Book of Negro Folklore*, p. 366. I have a number of other texts, one sent to me by Kenneth S. Goldstein from the recitation of E. H., a white truck driver from Texas, one from Roosevelt Wattley of Austin, Texas, and one collected by Debra Galoob in Longview, Texas.

reward, and it is his daughter who offers herself sexually and is rejected. The text, as printed, shows strong evidence of being bowdlerized. The common lines

> That's when the Captain's daughter came on deck;
> Hands on her pussy, and drawers 'round her neck.

becomes

> Jay Gould's millionary daughter came running up
>   on deck
> With her suitcase in her hand and her dress 'round
>   her neck.

The Hughes version lacks the dialogue between the shark and "Shine" and ends in a beautiful piece of modern irony.

> When all them white folks went to heaven,
> Shine was in Sugar Ray's Bar drinking Seagram's Seven.

It is impossible to date accurately the origin of this piece. The date of the sinking seems to indicate that it must be around forty-five years old. And, indeed, the story could be older, with a change in the name of the ship to make it more timely.

In *Gumbo Ya-Ya*[18] the authors report from the *singing* of one Carolina Slim a song about the *Titanic* which the singer claims to have written. The stanzas quoted are:

> I always did hear that the fi' of May was a wonderful day
> You believe me, everybody had somethin' to say,
> Telephones and telegraphs to all parts of town,
> That the great *Titanic* was a'goin' down.
> The captain and the mate was standin' on deck havin' a
>   few words
> 'Fore they know it, the *Titanic* had done hit a big iceberg.
> Had a colored guy on there called Shine, who came from
>   below,
> And hollered, "Water is coming through the fireroom do'."
> Shine jumped off that ship and begun to swim,
> Thousands of white folks watchin' him.
> Shine say, "Fish in the ocean, and fish in the sea,
> This is one time you white folks ain't gonna fool me."

18. *Gumbo Ya-Ya, A Collection of Louisiana Folktales*, compiled by Lyle Saxon, Edward Dreyer, and Robert Tallant (Boston, 1945), pp. 374-75.

This is certainly a not-too-remote relation of our toast. The authors possibly felt, as Hughes and Bontemps seem to have, that it would be improper to print anything so "raw," as they indicate that there were further verses. As the book is made up of material collected by the WPA, we can at least date the story in the same basic outlines as far back as the 1930's.

There is further secondary material to indicate that the story could be found in somewhat similar form even earlier. This can be deduced from a number of fragments from other sources. Carl Sandburg in *The American Songbag*[19] prints a Negro song about the *Titanic* which he claims was sung by American Negro soldiers during World War I. One stanza says:

> Up come Bill from de bottom flo'
> Said de water wuz runnin' in de boiler do'.
> Go back, Bill, an' shut yo' mouth
> Got forty-eight pumps to keep the water out!

In a minstrel song that was popular throughout the South in the 1920's, we find another momentary glimpse of the toast. In this song, usually called "The Travelling Coon,"[20] the hero is something of a trickster. His exploits seem to be derived from popular tall-tales.[21]

Found among the most common verses are the following:

> The coon got on the Titanic
> An' started up the ocean blue,
> But when he saw the iceberg,
> Right overboard he flew.

19. Carl Sandburg, *The American Songbag* (New York, 1927), p. 254.

20. This song can be found in many collections and on many records with practically identical texts. See: Howard W. Odum, *Rainbow Round My Shoulder* (Indianapolis, 1928), p. 235 (does not have verses quoted); Odum, *Wings on My Feet* (New York, 1929), p. 286; Newman I. White, *American Negro Folksongs* (Cambridge, Mass., 1928), p. 350; *The Frank C. Brown Collection of North Carolina Folklore*, Vol. III, *The Folksongs*, edited by Henry M. Belden and Arthur Palmer Hudson (Durham, 1952), p. 515.

I have also heard it on the following records: Victor 2095-7-B, as sung by Luke Jordan; Columbia 142028, as sung by Doc Walsh; OKEH 40237-A, as sung by Henry Witter; Riverside RLP 657, "Traveling Man," as sung by Billy Faier. Text on the latter from Walsh.

21. The most notable one included in all texts is the one about going to the spring to get water, a hole springing in the bucket, and how the traveling coon ran to the house, got another bucket and caught the water before it hit the ground (for a text of this, see 89. "Boasts, Brags, Exaggerations"). It is inter-

> The white folks standin' on the deck
> Said, "Coon, you are a fool."
> But 'bout three minutes after that
> He was shootin' craps in Liverpool.[22]

The problem presented by this material is whether these fragments are echoes of the toast in an old version, or the toast is made up of fragments derived from these sources. This is, unfortunately, a question unanswerable with the knowledge we are now able to gather.

One thing we do know is that there were a great many songs and ballads in broadsheet form concerning the sinking. The Lomaxes say of the event that it was "the most widely celebrated tragedy of that era, the event which seems to have caught the imagination of the Negro. . . . From the variety of ballads on this subject that have been discovered, we can only suppose that there must have been numerous songs composed and broadcast."[23] It was reported that one week after the event a blind preacher was seen on a train selling a ballad he had composed on the disaster.[24] There are three broadsheets of songs about the sinking in the Frank C. Brown Collection.[25] Besides these numerous creations, there are

esting to note the possible derivation of this song from the older song of tall-tales, "The Ram of Derby." The usual chorus to the minstrel song is:

> He was a travelling man.
> He was a travelling man.
> He was the travellinest man
> Finest was in the land.
> He was a travelling man
> He was known for miles around
> He'd never give up, no he wouldn't give up
> Till the police shot him down.

White, *American*, p. 350, notices that

> These lines seem to be based on the chorus of the modern minstrel song, current about 1905 to 1915: "He rambled, he rambled, he rambled all around town. He rambled, he rambled till the butcher cut him down."

This "modern minstrel song" must be either the very old song of "The Derby Ram" or the song very close to it known as "Didn't He Ramble" written by Will Handy on the "Derby Ram" pattern which has become a jazz classic.

22. White, *American*, p. 350.

23. John A. and Alan Lomax, *Negro Folk Songs as Sung by Leadbelly* (New York, 1936), p. 181.

24. A. E. Perkins, JAF, XXXV (1922), p. 223, as quoted in *Brown Collection*, Vol. II: *The Ballads*, p. 662.

25. *Brown Collection*, pp. 662-68. "A" text is a parody of "The Golden Vanity."

also parodies of previously existing songs which talk about the tragedy.

> Where wus you when the big Titanic
> Went down?
> Where wus you when the big Titanic
> Went down?
> Standing on the deck singing
> "Alabama Boun'."[26]

Most of these songs concerning the *Titanic* are moralistic in their nature. They say in effect, "See what God can do, even to the rich." Such common verses as:

> When that ship left England it was making for the shore,
> The rich had declared that they would ride with the poor.
> So they put the poor below,
> They were the first to go.[27]

do not necessarily contain any social message; rather, they are carrying the message of a God-fearing people.

Yet the Titanic disaster did evince social commentary in the songs which were written about it, especially in Negro renditions. This may have been because the story was circulated that Jack Johnson, the Negro Heavyweight Champion of the World, was not allowed on the boat and thus his life was saved, an irony which appealed to the Negro sense of humor. Leadbelly, in his song about the disaster says:

> Jack Johnson wanted to get on boa'd:
> Captain Smith hollered, "I ain't haulin' no coal."
> Cryin' "Fare thee, Titanic, fare thee well."

and later:

> Jack Johnson heard the mighty shock,
> Might'a' seen the black rascal doin' th' Eagle Rock.
> Cryin', "Fare thee, Titanic, fare thee well."
>
> Black man oughta shout for joy,
> Never lost a girl or either a boy.
> Cryin', "Fare thee, Titanic, fare thee well."[28]

26. White, *American,* p. 348.
27. White, *American,* p. 347.
28. Lomax, *Negro Folk Songs,* p. 182.

This irony may indeed account for the popularity which the story of the tragedy has had among the Negro.[29]

Yet this irony is only the germ of the one which is exercised in our toast. A great deal of the source of the humor in the piece depends also on the same triumphant ironic features that the Negro escapes while the whites all drown (with the crowning touch that "Shine" was already home and nearly drunk by the time news had arrived there). Yet this irony is made so much more effective by the fact that before the ship has gone down, Shine has been offered money and sex and refuses them.

In the figure of "Shine," the young Negro has found a character that exhibits in abundance many of the characteristics highly valued by him. He is more than a mere trickster with anxious repartee. He is to be regarded, both because of his actions and his name (generic for any male Negro), as a representative hero of his group. This toast may not be the only piece about him, but may simply be the most lively and memorable of them. Though I have not encountered any other full toast about Shine, pieces of others have come my way. "Kid" sometimes appends his Titanic toast with the following:

> Shine had two-cents in his pocket.
> He went to a place called "Dew-drop Inn."
> He asked the broads to give him cock* for a lousy fin.
> She took Shine upstairs and she gave him a fuck, and all this pats.
> He came out with the syphs, the crabs, lobstertoes*, and a hell of a case of the claps.
> He went to the doctor. Said, "Doctor, Doctor, can't you 'stand.
> Please remember I'm a fucked-up man."
> Doctor got his bag, rips in his tools.
> He says, "Sit here on my three-legged stool."
> He started hammering and cutting, breaking and sawing.

29. There seem to have been a number of white songs on the tragedy, but their currency in tradition is small indeed. See *Brown Collection*, pp. 663-66; Mellinger E. Henry, *Songs Sung in the Southern Appalachians* (London, 1933), p. 88; Mellinger E. Henry, *Folksongs From the Southern Highlands* (New York, 1938), pp. 426-27; Emelyn Elizabeth Gardner and Geraldine Jencks Chickering, *Ballads and Songs of Southern Michigan* (Ann Arbor, 1939), p. 295. Many of the above are related to the song very popular at campuses and camps, and which may be of Negro origin itself, as many early recordings testify; see *Folkways*, FP 221, #22, as sung by W. V. Smith.

Shine said, "Doc, is that the best you can do?"
He said, "Quiet, motherfucker, 'cause your nuts go too."

In a version which I collected in Texas, the descent into Hell, usually in "Stackolee" (with its relation to "The Farmer's Curst Wife"), is connected to Shine:

At half past four Shine came in the B & O,
And rolled up to the whore house door.
And said, "Come here all you whores, and don't you pout
'Cause I'm a peter-pushing papa, and a water trout.
I measures thirty-six inches across the chest,
And I don't borrow nothing but sickness and death.
I've got a tombstone disposition and a graveyard mind;
I'm one motherfucker that don't mind dying."
When Shine was dead from drinking his gin
The devil said, "You're a long time coming but you are
    welcome in."
He sent the devil for a glass of water.
When the devil came back, he was fucking the devil's
    daughter.
The devil stooped over to pick up a glass,
He rammed his dick in the devil's ass.
Two little imps standing against the wall
Said, "Get that black motherfucker out of here before he
    fucks us all."

Such additions make Shine into more of the badman than he previously appeared.

1A.

It was a hell of day in the merry month of May
When the great Titanic was sailing away.
The captain and his daughter was there, too,
And old black Shine, he didn't need no crew.
Shine was downstairs eating his peas
When the motherfucking water come up to his knees.
He said, "Captain, Captain, I was downstairs eating my
    peas
When the water come up to my knees."
He said, "Shine, Shine, set your black ass down.
I got ninety-nine pumps to pump the water down."
Shine went downstairs looking through space.

That's when the water came up to his waist.

He said, "Captain, Captain, I was downstairs looking
    through space,

That's when the water came up to my waist."

He said, "Shine, Shine, set your black ass down.

I got ninety-nine pumps to pump the water down."

Shine went downstairs, he ate a piece of bread.

That's when the water came above his head.

He said, "Captain, Captain, I was downstairs eating my
    bread

And the motherfucking water came above my head."

He said, "Shine, Shine, set your black ass down.

I got ninety-nine pumps to pump the water down."

Shine took off his shirt, took a dive. He took one stroke

And the water pushed him like it pushed a motorboat.

The Captain said, "Shine, Shine, save poor me.

I'll give you more money than any black man see."

Shine said, "Money is good on land or sea.

Take off your shirt and swim like me."

That's when the Captain's daughter came on deck;

Hands on her pussy, and drawers 'round her neck.

Says, "Shine, Shine, save poor me.

Give you more pussy than any black man see."

Shine said, "Pussy ain't nothing but meat on the bone,

You may fuck it or suck it or leave it alone.

I like cheese but I ain't no rat.

I like pussy, but not like that."

And Shine swum on.

He said, "I hope you meet up with the whale."

Old Shine he swim mighty fine.

Shine met up with the whale.

The whale said, "Shine, Shine, you swim mighty fine,

But if you miss one stroke, your black ass is mine.' '

Shine said, "You may be king of the ocean, king of the sea,

But you got to be a swimming motherfucker to outswim me."

And Shine swim on.

Now when the news got to the port, the great Titanic had
    sunk,

You won't believe this, but old Shine was on the corner,
    damn near drunk.

Arthur

1B.

It was back then a long time when the great Titanic was
    sinking away.
Shine, a little man, was off on the port side.
He come over and he said, "Captain, Captain, the water's
    over the first fireroom door."
He said, "Shine, Shine," he said, "Have no doubt,
For we got forty-nine pumps to pump that old water out."
Shine went down and came up again.
He said, "Captain, that damn water's still coming in."
Captain said, "Shine, Shine, have no doubt.
I told you we got ninety-nine pumps to pump the water
    out."
Shine said, "There was a time, your word might be true,
But this is one god damn time your word just won't do."
Shine jumped overboard, throwed two kicks and one
    stroke,
Was off like a motorboat.
Captain came up on deck. He said, "Shine, Shine, save
    poor me.
I'll give you more money than a man want to see."
Shine said, "There's money on land, money on sea,
But I keep on stroking, that money on land be best for me."
Captain's daughter came up on the deck
With her drawers in her hand, brassiere around her neck.
She said, "Shine, Shine, save poor me.
I'll give you more pregnant pussy than any black man
    want to see."
Shine said, "You know my color, and you guessed my race.
You better come in here and give these sharks a chase."
Shine kept a-swimming. Come past a shark's den.
Shark looked at Shine and invited him on in.
Shine said, "I heard about you. You the king of the ocean,
    the king of the sea,
But you got to be a stroking motherfucker to outstroke me."
When word got to Washing' times the great Titanic was
    sunk,
Shine was on Broadway, one-third drunk.

"Kid"

1C.

(Second Night's Version)

One day when the great Titanic was sinking away,
Captain was in his quarters one lonely night,
This old man came up the port side.
He said, "Captain, Captain, the water's over the first fire-
room door."
He said, "Shine, Shine, have no doubt.
We got forty-nine pumps to pump the water out.
Shine went down and he came up again.
He said, "Captain, look! That damn water's still coming in."
Captain said, "Shine, Shine, have no doubt,
Now we have ninety-nine pumps to pump the water out."
He said, "Captain, there was a time when your word might
be true,
But this is one damn time your word won't do.
So Shine he jumped overboard. He took two kicks, one
stroke,
He was off like a P.T. boat.
Captain came up on the deck. He said, "Shine, Shine, save
poor me.
I'll give you more money than any black man want to see."
Shine said, "You know my color and you guessed my race.
Come in here and give these sharks a chase."
Captain's daughter came up on deck,
Drawers in her hand, brassiere around her neck.
She said, "Shine, Shine, save poor me.
Give you more pregnant pussy than a black man want to
see."
Shine said, "I know you're pregnant, 'bout to have a kid,
But if that boat sink two more inches, you'll swim this
coast just like Shine did."
The Captain's wife came up on deck. She said, "Shine,
Shine, save poor me.
I'll let you eat pussy like a rat eats cheese."
Shine said, "I like pussy, I ain't no rat.
I like cock, but not like that."
Shine kept a-swimming.
Shine came past the whale's den.
The whale invited old Shine in.

Shine said, "I know you're king of the ocean, king of the
   sea,
But you gotta be a water-splashing motherfucker to out-
   swim me."
So Shine kept on stroking.
Now Shine met up with the shark.
Shark said, "Shine, Shine, can't you see.
When you jump in these waters you belongs to me."
Shine said, "I know you outswim the barracuda, outsmart
   every fish in the sea,
But you gotta be a stroking motherfucker to outswim me."
Shine kept a-swimming.
When the word got to Washington that the great Titanic
   had sunk,
Shine was on Broadway, one-third drunk.

                                        "Kid"

1D.

The eighth of May was one hell of a day
When the Titanic was sinking away.
Babies was crying and mothers was dying.
Boy, what a hell of a day,
The Titanic was sinking away.
Well on aboard that ship they had a man named Shine.
He ran up to the Captain, said, "Captain, Captain, don't
   your know,
There's a leak in your boiler-room floor?"
Captain looked at Shine, said, "Shine, Shine, have no fear.
Got three pumps to keep the water out of here."
Shine went down and closed the boiler-room door,
And he didn't fear no more,
Till the water come up to his waist.
He said, "Captain, Captain, don't you know,
You got nine holes in your boiler-room floor."
Captain said, "Shine, Shine, have no fear,
We got nine pumps to keep the water out of here."
He went down below. The water came up to his neck.
He said, "Captain, Captain, don't you know,
You got ninety-nine holes in the boiler-room floor?"
Captain said, "Shine, Shine, have no fear,
We got ninety-nine pumps to keep the water out of here."

He said, "Captain, Captain, I know your word is true."
He said, "But if you want the water out of here, you got to
    get down there and pump it till your ass is blue."
Shine jumped overboard and begin to swim.
Now the millionaire on board, with his daughter was pack-
    ing his trunk.
He land in the motherfucking porthole, damn-near drunk.
She went up on deck with her drawers below her knees.
She said, "Shine, Shine, save poor me.
I'll give much pussy as pussy can be."
Shine says, "Pussy on land, there's pussy on the sea,
But the pussy on land's the pussy for me."
So Shine started to swim, he begin to stroke.
He begin to wiggle like a motorboat.
And the Captain run up, said, "Shine, Shine, save poor me.
I'll give you much money as money can be."
Shine said, "Captain, that might be,
But you got to jump in this motherfucking water and swim
    like me."
He swam, he swam, he begin to stroke.
He was beginning to move like a motorboat.
Till he swum up to a shark.
He said, "Mr. Shark, of all the fishes in the sea,
I'll be damned if you can outswim me.
Your eyes may shine, your teeth may grip
          (couldn't remember any more)

Charley

1E.

The eighth of May was a hell of a day
When the Titanic was sinking away.
Yeah, what a hell of a day, when the news reached the
    seaport town
The Titanic was sinking down.
Shine went below deck, eating his peas
Till the water come up to his knees.
Shine went up on deck, said, "Captain, I was downstairs
    eating my peas
Till the water come up to my knees."
Captain said, "Shine, Shine, sit your black ass down.
I got ninety-nine pumps to pump the water down."

Shine went back down below deck, looking through space
Till the water came up to his waist.
Shine went up on deck, said, "Captain, I was downstairs
    looking through space
Till the water came up to my waist."
Captain said, "Shine, Shine, sit your ass down,
Got ninety-nine pumps to pump the water down."
Shine went down below deck eating his bread
Till the water came up to his head.
Shine went up on deck, said, "Captain, I was downstairs
    eating my bread
Till the water came up to my head."
He said, "Shine, Shine, sit your ass down.
Got ninety-nine pumps to pump the water down."
Shine took off his shirt and started to take a dive.
Captain's daughter came over to Shine.
Said, "Shine, Shine, save poor me.
Give you all the pussy eyes ever did see."
Shine said, "Pussy ain't nothing but meat on the bone,
You can fuck it, you can suck it, you can leave it alone."
Shine jumped in the water and met up with a shark.
Shark said, "Shine, Shine,
You miss one stroke, your black ass is mine.
Shine said, "You may be king of the ocean, king of the sea,
You got to be a swimming motherfucker to outswim me."
And Shine swim on.

Bobby

2. STACKOLEE

The history of the notorious badman Stackolee (or Stagolee) is indeed a curious one. Glancing at the various stories and songs concerning him, one can see that he was a "bully," a self-appointed guardian, the cock-of-the-walk of a neighborhood or a small town.

> Stagolee was a bully man, an' ev'ybody knowed
> When seed Stagolee comin' to give Stagolee de road.
> Oh, dat man, bad man, Stagolee done come.[30]

This kind of personage used to be common in Southern towns among the Negro community and is still flourishing in parts of the South. He has his roots in primitive tribalism (leadership by

30. *Journal of American Folklore*, XXIV (1911), p. 288.

prowess, or apparent control of people and/or nature), and his modern urban counterpart is the gang-leader. The bully is not responsive or responsible to white laws or society; he is a law unto himself, and his only obligation is to uphold, by his physical powers, the honor of the neighborhood, or town. In many cases, when he is not fighting, he may be terrorizing, in one way or another, his own neighbors; but even though he may be mean by nature, he seems to remain extremely attractive to women. (The portrait of "Crown" in "Porgy and Bess" seems to be an accurate picture of this type.)

In his guise as guardian, the bully is liable to attack from those that would depose him, either from the same neighborhood, or from another. He is a "bad man" both by nature and in the sense that his acts almost always violate the white man's laws. But he is not really to be judged by such morality, at least by his own people, as the apparent (approved) amorality of toasts and songs about Stack testifies.

Odum and Johnson describe Stack in terms of the bully. They say:

> The notorious character is sung as a hero of the tribe.
> His deeds are marvelous, his personality is interesting.
> He is admired by young and old in song and story and
> undoubtedly has an important influence upon the group.[31]

It is evident that Stack's most celebrated exploit (the one described in all of the ballads and toasts), the fight between Stack and Billy Lyons, was a fight between two bullies. "Bully" and "Billy" are so similarly pronounced that they could be easily interchanged; Billy's last name may originally have been "lion" (it is not untypical for a leader of this sort to take on the name of an animal), and this Billy Lyons may thus originally have been "Bully Lion."[32] "Lyon" is just as typical a spelling as "Lyons," and Richard

---

31. Howard W. Odum and Guy B. Johnson, *The Negro and His Songs* (Chapel Hill, 1925), p. 196.

32. It is interesting to note that in Onah Spencer's piece, "Stackolee," which is a semi-literary rehandling of traditional material (originally published in *Direction*, IV [Summer, 1941], pp. 14-17, and later printed by Botkin in *A Treasury of American Folklore* [New York, 1944], pp. 122-30, and Hughes and Bontemps, *Book*, pp. 361-63), there is a stanza:

> "Jailer, jailer," says Stack, "I can't sleep.
> For round my bedside poor Billy Lyons still creeps.
> "He comes in shape of a lion with a blue steel in his hand,
> For he knows I'll stand and fight if he comes in shape of man."

Dorson spells it as the animal.[33] One of the earliest versions of the song simply calls him "big bully":

> I got up one mornin' jus' 'bout four o'clock;
> Stagolee and big bully done have one finish' fight.
> What 'bout? All 'bout dat rawhide Stetson hat.
>
> Stagolee shot bully; bully fell down on de flo',
> Bully cry out: "Dat fohty-fo' it hurts me so."
> Stagolee done kill dat bully now.[34]

Most of the reported versions of the song involve the story of Stack killing Billy because the latter won Stack's Stetson hat. The earliest versions, however, are not so explicit. The two texts published by Odum in 1911 never specify any of the victims; in one it is simply:

> Stagolee started out, he give his wife his han';
> Goodbye, darlin', I'm goin' to kill a man."
>
> Stagolee killed a man an' laid him on de flo',
> What's dat he kill him wid? Dat same ole fohty-fo'.[35]

Most versions begin with some sort of introduction about Stack's badman characteristics:

> Stagolee, he was a bad man, an' ev'body know,
> He toted a stack-barreled blow gun an' a blue steel 44.[36]
>
> Stackerlee, he was a bad man,
> He wanted the whole round world to know
> He toted a 32-20
> And a smokeless 44.[37]

33. Dorson, *Negro Folktales in Michigan*, pp. 160-62. Also notice introduction of Billy Lion into the animal toast, p. 322.

34. Odum and Johnson, *The Negro and His Songs*, pp. 196-98. First printed, JAF, XXIV (1911), p. 288. Also reprinted, MacEdward Leach, *The Ballad Book* (New York, 1955), pp. 755-56; Dorothy Scarborough, *On the Trail of Negro Folksong* (Cambridge, Mass., 1925), pp. 92-93.

35. Odum and Johnson, *The Negro and His Songs*, p. 197.

36. John A. and Alan Lomax, *American Ballads and Folk Songs* (New York, 1934), p. 96.

37. "Negro Prison Songs," collected and annotated by Alan Lomax, Tradition Records, TLP 1020, Side B, Band 7.

> I remember when I was a little boy,
> Sittin' on my mother's knee,
> She often told me the story
> About that bad man, Stackerlee.[38]

There then usually follows a description of the gambling in which Billy wins the hat. Often it begins with a "discovery" verse:

> It was late last night
> I thought I heard my bulldog bark
> Stagolee and Billy Lyons,
> Squabblin' in the dark.[39]

and proceeds to the apparent victory of Billy. Stack gets his gun and comes back to get Billy, and he often pleads for him not to kill him.

> Stagolee found Billy,
> "Oh, please don't take my life.
> I got three children
> And a very sick little wife."[40]

The shooting itself is often described graphically:

> Stagolee shot Billy,
> Oh, he shot that boy so fas'
> That the bullet came through him
> And broke my window glass.[41]

In some versions there follows a trial scene, and in some others Stack is killed and goes to Hell. In some of these latter, he beats the Devil at his own game, either to be expelled or to rule in Hell.

There are quite a number of texts of the ballad in print. Odum's versions, printed in 1911, have served as the texts for many other books and collections.[42] The Lomaxes include two collated texts in *American Ballads and Folk Songs*.[43] Wheeler has a number of versions, one of which has Stack as the hero of "Bully of the

38. "Blues in the Mississippi Night," collected and edited by Alan Lomax, United Artists, UAL 4027 (end of Side A).

39. Lomax, "Blues in the Mississippi Night."

40. "Angola Prisoners' Blues," collected by Dr. Harry Oster and Richard B. Allen, Folk-Lyric Record, LFS A-3, Side A, Band 2.

41. Oster, "Angola Prisoners' Blues."

42. *New York Times Magazine* (June 5, 1927). Albert Friedman published a collated version of these texts in *The Viking Book of Ballads* (New York, 1956), pp. 381-82.

43. Lomax, *American Ballads,* pp. 93-99.

Town."[44] Alan Lomax, in his most recent volume, has a text of a chain-gang work song version.[45] Onah Spencer has a long text in his saga of "Stackalee," which has been reprinted by Botkin and by Hughes and Bontemps, but which presents special problems concerning its semi-literary rehandling. It is really only through the many recordings that one can fully realize the popularity of the ballad.[46]

Stack was not only a bully; he seems to have been of the roughest type, the levee-bully. His place of origin is not precisely known, but he is always associated with some town on the Mississippi. Most commentators place him from Memphis. Alan Lomax says unequivocally, "Legend has it that Stacker Lee . . . was the most dangerous Negro tough of Memphis in his time, and that he shot and killed Billy Lyons, because Billy stole, or, in some accounts, spat in Stack's milkwhite Stetson hat."[47] In a letter sending in a text of the song as sung earlier than 1910, the following remarks were made:

> The origin of this ballad, I have been told was the shooting of Billy Lyons in a barroom on the Memphis levee, by Stack Lee. The song is sung by Negroes on the levee while they are loading and unloading the river freighters, the words being composed by the singers. The characters were prominently known in Memphis, I was told, the unfortunate Stagalee belonging to the family of the Lee line of steamers, which are known on the Mississippi from Cairo to the Gulf.[48]

44. Mary Wheeler, *Steamboatin' Days*, pp. 100-102.
45. *Folk Songs of North America* (New York, 1961), p. 306.
46. Charles Finger, *Frontier Ballads* (New York, 1927), p. 91. Further printed references are: Sigmund Spaeth, *Weep Some More, My Lady* (New York, 1927); Robert W. Gordon, *Folk Songs of America*, National Service Bureau (New York, 1938), (printed from *New York Times Magazine*); Olive W. Burt, *American Murder Ballads* (New York, 1958).
  Recordings of the song include: Alan Lomax, *Negro Prison Songs from the Mississippi State Penitentiary*, Tradition Records, TLP 1020 (collected 1947); Frank Hutchinson, original issue, OKEH 45106 (w80-359A), recorded in early 1927 (this is on *American Folk Music*, Vol. I, *Ballads*, Folkways, FP 251); John Hurt, OKEH 8654; Johnny Dodds and his Chicago Boys ("Stack O'Lee Blues") DE-1676; Woody Guthrie, ASCH-347 (also Folkways 781); Alan Lomax, *Listen to Our Story*, BR-1024; Paul Clayton, *Bloody Ballads*, Riverside RLP 12-615; Cisco Houston, Folkways 42; Furry Lewis, Brunswick 59001; Ed McCurdy, Elektra 108; Ma Rainey, Riverside 12-108; Logan English, Riverside 12-643; Jesse Fuller, Good Time Jazz L-12031.
47. Notes to "Negro Prison Songs."
48. Lomax, *American Ballads*, pp. 93-94.

There were many such conjectures as to his birth and occupation. "His real name was Stack Lee and he was the son of the Lee family of Memphis who owned a large line of steamers that ran up and down the Mississippi. . . . He was a nigger what fired the engines of one of the Lee Steamers. . . . They was a steamer runnin' up an' down de Mississippi, named de Stacker Lee, and he was one o' de roustabouts on dat steamer. So dey called him Stackerlee."[49] Certain it is that there was such a steamer with his name;[50] Edna Ferber even included it in *Showboat*. Wheeler has a song about the boat.

The ballad and the toast stem from the same dramatic situation, the killing of Billy by Stack, but they do not share much else. In some versions of the ballad the shooting takes place in a barroom and the locale of the toast is the particular bar-cafe, "The Bucket of Blood." Gone is the controversy over the Stetson; the fight between bullies is sufficient rationale (based on the fact that Stack has shot Billy's brother). The ironic verse

> Stagolee tol' Mrs. Billy, "Ef you don't b'lieve yo man
>   is dead,
> Come to de barroom, see de hole I shot in his head."[51]

is also found in the toast, but the words are put into the mouth of the bartender's mother:

> She said, "You don't mean to tell me my son is dead."
> I said, "If you don't believe it, look at those mother-
>   fucking rockets in his god damn head."
>
>   (C text)

Only in the "C" text is any courtroom scene included and then it is for a different purpose than that found in the ballad.

The three texts of the toasts included here are similar in many respects. They all begin with a description of the times; a catalog of Stack's earthly belongings; the walk down the street; the entering of "The Bucket of Blood"; the serving of the unfortunate meal, and the consequent killing of the bartender; the arrival of the dead man's mother and her warning about the coming of her other son, Billy Lyons (or Benny Long); the deploying of the girl to keep Stack there by "taking him upstairs"; the arrival of Billy; the fight;

49. Lomax, *American Ballads*, p. 93.

50. See *Midwest Folklore*, 10:77. Also see Wheeler, *Steamboatin' Days*, pp. 102-103.

51. Lomax, *American Ballads*, p. 97.

and Billy's demise. Each adds little interesting scenes, such as the other characters in the bar in the "A" text. The endings of the "A" and "B" texts are conventional boasts which may well have traveled from the river with the stories of Stack. The ending of the "C" text is the conventional courtroom scene described in the introduction to this chapter.

Nothing like the toast has ever appeared in print. D. K. Wilgus has sent four texts from the Western Kentucky Folklore Archives which are very similar to the Philadelphia texts. Three of his texts have the same general plan of the "C" text of this collection. The fourth has the outlines of "A" and "B" with the boast at the end, and also has the type of signature to be found in Arthur's version of "The Monkey and the Baboon." There are two texts in the Texas Archives, one collected by myself from a student who had it from a Negro marine in San Diego in 1959. The other was collected by Debra Galoob and is printed in bowdlerized form in her article referred to above.

There are, however, two places in which toast-like pieces appear in print concerning the Stackolee story. The first of these is contained in an article by Richard Dorson, "Negro Tales." He includes two texts which show clearly that the ballad and the toast are related. His first text includes verses from the ballad, including the one about the bulldog barking and arguing in the dark, and goes on to a number of lines of boasts including the one commonly found in the toast about rattlesnakes crawling off and dying.[52] His second text is sometimes in verse form, sometimes in prose, and also includes verses from the ballad.[53] The prose passages show, by their occasional rhymes, some contact with a toast; this is also shown in the references to clocks and time, which is found often in the toast, but not, so far as I have found, in the song. Hughes and Bontemps[54] include a similar text that seems to be in toast form, but which has the story told in the ballad, and which ends with Stack running

52. These boasts are some widely known ones. JAF, 40:293, has the similar:

> I was born in a backyard
> Suckled by a bear
> I got nine sets of jaw teeth
> An' three coaches of hair.

See the rattlesnake boast in N. Howard Thorp, *Songs of the Cowboys* (Boston and New York, 1921), p. 17, in a song called "Buckskin Joe."

53. Dorson, *Western Folklore*, pp. 160-62.

54. Hughes and Bontemps, *Book of Negro Folklore*, pp. 361-63.

Hell after vanquishing the Devil and having an affair with his wife.
"Kid" gives a similar narrative about Stack and Billy in joke form:

> Now you know, everybody heard the joke about Stacko-
> lee. Well, they didn't tell you that Stackolee died and Billy
> died and they went to Hell. Devil said to Billy, "I seen
> you every day and I know you was coming. I knowed you
> was on your way." So he told Billy he could have all the
> fun he wants, just to keep away from his wife.
>
> So Billy was goofing around one day and got hold of the
> Devil's wife, started working. Got through, he got hold of
> the Devil's daughter, started to working. Got through,
> grabbed hold of the Devil's niece, he started working. He
> was running around Hell trying to catch the Devil's wife.
> She said, "Devil, get him down." When three little jumpy
> little bastards jumped out of the wall and said, "Get that
> motherfucker before he fucks us all."

2A.

Back in '32 when times was hard
I had a sawed-off shotgun and a crooked deck of cards,
Pin-striped suit, fucked-up hat,
T-model Ford, didn't even have a payment on that.
Had a cute little broad, she throwed me out in the cold.
I asked her why, she said, "Our love is growing old."
So I packed all my little rags, took a walk down Rampail
    Street.
That's where all the bad motherfuckers went down to meet.
I walked through water and I waded through mud,
Come a little hole-in-the-wall, they call the "Bucket of
    Blood."
I walked in and asked the bartender, "Dig chief, can I get
    something to eat?"
He throwed me a stale glass of water and flung me a
    fucked-up piece of meat.
I said, "Raise, motherfucker, do you know who I am?"
He said, "Frankly, motherfucker, I just don't give a damn."
I knowed right then that chickenshit* was dead.
I threw a 38 shell through his motherfucking head.
So a broad walked over, she said, "Pardon me, please.
Can you tell me where the bartender is, please?"

I said, "Sure, whore, behind the bar with his mind at ease."
She looked back and screamed, "No! My son can't be dead."
I said, "You don't think so? Look at the hole in that mother-
    fucker's head."
She said, "Who did this terrible crime, may I ask you
    please?"
I said, "Me, bitch, and my name is Stackolee."
She said, "Oh, I heard of you, Stack, from the tales of old.
Be here when my son Benny Long get back."
I said, "Bitch,* I'll be here till the world go to pass.
You tell your son, Benny Long, that I said, 'kiss my ass'."
Just then a cute little broad came over, a terrible smile.
She looked me up and down and said, "You look like you
    ain't had none, Daddy, in quite a while."
I said, "Now raise, bitch, don't hand me that shit.
I'm used to pussy quite a bit."
She looked at her watch, it was quarter to eight.
She said, "Come on upstairs, I'ma set you straight."
The bed gave a twist, the springs gave a twistle.
I throwed nine inches of joint* to the whore* before she
    could move a gristle.
We came back downstairs. They was fucking on the bar,
    sucking on the floor.
Just then you could hear a pin drip, for that bad-ass Benny
    Long walked in the door.
Now he walked over to the bar where his brother lay dead,
And quietly said,
"Who had nerve to put a hole in *my* brother's head?"
I jumped up and screamed, "Me, motherfucker, put your
    mind at ease.
I'm known as a bad motherfucker called Stackolee."
He said, "Oh, I heard of you, Stack, from tales of old.
But you know you done tore your ass when you fucked
    my hole.
I'ma give you the chance my brother never had. I'ma give
    you the chance to run,
Before I throw upen my bad-ass cashmere* and pull my
    bad-ass gun."
Just then some little short motherfucker, way over in the
    corner jumped up and hollered, "Somebody call the
    law."

Benny Long throwed a 45 shell through the motherfucker's
 jaw.
His broad walked over, she said, "Benny, please."
He beat that whore down to her motherfucking knees.
Just then everything got black, 'cause out went the lights.
I had that old bad-ass Benny Long in my 38 sights.
When the lights came back on and all the best,
I had sent that old bad motherfucker to internal *(sic)* rest.
Thirteen 38 bulletholes 'cross his motherfucking chest.
His boys jumped up and said, "Ain't this a shame.
Here's a man got our boss, Benny Long there on the floor
 dead.
This jive-ass motherfucker's reputation we haven't ever
 heard."
They dove in their coats and went down for this shit.
I said, "Cool* it motherfuckers, let me tell you a bit.
I was born in the backwoods, for my pet my father raised
 a bear.
I got two sets of jawbone teeth, and an extra layer of hair.
When I was three I sat in a barrel of knives.
A rattlesnake bit me and crawled off and died.
'Cause after I get up and leave, my ass-hole print leaves
 'danger'."

"Kid"

2B.

Back in '32 when times was hard
Had a sawed-off shotgun with a crooked deck of cards.
Had a pin-striped suit, old fucked-up hat,
And a T-model Ford, not a payment on that.
I had a cute little whore, throwed me out in the cold.
When I asked her why, she said, "Our love is growing old."
I took a little walk down Rampart Street,
Where all them bad-assed motherfuckers meet.
I walked through water and I waded through mud.
I came to a little-old hole-in-the-wall called the "Bucket
 of Blood."
I walked in, asked the man for something to eat.
Do you know that bastard gave me a stale glass of water
 and a fucked-up piece of meat.
I said, "Raise, motherfucker, do you know who I am?"

He said, "Frankly, I don't give a damn."
I know right then that sucker was dead.
I throwed a 38 shell through that motherfucker's head.
Now a cute little whore* came up and said, "Where's the
    bartender, please?"
I said, "Look behind the bar, baby, he's with his mind at
    ease."
She grabbed her head.
She said, "No, my son can't be dead."
I said, "No? Look at the hole in that motherfucker's head."
She said, "Who did this crime, may I ask you, please?"
I said, "Me, bitch,* and they call me Stackolee."
She said, "I heard of you Stack,
But you better not be here when my son Benny Long gets
    back."
I said, "Bitch, I'll be here when the world go to pass.
And you can tell Benny Long he can kiss my ass."
Still another cute little whore came up, said, "Where's the
    bartender?
Hi, there, baby, where's the bartender, if you please?"
I said, "Look behind the bar, he's with his mind at ease."
So she peeped at her watch, it was seven of eight.
She said, "Come upstairs, baby, let me set you straight."
Now we went upstairs, the springs give a twistle.
I throwed nine inches of dick* into that bitch before she
    could move her gristle.
Now we came downstairs big and bold.
They was fucking on the bar, sucking on the floor.
Then you could hear a pin drop. Benny Long came in.
He walked over where his brother lay dead, and he calmly
    said,
"Who had the nerve to put a hole in my brother's head?"
When I jumped up, I said, "Me, motherfucker, so put your
    mind at ease.
I'm that bad-ass so-and-so they call Stackolee."
He said, "I heard of you, Stack, from the tales of old,
But you know you tore your ass when you fucked my hole.
But I'ma give you the chance my brother never got. I'ma
    give you a chance to run,
'Fore I reach in my cashmere* and pull out my bad-ass
    gun."

Just then some old sucker over in the corner said, "Some-
    body call the law."
He stretched out and put a 45 shell through that mother-
    fucker's jaw.
A cute little whore came over and said, "Benny, please."
He blowed that bitch down to her knees.
And out went the lights,
And Benny Long was in both of my 38 sights.
Now the lights came on and all the best.
I sent that sucker to eternal rest,
With thirteen 38 bullet-holes 'cross his motherfucking chest.
This boy said, "Who is this sucker whose name we haven't
    heard
Got our boss laying there dead?
We ought to kill this motherfucker to fuck him up."
I said, "Cool it,* motherfucker, let me tell you a bit.
I was raised in the backwoods, where my pa raised a bear.
And I got three sets of jawbone teeth and an extra layer
    of hair.
When I was three I sat in a barrel of knives.
Then a rattlesnake bit me, crawled off and died.
So when I come in here, I'm no stranger,
'Cause when I leave my ass-hole print leaves 'danger'."

Arthur

2 C.

In 1938 when things was hard
I had a crooked pair of dice and a stacked deck of cards.
I waded through water and I waded through mud
Until I came to a place called the "Bucket of Blood."
Now I went in to get myself a little something to eat
And the waiter brought me back a muddy glass of water
    and a tough-ass piece of meat.
I said, "Say, motherfucker, do you know who this might be?
This is that bad motherfucker named Stackolee."
The waiter looked at me and said,
"I heard 'bout you from 'cross the way,
But I feed you hungry motherfuckers each and every day."
Now I pull out my gun and layed three rockets in his
    motherfucking head.
He fell out behind the counter dead.

Little lady came in and said, "Where's the waiter, please?"
I said, "He's laying behind the counter with his mind at
    ease."
She said, "You don't mean to tell me my son is dead."
I said, "If you don't believe it, look at those motherfucking
    rockets* in his god damn head."
She fell out on the god damn floor,
And here come walked up to me a pretty little whore.
Said, "Hello, Stackolee, I haven't seen you in a mighty
    long time."
She looked at the clock, it was about quarter to eight.
She said, "Come on upstairs and I'll see you straight."
Now I went upstairs and we begin to fuck.
I begin to push dick to this whore like a ten-ton truck.
And then everything was going 'long fine
When out walked Billy Lyon.
At first I thought it was the motherfucking law,
The way the hinges jumped off the god-damned door.
I looked around, said, "What the fuck this might be?"
He said, "You know you bad motherfucker, I know your
    name is Stackolee."
I said, "And by the way, what's your name, look so fine?"
He said, "Shut up, motherfucker, this is Billy Lyon."
Now some dirty bitch turned out the light,
But I had Billy Lyon in my god-damned sight.
One little bitch hollered, "Stackolee, please."
I shot that bitch clean to her knees.
The other one hollered, "Call the law."
I shot that bitch in the god-damned jaw.
Now three of them old Mississippi police came in all loud
    and raunchy.*
"Let's kick this motherfucker's ass and go on home."
Well I guess it was 'round nine o'clock, or somewhere
    'round ten
I was standing before some jive-ass* judge and ten other
    men.
One motherfucker said, "What may the charges be?"
One said, "Murder," one said, "Rape," one said, "Murder
    in the third degree."
Then the old judge said, "Well, how might he die?"
One said, "Hang him," one said, "Give him gas."

Little lady jumped up in the courtroom and said, "Run
    'lectricity through the rotten motherfucker's ass."
I grabbed that bitch by the seat of her drawers
And threw her out the courtroom door.
Judge said, "Stackolee, I see you're a man without any fear,
So I'ma give you ninety-nine years."
I looked at him, said, "Judge, ninety-nine ain't no god-
    damn time.
My father's in Sing Sing doing two-ninety-nine.

Charley

3 - 4. *THE SIGNIFYING MONKEY*

These toasts about the adventures of "The Signifying Monkey"
may be the last lively gasp of the Negro tradition of animal stories.
As in the famed series about "Brer Rabbit" or even "Anansi," the
animals act like animals often only to show the similarities of themselves to humans. As in these older tales, these toasts present a
milieu which is half natural-habitat, half world-of-man, and characters which sometimes act like the animals whose names they
bear and sometimes like human beings. The shift between these
oppositions is done without any sense of existing conflict at all.

Deep down in the jungles, way back in the sticks,
The animals had formed a game called "pool." The baboon
    was a slick.*
Now a few stalks shook and a few leaves fell.
Up popped the monkey one day, 'bout sharp as hell.

The animals seem equally at home in the "jungle" or on the street;
the monkey is equally adept at climbing trees and shooting pool.
Though he is portrayed as a tree climber, he is the sharpest of
dressers by human standards.

He had a one-button roll,* two-button satch.*
You know, one them boolhipper* coats with a belt in the
    back.

or

He had a camel-hair benny* with a belt in the back,
He'd a pair of nice shoes and a pair of blue slacks.
Now his clothes were cute little things,
Was wearing a Longine watch and a diamond ring.

136

The baboon is easily his match, though:

> The baboon stood with a crazy rim,*
> Charcoal grey vine,* and a stingy brim,*
> Hand full of dimes, pocket full of herbs,*
> Eldorado Cadillac parked at the curb.

Much like his predecessors, "Brer Rabbit" and "Anansi," the monkey is a trickster figure; his mode of life, his existence depends upon his agility, mental and physical. Though not solely the possession of the Negro, the trickster figure has figured very greatly in his folklore. The fact that the monkey fits into this type is patent. He is not only a "clever hero . . . smaller and weaker" and a "diminutive animal" but his adventure with the lion qualifies him for the epithet of "villain" or "rogue," often attached to the trickster figure.

There is a noticeable diminution of interest among the Negro for stories of the trickster type. The spider, the rabbit, the Marster and John cycles have all, for the most part, passed out of their lore, at least among the urban Negro. The monkey here is the last remnant of this type, and it is perhaps significant that he is killed in some versions of his adventure with the lion.

It is interesting to note that this "hero" is a monkey. In the minds of a certain segment of the white population of the world, the Negro has been associated with the monkey. Perhaps because of his African jungle heritage and the casual resemblance between some Negroid and some simian physical characteristics, the words "monkey" and "ape" have been used as derogatory words in relation to the Negro, and have achieved a meaning and notoriety not very different from "nigger." In much the same way that "nigger" has come to mean, among Negroes, any bad kind of Negro, so the word "monkey" has come to mean any Negro that will unduly play around, and especially for the amusement of whites. As one Negro youth is reported to have said, "If you can act big enough monkey, you can get anything you want (from whites)."[55]

Probably because of this concept, Negro children often feel mystically related to monkeys, and call each other "apes" or "monkeys" in jest (just as they humorously chide each other on being black). As we had a pet monkey ourselves, we were able to see much of this "identification." Beyond the common taunt found

55. G. E. Simpson and Y. M. Yinger, *Racial and Cultural Minorities* (New York, 1953), p. 470.

among children (and adults) of all races of "Look, there goes your brother," when the monkey passed, many of the Negro children developed a real kinship feeling with the monkey, erupting with such statements as, "Is he Negro?" (i.e., the monkey), or "He is colored, and I am a monkey." The same children would often look through a book of monkey pictures that we had and would comment on each, assigning someone's names to the pictures, such as "There's you." "There's her." "There's Lydia." "There's me." The identification was certainly a racial one, for certain monkeys were excluded from the name-attaching ceremony because they were "white monkeys," i.e., did not have such pronounced Negroid features.

Yet the character portrayed here is not a representative of the Negro in general. He is the "Signifying Monkey" and represents the recognition, by the Negro, of a certain type, found among every society (but especially noticeable to the Negro). This is the little-man type, the kind that tries to make up for his size by his mental and physical capacities, and he exercises these without consideration for anyone's welfare but his own.

Of the two toasts concerned with the doings of the monkey, the only texts in print are of the "Signifying Monkey and the Lion." Once again, our printed text comes from Hughes and Bontemps.[56] It is obviously rewritten to a slight degree, but preserves most of the feeling of the original. It has an interesting moralistic ending:

> Monkey, said the Lion,
> Beat to his unbooted knees,
> You and your signifying children
> Better stay up in them trees.
> Which is why today
> Monkey does his signifying
> A-*way-up* out of the way.

Richard Dorson prints a tale, "The Elephant, the Lion, and the Monkey," which tells the same story, with the change that the Monkey tells the Elephant the Lion is playing the dozens on him.[57] The toast must have a fairly wide distribution, for D. K. Wilgus has sent on two Kentucky texts very similar to the ones here printed, and a shorter text from New Jersey. Kenneth S. Goldstein has sent a fragmentary text as recited by Ernest Hobbs. Ed Kahn also sent

56. Hughes and Bontemps, *Negro Folklore*, p. 363.
57. Dorson, *Western Folklore*, 13:87-88.

a partial text. I have three Texas versions, two from Austin and one from Longview which was printed in bowdlerized form in Debra Galoob's article, "Back in '32 When the Times Was Hard," referred to above.

From an early race record, "Can't You Read," sent in to me by Mack McCormick as sung by Big Maceo (Maceo Merriweather, Bluebird 8772, Victor 3209, recorded June 24, 1941), the following verse occurs:

> Now the monkey and the elephant, they went out for a
>   little drive.
> Elephant hit the monkey right square in his eye.
> The monkey looked up with a tear in his eye.
> "Now lookahere, big boy, you oughta get someone your size.
> One of these days I'm gonna climb me a tree.
> Remember big boy, you got to march right under me.
> When you march under me you better march careful and
>   fast.
> I hear the wind abreakin' cause a . . ."

This record is probably a new issue of records made in January, 1930, by Lonnie Johnson and Spencer Williams (OKEH 8762) and Barbecue Bob (Columbia 14523-D) called "Monkey and the Baboon," and these seem to indicate the existence of this toast for at least three decades.

A recent pop record[58] is very close to many of the texts here, with the interesting etiological ending of the lion chasing the monkey into the tree and that is the reason why the monkey lives there (Motif A 2433.3.19). I am indebted to Bruce Jackson for sending me a highly bowdlerized prose text of "The Monkey and the Lion," printed in *The Lancer*, the Indiana State Prison inmate magazine, March 1946 (Vol. III, #3, p. 37).

There is a derivative verse, current in white tradition in the Eastern United States, which stems only in part from these toasts. The beginning is a direct borrowing:

> Up jumped Willie from a coconut grove,
> He was a mean cocksucker by the color of his clothes.
> He had a twelve-inch peg and a two-button stitch;
> Man, he was a cool looking son of a bitch.

58. Oscar Brown, Jr., *Sin and Soul*, CL 1577 (LP), Columbia 3-41977 (single).

but the subsequent action places the piece firmly in the fornication contest tradition. (See Toasts 10 and 11.) The ending is often the stock commonplace toast ending:

> Now when Willie died, he went to hell
> And he fucked the devil's wife, and he fucked her well,
> And on his grave this is seen,
> "Willie, the human fucking machine."

The texts of "The Monkey and the Lion" printed here are uniform, except in some small particulars of the fights and in respect to the variable ending. Text "C" has a continuation of the story which has been unreported elsewhere, in which the Lion and the Baboon have a boxing match, and the Lion ends in jail. In the latter part of this text, all pretense of the jungle is given up. In the last few lines, the Lion becomes "Billy Lion," the protagonist of the "Stackolee" story, and this fight may indeed have come from another "bully" story and have been an autonomous toast just added to this story for interest.

The story is strongly reminiscent of two international tale-types. Type 6 is a tale in which an animal captor is persuaded to talk and thus the captive is released. The monkey uses a very similar strategy for his escape. (See Motif K561.1.) Type 59 involves a strategy similar to the one the monkey uses in the early part of the toast. In this tale, "Jackal carries false challenges, etc., between the lion and the bull so that they kill each other" (see K213.2).

The texts of "The Monkey and the Baboon" also, for the most part, are similar. Except for the fragmentary text printed by Debra Galoob in her article referred to above, I have never seen a text in print. The Big Maceo record cited above also has a stanza which goes:

> Way back in nineteen hundred and ten
> The monkey and the baboon they came walking in.
> The monkey told the baboon "Let's shoot a game of pool"
> The monkey could shoot but the baboon wasn't no fool.
> Next thing came along was a little mule
> He said, "You know I'm so mad I even caint wear no shoes."
> Next thing came down was Mr. Cat.
> We're gonna have to put the stuff going on here like that.
> Next thing came, there was a little mouse.
> Let's all get drunk, break up the doggone house.
> Can't you read.

Can't you read.

If you keep on reading, I'm bound to put you out.

The Toast can be understood only by a knowledge of the strategy of the games of pool and cooncan. The pool game speaks for itself, the object obviously being to sink as many balls in their numerical order as possible without missing. To have a "run" like that described in this game is truly phenomenal, as is only seen among the "sharks."

Cooncan is a rummy game that is a favorite among the Negroes in this area (and throughout the South). It is very complicated, and as it is amply described in Hoyle, I will omit such description here. The dialogue that surrounds the cooncan game is the sort that one can hear during any game among the Negro. It is an attempt to "one-up" or "out-psych" the opposing players. For a fuller description of this type of badinage, see Chapter II.

3. *THE MONKEY AND THE BABOON*

3A.

1

Deep down in the jungles, way back in the sticks,
The animals had formed a game called "pool." The baboon
    was a slick.
Now a few stalks shook, and a few leaves fell.
Up popped the monkey one day, 'bout sharp as hell.
He had a one-button roll, two-button satch.
You know, one them boolhipper coats with a belt in the
    back.
The baboon stood with a crazy rim,
Charcoal grey vine, and a stingy brim,
Hand full of dimes, pocket full of herbs,
Eldorado Cadillac parked at the curb.
He said, "Mr. Monkey, if it ain't my friend.
We gonna play some 'Georgia Skin'."*
"Raise! That ain't my game.
Me and you can play some 'Cooncan'."*
"Why should we argue and fight, acting like a fool
We'll just step in the hall and shoot a game of pool."
So the baboon reached over to break the rack.
The monkey kicked him square in the ass and he snatched
    him back.

He said, "Unh, unh, not here."
So they was fussing and fighting over who was going to
    make the break.
The giraffe was the houseman. You know naturally he had
    a stake.
So he said, "We'll flip for it."
So he flipped a coin about three feet in the air.
The baboon was itching to try to make a pin.
It was a two-headed coin, the monkey had to win.
The monkey grabbed a stick, and the baboon snatched
    the chalk,
And around the table them two motherfuckers started to
    walk.
The monkey broke the rack. Got the one, two, three, four,
    and five.
Brought tears in the baboon's eyes.
Now the six, seven, and eight
Was a natural take.
The nine and ten
Flew right in.
The 'leven ball crossed corner, the twelve just as well.
The thirteen in the side pocket, combination, like a bat
    out of hell.
Baboon jumped up, said, "It's a god-damn shame,
I can't beat this ugly motherfucker in no kind of game.
We gonna play some 'Cooncan'."
The monkey told the baboon, "You know Brother Buzzard
    who live across the creek?"
He said, "I cooncanned him for a solid week."
He said, "But you ain't gonna act right,
'Cause it took all me and my blade could do to keep out
    of a fight.
But you go find yourself a stump to fit your rump,
I'ma cooncan you tonight till your asshole jump."
He said, "I'ma hold my jacks, spread my queens,
I'ma do switching in this old fucked-up deck the world's
    never seen.
I'ma hold my deuces, lay down my treys,
Get down on your motherfucking ass in a thousand ways."
He said, "Now skip Mr. Rabbit, hop Mr. Bear,
Look's shitty, but there's 'leven of them there."

"Kid"

2

Deep down in the jungles, way back in the sticks,
The animals had formed a game called "pool" and the
   baboon was a slick.
Now a few stalks shook and a few leaves fell
When up popped a monkey one day, 'bout sharp as hell.
With a one-button roll, two-button satch,
Boolhipper coat with a belt in the back.
The baboon said, "Well, Mr. Monkey, if it ain't my friend.
Let's play us some Georgia Skin."
He said, "Raise, motherfucker, you know that ain't my
   game.
He said, "Why should we stand and holler like a fool.
Let's step in the hall and play a game of pool."
The baboon reached over to break the rack.
The monkey kicked him square in his ass and snatched
   him back.
He said, "Not here." Well, while they was ready to go to
   blows
And throwing punches all around the poolroom floor,
They was fussing and fighting over who was going to make
   the break,
The giraffe was the houseman, you know damn well he
   had a stake.
He said he'd flip a coin to flip for the break.
He flipped one about two feet in the air.
The baboon's inches was trying to make a pin.
There was two in the corner, the monkey had to win.
The monkey grabbed the stick, the baboon grabbed the
   chalk.
'Round the table them two ugly motherfuckers started to
   walk.
The monkey broke the rack; he got the one and the two.
And looked at me and you.
He dropped the three and four,
And looked out the door.
The five and six
Was a natural fix.*
The seven and eight
Was a natural take.
The nine and ten
Flew right in.

The 'leven ball crossed corners, twelve just as well;
Thirteen in combination in the side pocket like a bat out
 of hell.
The baboon said, "Ain't this a motherfucking shame.
I can't beat this ugly motherfucker in no kind of game.
We gon' play some Cooncan."
The monkey looked at the baboon and said real sweet,
"You and me gonna walk 'cross the street.
Find yourself a rump to fit your stump
'Cause I'ma Cooncan you tonight till your asshole jump."
Said, "I'ma hold my deuces and dish my treys,
Get down on your dirty ass in a thousand ways.
I'ma hold my jacks and spread my queens.
Put a switch in this fucked-up deck, this world has never
 seen.
He said, "Hop, Mr. Rabbit, skip, Mr. Bear.
I know you think it's shitty, but there's eleven of 'em
 there."

"Kid"

3B.

Deep down in the jungle way back in the sticks
The animals had a pool room and the baboon was a slick.
But they didn't know, deep down in the jungle in the coco-
 nut grove
Lived a little pimp* monkey, you could tell by the clothes
 he wore.
He had a camel-hair benny with the belt in the back,
Had a pair of nice shoes, and a pair of blue slacks.
He said he think he'd take a little stroll.
In just a few minutes he passed the pool-room door.
Now the baboon was setting on the stool
Waiting for the next damn fool.
Celery seen, celery done,
Who wanted to try Brother Devil one?
He said, "Come here, Mr. Monkey, you come here late.
But you're just in time for one more break."
The monkey said, "Houseman, I want you to hold my gun.
I don't want to kill the motherfucker, I just want to shoot
 him one."

He said, "And by the way, while you're at that, I want you
    to chalk my cue.
If I break this motherfucker, there's gonna be a tip for
    you."
He broke the balls and ran the one, two, and three.
He said, "Hold this cue stick while I go and pee."
He pissed on the table, he shit on the floor.
Came back and run the three and four.
Now he shot the balls, and he shot 'em all, and turned
    around and shot the five.
Brought hot, scalding water from the baboon's eyes.
He banked the six and seven cross-side.
He took the motherfucking eight for a god-damn ride.
He shot the nine, he shot the ten.
He only had five more balls to shoot on in.
He shot the 'leven, he shot the twelve.
By that time, the baboon said, "To hell! Go to hell!"
He said, "Wait a minute, rack the ball."
He said, "Do you know how to coon?"
"Get you a rump to fit your stump
And I'll coon you till your ass-hole jump."
The monkey said, "Well, you ain't saying a thing."
So they started out. Brother Baboon said, "Monkey, when
    I fall out on you I'm gonna spread four queens
And this a king."
Well, the game's going 'long all right, he made a mistake.
And that's when this monkey made a hell of a break.
Now there was a spider on the wall, with a fly beside his
    head.
He saw that break and he dropped dead.
He said, "Jump, Brother Rabbit, and leap Brother Bear,
It may look like shit, but there's 'leven cards there."
He said, "Somebody go get this motherfucker's wife,
'Cause I'm just about to win his god-damned life.
I done won all his silver, done won all his gold.
If we play long enough, win his god-damned soul."

                                         Charley

3C.

Deep down in the jungle, way back in the sticks,
That's where the baboon was a slick.

Now a few stalks shook, and a few leaves fell,
And up jumped the monkey, sharp as hell.
Had a one-button roll, two-button satch.
You know, one of them boolhipper coats, you know, with
    a buckle in the back.
There was Mr. Baboon, he was sharp as a pin.
Charcoal gray vine with a stingy brim.
He had a pocket full of money, handful of herbs,
Eldorado Cadillac parked at the curb.
He said, "Mr. Monkey, if it ain't my friend.
Come on, Dad, let's play some 'Georgia Skin'."
He said, "Raise, motherfucker, that ain't my game.
Come on, let's play some 'Cooncan'."
He said, "No, don't be no fool.
Let's go in the hall and play a game of pool."
They was fussing and fighting 'bout who was going to
    make the break.
They asked the houseman, naturally he had a stake.*
The monkey grabbed the stick, and the baboon grabbed
    the chalk.
Around the table them two motherfuckers started to walk.
Now the monkey reached back
He broke the rack.
He sank the one, two, three, four, and five.
He brought tears to the baboon's eyes.
The six, seven, and eight
Was a natural take.
The nine and ten
Flew right in.
He played the 'leven in the corner and the twelve just as
    well,
Put the thirteen ball in the side, like a bat out of hell.
Knocked his stick on the floor,
Said, "Count 'em house, you'll find well over sixty-four."
The baboon said, "God damn, I can't beat this man in no
    kind of game.
Come on, let's play some Cooncan."
He said, "You know Brother Rabbit across the creek?
Well, I cooncanned him for a solid week.
But you ain't gonna act right,
'Cause it took all me and my blade to do to keep out of a
    fight.

146

Come on. I'ma find a stump to fit your rump
And I'ma cooncan you till your asshole jump."
He said, "I'ma spread my deuces, and dish my treys,
I'ma get down on you in all kinds of ways.
I'ma spread my jacks and dish my queens,
I'ma put a switch in the deck the world never seen.
So hop Mr. Rabbit and skip Mr. Bear.
It's gonna look mighty shady, but there's 'leven of them
    there."
If anybody asks you who pulled that toast,
Just tell them old bullshitting Snell, from coast-to-coast.
I live on Shotgun Avenue, Tommygun Drive,
Pistol Apartment, and Room 45.

                                                    Arthur

(To be said at end of "Monkey and Baboon" sometimes)

Now I was walking through the jungle the other day, come
    along a coconut tree
That old dirty motherfucking baboon tried to shit on me.
So I looked up and said, "Raise, Do you know what you're
    doing?"
He said, "Dig, kid, did you see me lose my money the other
    day?"
I said, "Yeah." He said, "Don't come fucking me in that
    kind of way."
He said, "Furthermore, due to that you're a slick, and I'm
    supposed to be smart,
You knowed I was going to shit, 'cause you heard me when
    I fart."

                                                    "Kid"

4. *THE LION AND THE MONKEY*

4A.

Down in the jungle near a dried-up creek,
The signifying monkey hadn't slept for a week
Remembering the ass-kicking he had got in the past
He had to find somebody to kick the lion's ass.
Said the signifying monkey to the lion that very same day,
"There's a bad motherfucker heading your way.
The way he talks about you it can't be right,
And I know when you two meet there going to be a fight.

He said he fucked your cousin, your brother, and your
    niece,
And he had the nerve enough to ask your grandmom for
    a piece."*
The lion said, "Mr. Monkey, if what you say isn't true
    about me,
Bitch, I'll run your ass up the highest tree."
The monkey said, "Now look, if you don't believe what I
    say,
Go ask the elephant. He's resting down the way."
The lion let out with a mighty rage,
Like a young cocksucker blowing his gauge.
He ran through the jungle with a mighty breeze,
Kicking gorillas in the ass and knocking giraffes to their
    knees.
Then he saw the elephant resting under his tree.
He said, "Get up, motherfucker, you and me."
The elephant looked up from the corner of his eye
And said, "Scram, chickenshit, fuck with someone your size."
The lion squatted and made a pass.
The elephant ducked and knocked him flat on his ass.
Then he jumped in his stomach and stepped in his face
And tore his ass hole clean out of place.
He mashed in his face like a forty-four,
Plucked out his eyes and dared him to roar.
The lion crawled through the jungle more dead than alive,
And swore to stop the monkey from signifying.*
Now that's when the monkey really started his shit.
"Jive-king* of the jungle, ain't you a bitch,
All swelled up like you got the seven-year itch.
You was up there all jobbing and jiving and swinging
    your arms
While the elephant was hitting you like a young King
    Kong.
Going around talking about you can't be beat.
Well I want you to know that me and my wife had a
    ringside seat.
And another thing. Every time me and my old lady try to
    get a little bit,
You come 'round here with that roaring shit.
Git away from my tree before I pee."

The lion looked up and said, "Mr. Monkey, if you piss on me
While under your tree I pass,
I'll climb that tree and kick your motherfucking ass."
The monkey said, "Mister Lion, if I piss on you while you
    pass,
You'll climb this tree and *kiss* my ass."
The monkey started jumping up and down.
His foot missed the limb and his ass hit the ground.
Faster than a streak of lightning and a bolt of heat,
The lion was on the monkey with all four feet.
Then the monkey's wife started her shit,
"See that, monkey, that's what you git
Going around signifying and shit."
The monkey said, "Now look! You shut up, because there's
    one thing I'll never be able to see.
That's how I leaped and missed a whole damn tree.
Bitch, I believe you pushed me."
The monkey looked up with tears in his eyes
And said, "I'm sorry, Mister Lion, I apologize."
The lion said, "There ain't no use for you to be crying,
Because I'm going to stop you from signifying.
Now before I put you away to rest,
I want to hear your dying request."
The monkey said, "Get your motherfucking feet out my
    eyes and my nuts out of this sand,
And I'll wrestle your ass all over this land."
Then when the lion got ready to fight
The monkey jumped up and went clean out of sight.
But in the distance you could hear the monkey say,
"As long as these weeds and green grass grow,
I'm going to be around to signify some more.
And another thing, Mr. Lion, you ain't no hell by the way
    you creep,
'Cause I know where three elephants sleep."

                                            Arthur

4B.

Deep down in the jungle so they say
There's a signifying motherfucker down the way.
There hadn't been no disturbin' in the jungle for quite
    a bit,

For up jumped the monkey in the tree one day and laughed,
"I guess I'll start some shit."
Now the lion come through the jungle one peaceful day,
When the signifying monkey stopped him and this what
    he started to say.
He said, "Mr. Lion," he said, "A bad-assed motherfucker
    down your way."
He said, "Yeah! The way he talks about your folks is a
    certain shame.
I even heard him curse when he mentioned your grand-
    mother's name."
The lion's tail shot back like a forty-four,
When he went down the jungle in all uproar.
He was pushing over mountains, knocking down trees.
In the middle of a pass he met an ape.
He said, "I ought to beat your ass just to get in shape."
He met the elephant in the shade of a tree.
"Come on long-eared motherfucker, it's gonna be you
    and me."
Now the elephant looked up out the corner of his eye,
Said, "Go on bird-shit, fight somebody your size."
Then the lion jumped back and made a hell of a pass.
The elephant side-stepped and kicked him dead on his ass.
Now he knocked in his teeth, fucked-up his eye,
Kicked in his ribs, tied-up his face,
Tied his tail in knots, stretched his tail out of place.
Now they fought all that night, half the next day.
I'll be damned if I can see how the lion got away.
When they was fussing and fighting, lion came back
    through the jungle more dead than alive,
When the monkey started some more of that signifying
    jive.*
He said, "Damn, Mr. Lion, you went through here yester-
    day, the jungle rung.
Now you come back today, damn near hung."
He said, "Now you come by here when me and my wife
    trying to get a little bit,
T' tell me that 'I rule' shit."
He said, "Shut up, motherfucker, you better not roar
'Cause I'll come down there and kick your ass some more."
The monkey started getting panicked and jumped up and
    down,

When his feet slipped and his ass hit the ground.
Like a bolt of lightning, a stripe of white heat,
The lion was on the monkey with all four feet.
The monkey looked up with a tear in his eyes,
He said, "Please, Mr. Lion, I apologize."
He said, "You lemme get my head out the sand
Ass out the grass, I'll fight you like a natural man."
The lion jumped back and squared for a fight.
The motherfucking monkey jumped clear out of sight.
He said, "Yeah, you had me down, you had me last,
But you left me free, now you can still kiss my ass."
Again he started getting panicked and jumping up and
    down.
His feet slipped and his ass hit the ground.
Like a bolt of lightning, stripe of white heat,
Once more the lion was on the monkey with all four feet.
Monkey looked up again with tears in his eyes.
He said, "Please, Mr. Lion, I apologize."
Lion said, "Ain't gonna be no apologizing.
I'ma put an end to his motherfucking signifying."
Now when you go through the jungle, there's a tombstone
    so they say,
"Here the Signifying Monkey lay,
Who got kicked in the nose, fucked-up in the eyes,
Stomped in the ribs, kicked in the face,
Drove backwards to his ass-hole, knocked his neck out of
    place."
That's what I say.

"Kid"

4C.

Deep down in the jungle where the coconut grows
Lives a pimp little monkey, you could tell by the clothes
    he wore.
He had a camel-hair benny with a belt in the back,
Had a pair of nice shoes and a pair of blue slacks.
Now his clothes were cute little things,
Was wearing a Longine watch and a diamond ring.
He says he think he'd take a stroll
Down by the water hole.
And guess who he met? Down there was Mr. Lion.

The monkey started that signifying.

He said, "Mr. Lion, Mr. Lion, I got something to tell you
    today."

He said, "This way this motherfucker been talking 'bout
    you I know you'll sashay."

(He told the lion)

He said, "Mr. Lion, the way he talking 'bout your mother,
    down your cousins,

I know damn well you don't play the dozens.

He talking your uncle and your aunt's a damn shame.

Called your father and your mother a whole lot of names.

I would'a fought the motherfucker but looked at him with
    a tear in my eye.

He's a big motherfucker, he's twice my size."

The lion looked down with a tear in his eye,

Said, "Where's this big motherfucker that's twice my size?"

That little monkey said, "I'll show you the way."

He went down and the elephant was standing by a tree,

And the lion said, "Hey, motherfucker, I hear you been
    looking for me."

Elephant looked at the lion and said,

"Go on chicken-shit, pick on somebody your size."

The lion made a roar.

The elephant side-stepped and kicked his ass on the floor.

The lion looked up with a tear in his eyes.

Says, "I'm gonna beat you, motherfucker, though you're
    twice my size."

He looked back and squared off to fight.

The elephant kicked his ass clean out of sight.

Came back for ride or roar.

Elephant stomped his ass clean on the floor.

The elephant looked about, said, "What the fuck is this?"

The lion said, "You know you's a bad motherfucker, put up
    your fists."

They fought three days, and they fought three nights.

I don't see how in hell the lion got out of that fight.

Coming back through the jungle more dead than alive,

Here goes the monkey in the tree with that same signifying.

He said, "Look at you, you god-damn chump.

Went down in the jungle fucking with that man

And got your ass blanshed* and drug in the sand.

You call yourself a real down king,
But I found you ain't a god-damned thing.
Get from underneath this god-damned tree
'Cause I feel as though I've got to pee."
The lion looked up, said
"That's all right, Mr. Monkey, if that's the way you want
    to play
The sun's gonna shine in your ugly ass some day."
Monkey looked down, said, "Long as the trees grow tall,
    the grass grows green,
You's the dumbest motherfucker the jungle's ever seen."
Said, "You motherfucker, I heard you down there pleading
    for your life.
At the very same time I had my dick in your wife.
You motherfucker, when that man knocked you over the
    hill,
I was gonna throw a party 'cause I thought your ass got
    killed."
The lion strode through the jungle to pick himself up.
The monkey called him back, said,
"Hey, you motherfucker, and oh, by the way,
Don't you come 'round here with that hoorah* shit,
Everytime me and my wife get ready to get a little bit."
Monkey started jumping up and down.
The left foot slipped and his ass hit the ground.
Like a bolt of lightning, like a streak of heat,
The lion was on him with all four feet.
Monkey look up with a tear in his eye,
Said, "Mr. Lion, I'se just kidding, but I apologize."
He said, "No, you're a signifying motherfucker and you
    always will.
You gonna fuck around some day and get somebody
    killed."
The monkey jumped back, and said, "Get your feet off my
    chest and my head out the sand
And I'll get up and beat you like a natural-born man."
Now the lion squared back, he was ready to fight,
But the poor little monkey jumped clean out of sight.
He said, "I told you, long as the trees growed tall, grass
    growed green,
You's the dumbest motherfucker the jungle ever seen.

Dumb motherfucker, I done tricked you again."
So the lion said, "All right, Mr. Monkey, if that's the way
    you want to play.
The sun's gonna shine in your ass some day."
Now what do you think? Down on Rampart Street
Who did Mr. Lion chance to meet —
The signifying monkey.
He stomped to the right and he stomped to the left.
Stomped the poor monkey clean to death.
Now I know some people think there is where the story
    ends.
But I'm gonna show you when it just begins.
You know how news travels in the jungle far and fast,
When it reached the monkey's baboon cousins at last.
He looked in the mirror with a tear in his eyes,
He says, "I'll get this motherfucker, he's just about my size."
He told his main whore* he had to go,
Down to the coconut grove to the water hole.
He packed up his whiskey and his bottle of gin,
He had a long ways to go, but a short time to make it in.
Coming through the jungle, swinging on the limbs,
Come the baddest motherfucker the jungle ever seen.
So by the time he got down to the coconut grove,
All the animals having a party 'round the water hole.
So Brother Lion was there, him and his wife,
When the baboon came up. In his hand he was carrying
    his knife.
He said, "Hey there, bad motherfucker, you did my
    cousin in.
Now I come down here to fight, to do you in."
So the lion said, "Look here, Mr. Baboon, I don't want to
    fight,
I want you to get your ass out of my sight."
He said, "Tomorrow I want you to come down here early
    in the morning.
And be ready to fight."
So the lion went on home, preparing for the next day.
He knowed he had to fight, he had to fight in a hell of a
    way.
So now coming back to the fight, turn back down to the
    coconut grove.

Who was standing there looking so outright and fine,
But old brother Monkey and Billy Lion.
While over there with real bad sight,
They naturally had to pick on Brother Bear to referee
    the fight.
So he introduced them.
He said, "In this corner we got Brother Lion,
He been bit by a tiger, scratched by a lion,
Tied in a barrel of lye, shot in the ass with a forty-five.
He's a bad motherfucker, but he don't want to die.
And in this corner we got Brother Baboon.
So far he's done licked every ass from earth to the moon.
He's better known as Big Jim,
He's the baddest motherfucker that ever swing from a
    limb."
So when Brother Bear jumped back off the grass,
Signal for the two motherfuckers to tear their ass.
Now they begin to fight and they begin to scuffle.
Soon the lion's jaw begin to ruffle.
After awhile I saw a mighty right to the lion's chin.
And everybody thought the lion had come out to an end.
But now when the bell rang for the first round,
The lion went back to his corner.
In his corner they were using Hadacol,
While in the baboon's corner they were saying a prayer to
    the Lord.
Everybody thought that Big Jim was through.
But when they came back out, that's when it turned to.
Brother Lion hit Brother Baboon to the face, one to the
    ribs,
Kicked him in the mouth, bust all his jibs.*
Hit him in the ribs, hit him in the head.
That time the lion fell out for dead.
Brother Lion's wife jumped up in a mighty roar,
Said, "You just knocked my husband down to the floor."
She said, "I'ma have you put in jail.
And there ain't nobody here gonna go you bail.
So the monkey is standing on the corner with the same old
    signifying,
Said, "Don't worry, I got a friend and his name is Billy
    Lion.

He's the richest man 'round here in town. He'll get you
    out."
But where it ends, the baboon's still in jail,
And the monkey not trying to get a dime to go his cousin's
    bail.

Charley

4D.

The monkey said to the lion, one bright summer day,
"There's a big motherfucker across the way,
You and him will never be right
Because I know when you get there, there'll be a hell of
    a fight.
Now here is something I really has to say.
He talks about your mother in a bitching way.
He called her a no-good bitch and he meant it for a fight.
You ask my opinion, I'll say, 'Man, it wasn't right'."
Off drove the lion in a terrible rage,
Creating a breeze which shook the trees
And knocked the giraffe to his knees.
He confronted the elephant up under the tree,
And said, "Motherfucker, it's you or me."
He drove at the elephant and made his pass.
The elephant knocked him flat on his ass.
He kicked and stomped* him all in his face.
He busted two ribs and pulled his tail out of place.
They cursed and fought damn near all day.
I still don't see how that lion got away.
He dragged himself back, more dead than alive,
When the monkey started his signifying.
"Well, I be damned, kid, you don't look so well.
Looks to me like you've been catching hell.
When you left here the whole forest rung.
Now you come back damn near hung.
That elephant sure kicked the shit out of your ass,
But that bad, bad cocksucker sure put you in your class.
You've got more scratches on your ass than a dog with the
    seven-year itch.
You say you're King of the Jungle, now ain't that a bitch.
Every night when I'm trying to steal a bit
Here you come with your ratcoon shit.

Now motherfucker, if you make another roar
I'll jump down and kick your ass some more."
The monkey laughed and jumped up and down.
He missed a limb and his big ass hit the ground.
Like a bolt of lightning or a flash of heat,
The lion hit the monkey with all four feet.
The monkey screamed and rubbed his eyes,
And said, "Please, Mr. Lion, I apologize."
"Shut up, motherfucker, and stop your crying,
'Cause I'm gonna kick your ass for signifying."
The monkey's last words as he was dying,
"I tore my ass by signifying."
Now the monkey is dead and in his grave.
No more meddling will he crave.
On his tombstone, these words are wrote,
"He's dead as he lived, by his signifying shit,
Now take my warning and stay in your class,
Or you'll get knocked right square on your ass."

Harry

5. *SQUAD TWENTY-TWO*

Judging by the streets mentioned in this toast, this is a local production. South and Lombard Streets are the two major east-west arteries in the neighborhood.

The attitude toward the police expressed here is the prevalent one among the Negroes of this area. Due to long history of very bad incidents, there is much antagonism between the police and the inhabitants of the neighborhood.

I ran over to Lombard Street to get my gat.°
I ran back to South Street, put on my hat.
While I was walking along who did I run into but a little
    old boy who was holding a ten-spot in his hand.
So I grabbed that motherfucker and away I flew,
And guess who I run into?
Those bad motherfuckers from Squad Twenty-two.
Now in the back was my man.
He didn't even raise his hat or tip his hand.
So they put me in the wagon and they took me on down
    to the county jail.

I didn't have a punk,* fag,* or sissy* to go my bail.
So a guy in the cell told me the thing to do,
Was to get in tight with the captain of Squad Twenty-two.
I talked my shit and I talked it well.
He let me out of jail, so I flew home like a bat out of hell.
Now I run back to South Street to put down my gat,
And back over to Lombard Street to put down my hat.
Now I takes the short-cut home and jumps into bed,
And this is what the rotten bitch I live with said,
Said, "Charley dear, wonderful one,
While you was gone I dreampt you got shot in the ass by
    a big gun.
And by the way, the man that was carrying the gun was
    from Squad Twenty-two."
Now my blood began to boil, my ass began to itch.
I jumped up and shot that rotten bitch.
Now I know you fellows think that's the wrong thing to do,
But I don't want to hear another motherfucking word
    about Squad Twenty-two.

                                                    Charley

6. *A HARD-LUCK STORY*

The only other text of this which I have encountered was sent to
me by Bruce Jackson and comes from his Indiana prison collection,
though it is closely related to other stories reciting the hardships of
being without money. The structure of this shows that it relies for
its effect on the final line (the most constant feature of these versions) and the demands which will remind many of the impossible
tasks contained in "The Elfin Knight" (Child 2).

6A.

Look out, bitch, and don't say a word,
'Cause I'm beating your ass about some shit I heard.
Long time now you been pulling this shit.
I'ma give you an ass-whipping you never will forget.
I send you to the store ask for butter, you bring back lard.
I'll lay beside you, my dick won't get hard.
You got a nerve to ask me for a dime.
You're kinda pigeon-toed, knock-kneed and blind.

Receiving the call off of each and every line,
That your grandmammy's pussy done run your grand-
    pappy's line.
You got a nerve to ask me for a dime.
You got to walk the water, like Christ walked the sea,
Hold both thunder and lightning and bring it back to me.
Then I'll introduce you to a friend of mine.
He might lend you a nickel, he won't lend you a dime.
By that you know, you ain't no more bitch of mine.

Arthur

6B.

I was once a man with plenty of wealth,
Going 'round showing my friends plenty good time.
And so one day when I realized I didn't have a thing,
I decided to walk down the street and ask a friend of mine,
To loan me a dime.
He said, "You're a friend, a friend it's true
But to get one of these thin dimes, here's what you're
    gonna have to do."
He said, "You have to walk the waters, like Jesus walked
    the sea.
Got to hold both thunder and lightning and bring it back
    to me."
He said, "Put the Empire State Building down in a sack.
Jump up a camel's ass and snatch the hump out of that
    motherfucker's back."
He said, "When you receive a letter from your grand-
    father, saying your grandmother's pussy's running
    blind(?)
Your mother's sick and your father's dying.
Then I'll introduce you to a friend of mine
Who might loan you a nickel, but not a dime.

"Kid"

6C.

When I was rich, I was right.
I used to spend my money just like I was white.
One day I got broke.
Not a friend did I have.

But you know what all good hustlers do.
They always keep a quarter too.
So I was walking down Rampail Street,
When two chock whores I chanced to meet,
They said, "Hello, Charley, I haven't seen you in a mighty
    long time.
Stand me maybe a dime?"
I said, "Before I give you a dime, this is what you got to do.
You got to go up on the Empire State Building and jump
    clean down on your head.
Then say, 'Charley boy, I ain't dead.'
You got to swim a ocean, 'round and around.
From the Pacific, you got to swim the deep sea channel
    and tell me you ain't drowned.
You got to eat ten links* of cat-shit, and you better not
    frown.
You got to go way up high,
And find the rock that David killed Goliath,
If you do all this in a half-hour time,
Might loan you a nickel but not a god-damn dime."

Charley

The next three toasts are further "bad man" stories, but of a different sort from "Stackolee." These are the stories, not of bullies fighting each other, but of modern criminals outwitting the police or dying at their hands. Even when they do die, they do it with a kind of glory, boasting as they go. And in many ways, we could think of these toasts as extended boasts.

Just as in so many other aspects of the neighborhood, one can see here the strong effects of popular entertainment mediums. Dillinger, Slick Willie Sutton, the Dalton Brothers, the James Brothers, Geronimo are the heroes of these pieces. And the Jesse James portrayed here is not the modern Robin Hood of the ballad; he is just as mean as any of the others.

Many of the lines will be familiar. Jesse winds up at the same bar at which "Stackolee" killed Billy, and he seems to be uttering the same dialogue. Both the "MacDaddy" and the "Big Man" toasts contain the stock courtroom scene. The final lines of "MacDaddy" are also associated with the "Stackolee" tradition.

"The Big Man" may be a strictly local toast, as evidenced by the reference to Fifth and South. "Kid" claimed to have written this one, but he claimed to have written "The Titanic," also, as well as others. The final curse is certainly not local; it is part of a longer one which is widely known.

7. THE BIG MAN

I met a cute little girl, she took my heart,
So I decided my life I wanted to share a part.
Now the fellows told me, "Now look here, Kid,
She wasn't no good for me."
I didn't care what the boys had to say,
I went down to the judge to read the matrimony one day.
So I come off from work and I was tired.
I come in the house and I see my best friend laying my
  bed inside.
So I shot him in the head and she ran out down the street.
I cut her in the throat, chopped off her feet.
So 'round about two o'clock that morning, I was standing
  on Fifth and South,
My man walked up saying, "Kid, is you the one that busted
  your lady in the mouth?"
I said, "That's me." He said, "Come on, I got a warrant for
  your arrest."
He just read a few lines, then he stopped, and he wouldn't
  say a word.
Now tomorrow morning, after the judge read it, you heard.
So the judge looked down at me, my wife started to
  crying,
Mother-in-law jumped up, she began to shout,
My lawyer said, "Sit down, bitch, you don't know what the
  trial's about."
The judge told me, he said, "Kid, I'ma give you some time.
Here go fifty-five years to get that whooping* off your
  mind."
I said, "Fifty-five years ain't no time,
I got a brother in Sing Sing doing ninety-nine.
If you think that's a kick, here's a better.
I got an uncle in Alcatraz waiting for the chair."
So he took me up and he gave me cell number 32.

So right up 'bout four, five years had passed,
When I got a letter from that old nasty bitch.
She said, "Kid, I came to your trial,
Now I didn't come there to place a bet.
Just came to see how much time your ass was going to get."
She said, "Things out here sure is hard.
I'm out here on the street, trying to make a bite,
Fucking, eating chicken every night."
So it got on my nerves, made me mad,
So I got my pencil and paper, my scratch pad.
I wrote her back a letter, and here's what I said.
"For your dirtiness towards me that can't be accounted for.
May the crabs grow 'round your body and start to eat.
May the lice grow up around your back, eat down to your
     feet.
May you get corroded, and blood run from your nose.
Then before your life's a wreck, may you fall backwards to
     your asshole.
                                        Your motherfucking man."
                                                        "Kid"

8. *THE GREAT MAC DADDY*

I was standing on the corner, wasn't even shooting crap,
When a policeman came by, picked me up on a lame rap.
He took me to the jailhouse, 'bout quarter past eight.
That morning, 'bout ten past nine,
Turnkey came down the line.
Later on, 'bout ten past ten,
I was facing the judge and twelve other men.
He looked down on me, he said,
"You're the last of the bad.
Now Dillinger, Slick Willie Sutton, all them fellows is
     gone,
Left you, the Great MacDaddy to carry on."
He said, "Now we gonna send you up the way. Gonna send
     you up the river.
Fifteen to thirty, that's your retire."
I said, "Fifteen to thirty, that ain't no time.
I got a brother in Sing Sing doing ninety-nine."
Just then my sister-in-law jumped up, she started to cry.

I throwed her a dirty old rag to wipe her eye.
My mother-in-law jumped, she started to shout.
"Sit down, bitch, you don't even know what the trial's
    about."
'Pon her arm she had my six-button benny.
Said, "Here you are MacDaddy, here's your coat."
I put my hand in my pocket and much to my surprise,
I put my hand on two forty-fives.
I throwed them on the judge and made my way to the door.
As I was leaving, I tipped my hat to the pictures once more.
Now outside the courtroom was Charcoal Brown.
He was one of the baddest motherfuckers on this side of
    town.
The juries left out, and the broads gave a scream,
I was cooling 'bout hundred-fifteen miles an hour in my
    own limousine.
Rode here, rode there, to a little town called Sin.
That's when the police moved in.
We was fighting like hell till everything went black.
One of those sneaky cops come up and shot me in the back.
I've got a tombstone disposition, graveyard mind.
I know I'm a bad motherfucker, that's why I don't mind
    dying.

"Kid"

9. *JESSE JAMES*

9A.

When the west was at its best
And every time a locomotive hit a rump-stump bump
And was unable to go any further
Jess and his brother Frank would take over.
"Frank, you guard the rear
While I stomp the shit out the engineer."
Man jumped up, said, "You can have my money, but spare
    my life."
He said, "I don't want neither, I want to fuck your wife."
He said, "Do this, well I'd rather be dead."
That's when Jesse sent four rockets through his head.
Fucked the wife, fucked her well,
Fucked her till her pussy swelled,

Got Frank to wipe the chicken-shit from around his dick.
But don't get me wrong.
The James Brothers weren't the only badmen on the train.
There was the Dalton Brothers, four of a kind.
They shot a motherfucker for a raggedy dime.
There was John Dillinger in the corner, counting his gold.
He shot his motherfucker when he was ten years old.
There was a bad motherfucker in the corner we all should
    know.
His name was Geronimo.
A man jumped up and said, "Call the law."
Jesse sent two rockets through that motherfucker's jaw.
He looked over at the conductor.
He said, "Conductor, don't you breathe or shit."
Conductor went to move, dead he lay.
Jesse dived out the window, swam through water, swam
    through mud.
He was looking for the place they call the "Bucket of Blood."
He went in the bar expecting to eat.
The bartender gave him a muddy glass of water and a
    fucked-up piece of meat.
He pulled out a gun, he shot the bartender from front to
    back.
Lady came in, said, "Where's Pete?"
Said, "Pete's behind the bar, fast asleep."
She said, "Pete ain't dead, Pete ain't dead."
He said, "Just count the six bullets in that raggedy mother-
    fucker's head."
She said, "My son Pete's dead, I can't go on."
Jesse put his foot on her ass and aimed her for the door.
He punched and shot a cat.
Shot a dog from front to back.
He was in this bad old Texas town, where the dudes go
    down.
"You just pack your rags and leave this town."
              (Couldn't remember rest)

                                Freddie

9B.

It was a nine o'clock jump
When the train hit the stump.

Jessie said, "Frank, you take the back and I'll take the
    front."
Now on the train, there were bad cats on there,
From everywhere.
There was John Dillinger who was on the run.
Just broke jail with a wooden gun.
There was Pretty Boy Floyd, he wasn't nothing but a name.
He used to get all the money for old fucked-up dames.
Now there was Baby-Face Nelson, he was bad show.
He knocked down a police station, kicked in the president's
    door.
Now on the train there was some bad motherfuckers on
    there that everybody know.
Bad-ass Apache called Geronimo.
Jesse James said, "Everybody reach, and reach in the air.
And put that money in the sack here."
So he got to Geronimo, he slapped him in the mouth, ain't
    that real bad.
He said, "Now I want everything you have."
Geronimo looked at him, said, "Jesse, you don't scare me,
    not a damn bit."
And that's when Jesse put a 38 shell in his chest so hard
    it made him shit.
Geronimo looked up, on his dying breath,
He said, "Jesse, you didn't have to act like that.
If you had asked real nice I'd put a dollar cue* in that
    old fucked-up hat."

"Kid"

The next three pieces are of the familiar pattern of the fornication contest. That this is common lore in the Anglo-American
tradition, one need only glance at the most recent and available
collection of such lore, *Count Vicarion's Book of Bawdy Ballads.*[59]

10. *SCHOOLTEACHER LULU AND CRABEYE PETE*

Schoolteacher Lulu come to town,
Ninety-nine men couldn't fuck her down.
In that town lived Crabeye Pete.
Crab to his head and dick to his feet.

59. Paris, 1956 (edited by the British modernist poet, Christopher Logue).

All the pimps and the conventionists holding a convention
in town,
Betting that Crabeye Pete would fuck Lulu down.
They was hold a convention at Carnegie Hall,
Come one, come all.
Now they was standing around 'bout noon,
Here comes Pete from the greasy spoon.
Now they got on the ground, they begin to fuck,
And my man was pushing dick to her like a ten-ton truck.
Lulu threw the bulldog curve.
Pete held on but he lost his nerve.
Then she threw the bulldog twist.
Pete held on but he broke a motherfucking wrist.
They fucked and they fucked and they fucked and they
fucked.
Pete was still trying to put that dick to her like a ten-ton
truck.
But when it was all over poor Pete was dead.
So we took Pete up on the mountain and burried him deep
in the sand.
And on his grave we described, "Here Lies the World's
Greatest Fucking Man."

Charley

11. *GUNFIGHT AT O.K. CORRAL*

Now here's a story, a story of old,
When the men were men, and the women were bold.
It was back in a town that was peaceful and quiet
When one lonely night a man came walking down the
street.
He had about a yard and a half of joint hanging down by
his feet.
He walked to the hotel, and he asked the fellow sitting
quiet,
"Pardon me, mister, is this where the broad named Big
Whore lays her head?"
He said, "Well, tell her I'll see her tomorrow morning at
O.K. Corral, we'll start our bread."
That morning about nine past nine, Butterbean Susie let
out a fart,
To let them know the fucking was to start.

Just then, 'bout ten past ten,
Everybody knowed the fucking was about to begin.
Just then the earth gave a quiver, the ground gave a crut,*
Everybody in town knew Big Dick had busted his nut.
Big Whore Sue screamed and grabbed her head,
Big Dick wiped the blood off his dick, said,
"Get the bitch, 'cause this whore is dead."
He got up, put his thing down his pants, gently at ease,
Got up and wiped the dirt off his knees.
As he was strolling out of town, he tipped his hat,
He said, "I fucked many and I fucked 'em well,
But everyone I fucked have caught hell."

"Kid"

12. *JUST LOOKING FOR A JOB*

Now I was walking down the road one day 'cause things
    was hard.
I was just looking for a motherfucking job.
I knocked on this here door,
And what do you think, here come a pretty little whore.
She had on a nice little evening gown.
She said, "What you doing, hanging around?"
I said, "Well, Miss, I don't mean no harm."
I said, "I'm just coming 'round looking for a job."
She said, "Oh, a job."
She said, "Perhaps you could have the deed to my house or
    the deed to my car.
The job I want you to do ain't too hard."
She said, "Come on and sit down over here."
I said, "Well, would you tell me what might this here
    job be?"
She said, "Well, you got to get down on your knees
And eat this pussy like a rat eating cheese.
You got to get way down in it and blow it like Louis blow
    his horn.
You got to peck all around, like a rooster pecking corn."
I said, "Hold it! Wait a minute, bitch, you're talking too
    fast.
The next thing you know, you'll have my foot in your ass."

167

I said, "I'm not a rooster, so I can't peck corn
And I ain't Louis, so go blow your own horn."

Charley

13. *THE FREAK'S BALL*

The next four rhymes are all versions of what is usually callea
"The Freak's* Ball" (i.e., a party held by homosexuals). It seems to
have wide currency among Negroes, as I have encountered two
texts from Texas Negroes. "D" shows a distinct relationship to the
"Darktown Strutter's Ball" and may reflect a real ancestry for
this piece.

13A.

Lucy Lacy fucked Dick Tracy and Tessy Trueheart had
a fit.
Now Bullshit Benny fucked B. O. Plenty and Gravel Gerty
had a bowl of shit.
Well, the shit was so thick, it made Dracula sick
And the walls were full of slime.
While they was laughing and joking, the door flew open
And in walked Frankenstein.
He looked around to try his luck.
Grabbed the shortest broad in the crowd and started to
fuck.
While he was twisting and twirling
His hips hit the wall, his ass hit the ceiling,
His tongue got hot, his head got stiff,
His neck started to wibbling and then that was it.
He looked around and he grabbed the smallest bitch in
town.
He said, "I'll tell you what to do.
Now you put your left leg over my right shoulder,
And your right leg over my left shoulder and wiggle your
ass in time.
'Cause I'm booty struck, and got to fuck
And I got grinding on my mind."

"Kid"

13B.

Call up fast-fucking Fanny
To tell her gray-assed Mammy

We gonna have a ball
Down the bulldagger's hall.
There's gonna be thirty-nine cockheads fried in snot,
Two or three pickled dicks tied in a knot.
There's gonna be long cock, short cock, cock without bone.
You can fuck a cock, suck a cock, or leave a god damn
    cock alone.
There was Gravel Gerty and in walked Frankenstein.
He grabbed the littlest woman in the bunch.
He said, "Put your left leg on my right shoulder, and
    wiggle your ass in time.
'Cause I'm booty* struck, and got to fuck, and got grinding
    on my mind."

Arthur

13C.

Tell Bulldagging* Fanny
Tell her gray-assed Granny
Tell her no-good Mammy
That we're gonna have a ball
At the Bulldagger's Hall.
It was the first fuck fight
To broad daylight,
Without eating a bite.
Then we're going to have breakfast.
I'm gonna have fried snot,
Roast cock,
Three pickled dicks tied in a knot.
Come 'long lunch, I don't want no collard greens.
Just a bowl of catshit, some muddy beans.

"Kid"

13D.

Bullshiting Willie told cocksuckering Sammie,
To come on down and bring his motherfuckering mammy,
Come on down and don't be late,
We're going to be there when the band starts playing,
Come on down and don't miss the fun,
We're going to be there when the band shits all over the
    floor,
And the leader grabs his self a fat whore.

These old girls are going to fuck and fight
Till the broad daylight.
Tomorrow night at the cheap cocksucker's ball.

From Manuscript

14. *JODY THE GRINDER**

Whether "Jody" as a character was invented by inhabitants of
the prisons or the Army, he is the man who is home sleeping with
your wife. Lomax (FSNA), 595, prints the song "Sound Off" with a
Jody verse. This song is often called "Jody's Song" and other similar
ones "Jody Calls." For a jail-house mention, see Library of Congress
Record, AAFS L4 (A3), "Joe the Grinder." Other, but short, Jody
rimes came from this group.

Now in nineteen hundred and forty-four
The World War Two was over for sure.
Now a two-timing bitch with an old-man overseas,
Said, "Wake up, Jodie. Wake up, please.
This shit is over, Japan is fell."
Now Jodie woke up, his eyes all red.
He said, "What's that, whore, I just heard you said?"
She said, "Don't look at me like I did a crime.
You've heard me the first god-damn time."
He said, "No, that what you're talking can't be right.
'Cause the last I heard, the Japanese had just begin to
    fight."
She said, "There was a time the Japs wouldn't quit,
But Uncle Sam dropped an atomic bomb and changed all
    that shit."
She said, "Wise up, honey, just don't you get mad.
I think it's time for you to pack your rags and find another
    pad."
She said, "Anyway, see who's at the door."
"Knock, knock, I'm already in.
Take a shot of my bad-ass gin."
He said, "While I was overseas fighting the enemy, and
    digging that salt,
You was taking my checks and cashing them and taking
    my bitch to the Allotment Ball.
Now here's something I can't miss.
Take my motherfucking Longine off your wrist."

He said, "Hold it, motherfucker, don't start that talking
    that jive.
Let me throw you an introduction to my army forty-five.
What? Who am I? I know your name is Jodie the Grinder
    and you don't give a damn.
But, bitch, tell this no-good motherfucker just who I am."
"Well, honey, if you must know.
Jodie the Grinder, meet G.I. Joe."

"Kid"

15. *THE OLD POOH-POOH*

This is the old bawdy song, "Ring Dang Doo" in corrupted form
as performed as a toast.

There was a girl named Jane
Who took this fellow
Down to the cellar
Fed him whiskey, wine and gin
And give him a piece of that old pooh-pooh.

Her mother cried from within her bed,
Said, "Jane, what is this nasty thing you're doing.
You pack your rags and your bloomers too,
And you make your living off your old pooh-pooh."

Jane went to the big city,
She tacked a sign up on the door.
"Two cents a ride, four cents a trip."
They came in twos, they came in fours.
To be correct, they came in scores.
There even was a guy named Traps
Who had the claps,
The siphs and the blue-balls, too.
He even got a piece of that old pooh-pooh.

When she died in Carnegie Hall
They pickled her ass in alcohol.
They paraded her cock on Fifth Avenue.
And that was the end of the old pooh-pooh.

Freddie

16. *I JUST LEARNED TO DANCE*

Pardon me chicks, kats and hens,
No not now, I'll tell you when.
I am not at all trying to be real bold,
Because I just learned to rock and roll.

I also learned the latest Chinese hop,
Rattle, Shake, Crawl, and Flop.
Come on out and step over the floor,
And while the night is young let's hit the door.

I can even do the Norfolk dance.
Stand back chicks and see me prance.
And just to show you that I'm no hick,
Let me meet some real cute chick.

Now I will tell you the whole truth,
I come here looking for a chick named Ruth.
Move back your chairs and let everyone see,
That I can shake like a limb on a tree.

I dropped in here very full of pep
In order to do the hog-pen step.
That kat you see leaning against the wall,
Is not afraid the building will fall.

He sure does look like a very mean kat.
Standing there will make him really fat.
That kat sure is playing it cool.
You can see he ain't nobody's fool.

Sorry chicks, I got to run.
Goodnight, I sure had fun.
I'll be digging you again some time,
When I'm not so full of blackberry wine.

From Manuscript

17. *FRESH OFF THE FARM*

If you know a girl named Mable,
Take her around to Jacks, stable.
Tell her to stoop down slow and lay back fast
And give me that ass,

Because I am going to give it right back just like it has
     high power gas.
You are going to stay in this hay,
So keep cool, and listen to what I have to say.
"Are you ready?" Don't be afraid, I will do you no harm,
Because you are fresh off the farm.
Just rap your legs around my back,
And act like you are squzzing a cow's sack.
Have you ever been to Arkansaw?
Well I am, going to teach you how to screw like a first-
     class whore.
I can tell what you ate
By my dick probing in your belly, and the head of my
     dick is like a seeing-eye worm used for fish bate.

From Manuscript

CHAPTER V

THE JOKES

I HAVE ISOLATED THE OTHER NARRATIVES OF THIS GROUP FROM THE toasts because of the unique nature of the form and subject matter of those pieces, and because these other stories are in much more common joke and anecdote form. However, the tropism toward rhyme, observable so clearly in the toast, is also felt here in these short narratives, but to a lesser degree.

The Uncle Remus collections, and those that followed them showed that the Negro had a predilection for stories in *cante fable* form. This observation is borne out in both West Indian and recent African collections. In relation to the latter, Kenneth and Mary Clarke recently said, "Unfortunately, even in African materials, adequate indication of song is lacking in many of the collections made in the late nineteenth and early twentieth centuries before good portable recording equipment was available. Missionaries and others, whose knowledge of the native languages was limited at best, and whose knowledge of native music was even weaker, tended to distort or even to omit the musical portions of the tales they collected."[1]

In a fascinating early study of the ballad in Jamaica, Martha Warren Beckwith shows how the sung narratives of the British

1. *Introducing Folklore* (New York, 1963), p. 56.

tradition fared in the West Indian climate. She found an old man, one Forbes, who knew the ballad of "Little Musgrove" (Child 81). Here she describes his treatment of the song:

> Now when old Forbes first gave me the story of *Little Musgrove*, he strung the verse upon a connecting thread of prose to carry along the action. Only when confronted with the phonograph did he sing the verses straight through without interruption.
>
> That his method was not adopted by chance is proved by the fact that other collectors both in Jamaica and in the Bahamas have taken down ballad stories dictated in the same form, and that I myself secured two other ballads which were recited in this fashion, . . .[2]

Though she clearly does not fully understand it Beckwith has recognized an important pattern in West Indian Negro story-telling, a clear tropism toward the *cante fable* form.

Halpert comments upon the cause of this tropism in Miss Beckwith's article:

> . . . the popularity of the form with English-speaking Negroes is due to a joint cause: not only that, as Miss Beckwith has shown, the pattern is well known in Africa, but also that, as seems quite likely, it was a British folk-tale pattern and one that would be adopted even more readily than the ballad.[3]

He further points out that, "When the *cante fable* is found undistorted, . . . the interspersed verse or song usually is the dramatic core of the tale. Frequently it is the most memorable part."[4] at the same time as indicating that on Miss Beckwith's authority, this was the situation in Jamaica. In Miss Beckwith's words:

> The stories contain, or usually turn upon, a song which belongs to the dialogue or is used as an ejaculation. Often its use becomes more dramatic by putting it into the lips of a fiddler or of a singing bird; but whether so presented

2. "The English Ballad in Jamaica: A Note Upon the Origin of the Ballad Form," *PMLA*, XXIX, p. 456.

3. Herbert Halpert, "The Cante Fable in Decay," in *Folklore in Action*, Essays for Discussion in Honor of MacEdward Leach (Philadelphia, 1962), p. 141.

4. Halpert, "Cante Fable," p. 147.

or not, it is always there to emphasize an emotional moment and express a wish, call, or magical formula; and its repetition from time to time in the story gives the song the value of a chorus or refrain.[5]

The burden of Halpert's argument is that verses tend to remain even after stories have been lost, and that this represents "the *cante fable* in decay." He gives a number of examples from his New Jersey collection to justify this contention. In the case of the Negro tale in this country, however, this is not so much the case. The *cante fables* in the Uncle Remus collections, for instance, often have nonsense refrains (seemingly from the African), or are little songs put into Br'er Rabbit's mouth as jokes or as clever commentary, quite often having little to do with the story. This then is the *cante fable* in decay among the American Negro.

However, in the Camingerly stories, the repeated verse or song functions in a much more structural manner, very much in the stronger *cante fable* tradition. These are jokes, short, terse, witty stories, reliant upon a punch-line type ending. In a great number of the Camingerly *cante fables* it is the song or verse which supplies the material for the witty and humorous ending. This is most clearly seen in such stories as "The Curser Outcursed," "The Judge Replies," and "Open Them Doors."

This pattern is felt beyond the jokes which can be clearly classified as *cante fables*. There are many included which use the same kind of repetition of phrase in order to build up to the punch-line ending. This is true, for instance, in "The Preacher and His Song," where the repeated line "Oh Lord, would you drop me fifty cents?" is changed in the end to "Lord, lookahere, I don't want this shit; all I want is my fifty cents."

Many further stories use the same kind of wit (the punch-line as a perversion of a previous line) but the phrase changed is not one which has been repeated but rather one which has come just before. The first story, "The Preacher and the Pickles" involves just such a device in rhyme. Not in rhyme is the ending of "Coming or Going." Occasionally just the cleverness of a rhyme is sufficient for an ending, as in "Washday in the Woods."

Just why the *cante fable* and other related witty forms are found in such profusion in this group, while exhibited in more decay in other American Negro collections, remains a problem. It is impos-

5. Beckwith, Martha Warren, *Jamaica Folk-Lore* (New York, 1928), p. 458.

sible to answer it fully at this point, but one can point to the important tropisms of rhyme, joke form, and word-wit in general operating so importantly in this group. In fact, the *cante fable* may not have decayed ever among the Negro in regard to jokes, especially bawdy ones. They have simply never received scholarly collection, interest, perusal before.

A further problem confronts us, a consideration of the full relationship of these stories with those previously collected from the Negro, especially in the South. In this, we are immediately confronted with Richard M. Dorson's dictum on the subject:

> Southern Negro lore had moved north, indeed, but only with migrants cradled and nurtured in the yeasty Southern traditions, or with the few still-living children of slaves. Northern-born Negroes, growing up among cities and factories, supercilious toward their Southern brothers, had severed and discarded their folk heritage, and new migrants grow farther from it as they take on Northern attitudes.[6]

It is quite true that the Negroes who have been born in Philadelphia, or reared there, know little of the tradition of animal stories that has flourished in the South. But judging by many of the stories presented here, there are many of the older stories which they have retained from their Southern background. "The Coon in the Box" is one of the oldest and most ubiquitous stories collected among the Negroes of this country. The preacher tale is not only one of the oldest type of tale to be found among the American Negro but it is of broad international provenience. These are found in abundance.

But as Dorson points out, along with these older echoes, a new voice is heard in Negro narratives.

> Unrecognized until very recently, a whole body of jests, some bitter, some mocking, some merely wry, have vented the hurt of colored Americans at their un-American treatment. These tales of protest frequently revolve about a generic character called "Colored Man," who is discomfited and humiliated by White Man, but whose very arrogance he can sometimes turn to account.[7]

6. *Negro Folktales in Michigan*, p. 18.
7. *American Folklore*, pp. 182-83.

The existence and importance of this kind of story was examined briefly in Chapter Three. The germ of such stories certainly existed in the old cycle of "Marster-John" tales, which often had John, the slave, outwitting his master and either gaining his freedom, or getting approval of his slothful work habits. The ones that Dorson mentions are direct descendants of this sort of narrative, for the Negro in them turns the white man to account through verbal tricks. There are a number of that sort of story in this collection, notably the ones included under "Chinaman, Jew, Colored Man."

There are certain procedural methods which I followed in the presentation of the materials here. The headnote idea, begun in the introductions to the toasts, is broadened here. They give a brief survey to assist in making comparative study. Further, as before, Legman's comments are included *verbatim*. Because certain books and journals are constantly referred to in the headnotes, I have used certain shorthand methods to refer to them. These works are:

Baughman	Ernest W. Baughman, *A Comparative Study of the Folktales of England and North America.* (Unpublished thesis.)
Botkin (TAA)	Ben A. Botkin, *Treasury of American Anecdotes.*
Brewer (Brazos)	J. Mason Brewer, *The Word on the Brazos.*
Dorson (AF)	Richard M. Dorson, *American Folklore.*
Dorson (NFTM)	Richard M. Dorson, *Negro Folktales in Michigan.*
Dorson (NTPB)	Richard M. Dorson, *Negro Tales From Pine Bluff, Arkansas.*
Fauset	Arthur Huff Fauset, *Folklore From Nova Scotia.*
Hurston	Zora Neale Hurston, *Mules and Men.*
JAF	*Journal of American Folklore.*
Jones	Charles C. Jones, *Negro Myths from the Georgia Coast.*
MWF	*Midwest Folklore.*
PTFLS	*Publications of the Texas Folklore Society.*
Parsons (Cape Verde)	Elsie Clews Parsons, *Folklore From the Cape Verde Islands.*
Parsons (FLSI)	Elsie Clews Parsons, *Folk-Lore of the Sea Islands.*

Randolph (Devil's)	Vance Randolph, *The Devil's Pretty Daughter*.
Randolph (Sticks)	Vance Randolph, *Sticks in the Knapsack*.
Randolph (Church House)	Vance Randolph, *Who Blowed Up the Church House?*
Roberts	Leonard Roberts, *South From Hell-fer-Sartin'*.
SFQ	*Southern Folklore Quarterly*.
Southern Workman	*Southern Workman and Hampton School Record*.
Tidwell	James N. Tidwell, *A Treasury of American Folk Humor*.
WF	*Western Folklore*.

Full reference notations for these works can be found in the bibliography.

Asterisks (*), as in the last chapter, refer to further material in the glossary. Motif numbers refer to Stith Thompson, *Motif-Index of Folk-Literature;* tale-type numbers to Aarne-Thompson, *The Types of the Folktale*.

18. *THE PREACHER AND THE PICKLES*

These first two stories concerning the preacher emphasize his gluttony. Both seem to owe their existence more to the witty final lines than to the power of the narratives as a whole.

Mrs. Jones, she was a widow. So the preacher, he'd been trying to get Mrs. Jones for a long time. So he come over one day. He said, "Mrs. Jones," he said, "I think I'll come over to your house for dinner if you would invite me. I'll come over there and we'll set down, and eat a little dinner, we'll sit down and talk. We'll talk 'bout the Bible." So she said, "O.K., well come on over on Sunday."

But she had a little boy, he had a bad habit. Of farting. You see he drink a lot of milk, you know and it would make him fart. His mother would try to stop him from drinking milk you know, when she was going to have company, but he was sneaking and drinking anyhow. So this Sunday she was going to stop him, 'cause she knew he was going to sneak in and get it, 'cause she had a cow. If she didn't give it he'd go out to the cow and get it from the cow. So he drank this milk, so his mother said, "Well, I know what I'll do.

I'll take a pickle and stuff it up his behind." So she told him to get dressed; he went and got washed. She called him in the room, she said, "Come here. Pull down your pants." So she took this pickle and stuck it up his behind. She said, "Now that'll keep you from farting." He said, "Yes, Ma'am."

Well, this here preacher liked pickles. So he ate all the food. So he started eating the pickles. So he said, "Unh, I sure wish you had another one." So his mother said, "We haven't got another one in the house." Little boy hustling his mother. She said, "Stop, boy!" He went and got the pickle out of his ass-hole, washed it off, dipped it down in the pickle jar. Took it on the fork, back there, he said, "Here's one more." Preacher he laid back in his chair and he said, "That was a whooper and a whopper." Little boy looked at him and said, "You a god-damn liar, it was my ass-hole stopper."

Charley

19. *THE PREACHER IS CAUGHT*

Now you know, captain's come home from a hard day's work, he peeked into his kitchen window, and there was the preacher. There was the preacher taking one bite off of the chicken leg, throwing it away. Took a bite off a chicken wing, throwed it away. Took a bite off the breast and he throwed it away. The guy walked around the block and he came back again. He didn't see the preacher. Went in the front room, wasn't nobody in the parlor. Went down the cellar, nobody in the cellar. He went upstairs and opened the door, and there was deacon. But he wasn't at prayer meeting. But he was on his knees. He had whole mouth full of cotton.* He said, "Hold it, deacon. Unnh unnh. You got to get up from there." He said, "I come by the first time, I didn't mind what I seen." He said, "Now look. I'ma put you straight. I don't mind you fucking up my eating, but god damn, don't eat up my fucking."

"Kid"

20. *THE PREACHER AND HIS SONG*

Motif X 435 (The boy applies the sermon), X 410 (Jokes on parsons), related to J 1262.5.1 (Whoever gives alms in God's name will receive tenfold: preacher's wife gives sweetmeats away).

Little boy asked his father for fifty cents one day, so he could take his girl to the movies. This boy's father was a preacher. Boy's

father he had a little church. So he told his son, "O.K., son, here's
fifty cents." He said, "Now you spend this fifty cents wisely. But
I want you to come to church today before you go to the movies.
"O.K., daddy, I'll be there."

So he was in church preaching. So the time for collection and
he started hollering, "Oh, I want everybody to dig in their pockets
deep, put some money in the church. Yes, sir." Everybody says,
"Amen." Congregation hollered, "Amen." " 'Cause if anyone in my
family was here, and didn't put no money in the church, I'll skin
'em alive." But at the same time he was waving at his son not to
put his money in the church.

His son being a young boy figured that his father meant to put
the money in there, and when he get home he get fifty cents back.
So when the basket got 'round to his son, he put his fifty cents in
the basket.

So service was over, little boy went on him, said, "Dad, eruh,
could I have my fifty cents back?" So he said, "What fifty cents?"
He said, "Fifty cents I put in church. You was waving at me telling
me to put my money in the church." Said, "Now I figured, when
I get back home, eruh, you'd give my money back."

So his father said, "Look, boy. All you got to do is to have faith
in the Lord. All you got to do is to have faith in the Lord, un hunh,
and you get your money back." So he said, "You got to pray."

Well, the kid didn't know he'd messed, so he figured his father
was right. Went up in the steeple. Start praying. Said, "Oh, Lord,
please drop me my fifty cents. Lord, drop me my fifty cents." And
every time he'd ask Him for fifty cents he'd hold his hand out. So
just then a little bird flew over top him. He said, "Oh, Lord, would
you drop me my fifty cents." So just then the bird shit in his hand.
He said, "Lord, lookahere. I don't want this shit. All I want is my
fifty cents."

Charley

21. *THE PREACHER IS LOST*

Same punch-line as the last but a different story.

One day this preacher was taking a walk in the woods. Just
walking, not concerned with where he was going or nothing. So he
was walking and walking, started to turn to go back. When he

went back, he couldn't find his way out. So he said, "Well, I'm not worried, God gonna show me my way out." So he kept on walking. Walked till night come. "I ain't worried, 'cause God's gonna show me my way out." So he walked all night. Bright and early next morning, he still walking. He walked up against this log, and he kneeled down. He hold his hands out, and he said, "God, please show me my way out." Just then a bird flew over and shit in his hand. He said, "God, don't hand me no shit, I'm really lost."

Freddie

22. THE PREACHER AND THE FARM WOMAN

Once again, the same idea is conveyed by the punch-line. See Motifs Q 21.1 (Old Woman gave her only cow believing she would receive a hundred in return from God. A bishop hearing of her faith sends her 100 cows.) and J 1262.5 (Parishioner hears preacher say that alms are returned "100 to 1"). This story is close to both.

This was another about a preacher. I don't know why they do this to preachers. There was this preacher going around and he was going to different people's houses saying, "Sister or brother, you contribute five or ten dollars to the church and the Lord's gonna see that you get it back and then some."

So he went to this woman. They lived in the country, you know. She had cows and things. You know, bulls and pigs all over her place. So this morning when the preacher come there, he said, "Sister, say would you help the church get started by contributing five dollars?" So she said, "Well, I don't know." He said, "Well, Sister, if you do, you'll get your five back and about twenty-five more." So she said, "Well, O.K., reverend, I'll do that."

So, this was like maybe on a Friday, so Monday morning when she got up, sweeping her back porch up, old bull come up there and dumped his load on her steps. She swept it away and she didn't say anything. But that evening she set there, and she was waiting to get her five back and then this twenty-five.

So this went on every morning. She get up and sweep her porch, and she still never heard anything from this reverend. So next morning when she got up and she saw this pile down there, she looked up at the sky and she said, "Lord, I don't want no bullshit. I just want my five dollars back."

Charley

23. *THE REVEREND AND THE DEACON'S CONTEST*

Stories on the sexual promiscuity of the clergy are legion. Boc-caccio abounds with such stories, heightened in interest because of the supposed practice of priestly continence. Motifs J 1264 (Repartee concerning clerical incontinence), similar to J 1269.1 (The Parson's share and the Sexton's) in idea. Legman — The story, with the same details as here, appears in many French 1920's jest books.

The reverend and the deacon was sitting in church. The deacon said, "Reverend, I bet I have did it to more women in this congregation than you have." And the deacon said, "Shit, that what you think." He said, "Now I tell you what to do. When the church service starts, all that you did it to, say 'eeny meeny' and all that I did it to, I'm gonna say 'eeny meeny'." "All right, that's a deal."

So the congregation started about 8 o'clock, you know. They all started walking in. Reverend came in. The first two sisters come in, the reverend said, "Eeny meeny." Second two sisters came in, deacon said, "Eeny meeny." So then long come 'round about 10 o'clock, they still coming in, and the deacon's wife walked in. Reverend said, "Eeny meeny." The deacon said, "Hold it, reverend, I told all that you done did it to, you say 'eeny meeny.' But that's my wife." He said, "That's why I said 'eeny meeny'." "And that's my mother in back of her, my four daughters, my granddaughter, my mother-in-law, my three aunts, and my great-great grand-mother." Reverend said, "Well, eeny, meeny, meeny, meeny, meeny, meeny, meeny, meeny." Other words he done broke them all.

"Kid"

24. *HIS PRAYER IS UNHEEDED*

One day a preacher was walking across a bridge. He was the kind of preacher that always cussed a lot. He was walking across the bridge and he heard the train coming. And when he turned, he slipped and hit the side of the bridge. Hanging on the bridge, he looked down to see the water below. So he started praying. He said, "God, don't let me fall in this water." Just then his left hand started to slip. He was hanging by his right hand, still praying. "God, don't let me fall in this water. I'll never say another cuss word." So his right hand slipped and he fell in the water. Water came up to his knees. He said, "Ain't this a damn shame, I done all this damn pray-ing, and this water up to my motherfucking knees."

Freddie

25. OPEN THEM DOORS

Motif K 1961.1.2.1 (Parody sermon). Fauset, 93, has a similar brick-throwing incident in the middle of a sermon. Legman — . . . any connection with the song recorded by Jelly Roll Morton . . . called "Buddy Bolden's Blues"? "Thought I heard Buddy Bolden shout,/ 'Open up them doors, let that bad air out'."

25A.

One time this preacher was preaching in the church on how the Holy Ghost came into church, and enlightened the people. So he said,

> Open them doors, and open them wide,
> Let the gospel come inside.

So they opened the door. So bye-and-bye he said it again:

> Open them doors and open them wide,
> Let the gospel come inside.

So these two bums was coming past. So the preacher said,

> Open them doors and open them wide,
> And let the gospel come inside.

The bums threw in there and hit him with a brick. He said,

> Close them doors and close them quick.
> 'Cause some son of a bitch done hit me with a brick.

"Boots"

25B.

This is about this preacher. You know he used to go from city to city visiting churches and preaching, you know. And so some-body told him one time, "Well, you're gonna get enough." Well, he wasn't really a preacher, you know, but I mean, he was a self-styled preacher. He was a preacher on his own. So somebody told him, "You're gonna get enough going around trying to preach." So he told him, "No, my word is God's gospel," or some jazz* like that.

So he goes to this church one night, and every time he would start to preach a sermon, he would get loud. Tell 'em to open the doors and the windows. So this particular night, this Sunday night, he goes to this church and it's crowded, so he said,

> Open the door and open it wide,
> Let my voice be heard outside.

Some little kids were sitting out there, and these little kids got tired of hearing this jazz about he was what God sent, and this, that, and the other. So the little kids hurled a brick in there and hit him on the side of his head. He said,

> Shut that door and shut it quick.
> Some son of a bitch done threw a brick.

Freddie

26. WHAT DID JOHN SAY?

This is Tale-Type 1833 A, "The Boy Applies the Sermon." Motif X 435.1. For other American Negro texts of this popular story, see Dorson (NTPB), 255; Fauset, 94-5 (Nova Scotia); JAF 47:314; Parsons (FLSI), 127-8; SFQ, 19:112. For a close variant where a sermon causes a thief to own thievery, see Dorson (NFTM), 170; Fauset, 98.

Once this preacher was preaching, and he drunk a lot. So he told this bootlegging son that he wanted him to go to his father and send him a pint of goathair. So the boy went over there to his father, John, and he told him, said, "Pop, reverend over there told me to tell you send him a pint of goathair." He said, "You tell that motherfucker I ain't sending him shit till he pay me for that last pint."

So the boys went over there and sat in back. The church had started. "Oh, damn. I got to wait till the sermon is over." It just so happened he was preaching about John. So he asked one time, "What did John say?" So the little boy was sitting there. Said, "I know daggone well, the preacher didn't ask me what John say, and all these people in the congregation." Preacher said, "What did John

say? I ain't gonna ask you but one more time. I want to know."
Little boy said, "Well, if he ask me again, I'm gonna tell him." He
said, 'What did John say?" Little boy said, "John say he ain't gonna
send you a god damn thing till you pay him for the last pint
you got."

"Kid"

27. YOU SEEN WILLY?

*Dorson (NFTM) lists this as an "oikotype of Type 326." It is
close to Motif J 1495.2 ("When Caleb Comes"). Also E 281 (Ghosts
Haunt House), H1411 (Fear Test: staying in haunted house). For
other American reportings of this fairly common story, see: Dorson
(NFTM), 128-9; Dorson (NTPB), 78; Botkin (TAA), 222 (from
Alben W. Barkley, That Reminds Me, p. 37); JAF 40:258-9 (Ala.);
Randolph (Church House), 163-4; Roberts, 109-134 (13 variants).
Legman — A modernized "telephone" variety of this exists, in which
the supernatural element is rationalized — or, rather, irrationalized!
— as "mere nonsense." I have seen this on the vaudeville-nightclub
stage, and believe it was also used in a movie: The phone rings
repeatedly with people asking for Joe — person answering gets
angrier all the time, shouting that "Joe ain't here!" Last caller says
(sepulchral tone in the theatre, with hidden micropone — thus actually a Hamlet-type ghost, though presumably only the voice-at-the-
other-end [side!] -of-the-wire): "Hello, this is Joe. Been any calls
for me?" . . . The item about the hot-coals . . . .: a standard sort of
"trait" . . . in ghost stories.*

This little old preacher he was coming down the road one day.
So he passed this here farm house. So he went over, said "Er uh,
say, er uh, do have any rooms to put me up over night? I got my
own food and everything. I just want a place to stay." She said,
"Well, you go on down there to the shed house. Tell me it's a little
haunted, but I guess you can make it over there." "Oaah. Well,
could I borrow your frying pan, so I can fry my pork chops?" So
she said, "Yeah."

So the preacher went on over to the shed house, so long 'bout
12 o'clock he started reading his Bible under the candlelight. So
here comes this ghost. He said, "Er uh," tapped the preacher on the
shoulder, he said, "You seen Willy?" He said, "No, I ain't seen

Willy." So the ghost looked over, and went away rattling his chains and all. Came back 'bout five minutes later. He said, "You seen Willy?" So he said, "No, I ain't seen Willy." So *he* left.

So here comes another ghost in. So he said, "Hey there, have you seen Willy?" Reverend said, "No, I ain't seen Willy." So he grabbed the frying pan, drink the hot grease, ate the pork chop, grabbed some of the hot coals to wipe his ass. The preacher looked up and said, "Well, god damn, you ain't Willy. Let me get the hell out of here."

Freddie

28. *I'M HAULING SAND*

This most nearly resembles the appearance of the ghost as it slowly drops down the chimney. As such, it can be considered with that story as a humorous outgrowth of Type 326 (or more precisely a humorous relative). Motifs J 1495 (Person runs from actual or supposed ghost); E 293 (Ghosts frighten people deliberately); H 1411 (Fear Test: staying in haunted house); E 281 (Ghosts haunt house). See Dorson (NTPB) for a similar story.

28A.

The reverend and the preacher they were in church, the congregation was talking 'bout ghosts, so they wanted to prove to them there wasn't no such thing as ghosts. So they picked the hauntedest house they could find, and they said they'd spend the night there.

So they was sitting down, reading, all of a sudden they heard someone say:

Coming up the back road
And I'm hauling sand.

Deacon looked out the window. He said, "You hear that, Rev?" Rev said, "It wasn't nothing." He turned the page in the Bible.

Coming through the kitchen room
And I'm hauling sand.

Deacon said, "You hear that, Rev?" Rev said it wasn't nothing. He turned the page.

> I'm standing in the hallway
> And I'm hauling sand.

Deacon said, "Did you hear that, Rev?" Rev said it wasn't nothing and he turned another page.

> I'm standing in the front
> And I'm hauling sand.

Deacon said, "Rev, you see anything?" Rev looked around the room, he said, "I don't see nothing. Just somebody playing a trick on us."

> I'm standing in back of the reverend
> And I'm hauling sand.

Deacon said, "Rev, I don't see nothing." Rev didn't say nothing.

> I'ma put my hand on the reverend's shoulder
> And I'm hauling sand.

And the hand hit the reverend's shoulder, and he didn't see nothing. He got up, put his Bible down, put his hat and coat on, broke out the door. Deacon said, "Rev, where you going?" Said, "I'm going out the front door and I'm hauling ass."

"Kid"

28B.

Now this preacher, he come from out of church. They just got through praying and everything. Somebody come to his house that was haunting him which said,

> Coming up the sidewalk, swift and sound,
> Doowah, Doowah.

So the preacher turned around, he looked to see where it was coming from. He couldn't see it. Looked out the window and everything and he still couldn't see it. So it say:

> Coming through the front door, swift and sound,
> Doowah, Doowah.

The preacher got scared then, you know, 'cause he didn't know what was going on. So he goes to the door and see what happening.

> Coming up the front porch, swift and sound,
> Doowah, Doowah.

So all of a sudden the preacher he turned around and said:

> Going out the back door, hitting ass,
> Doowah, Doowah.

Freddie

29. BEAR MEETING AND PRAYER MEETING

This tale is common in the U. S., both in song and story forms. As a minstrel-type song it seems to have achieved some degree of popularity. Brown III, 511-12, *prints two variants;* Dorson (AF), 196 *alludes to a text;* Parson (FLSI), 177, *has one stanza from the South Carolina Sea Islands;* White (210) *prints it from Alabama;* Ford, Traditional Music of America, 301-2 *from the Ozarks; and it is mentioned both in the Shearin Kentucky syllabus (31) and the Davis, Virginia compendium (336). In tale form, we have texts from:* Botkin (TAA), 120 *(from* Wit and Humor of the American Pulpit [Philadelphia, 1904], *pp, 94-96);* PTFLS, 10:36 *(Texas);* SFQ, 18:129 *(Ala.);* Tidwell, 132 *(from* SFQ). *Most of these are Negro texts. The verse-sermon in the story suggests its connection with the song.* Jones, 66-68, *prints a related exemplary story that may be the immediate ancestor of this.*

Well, the deac and the rev was in the woods one day. The deacon and rev was breaking some wood together, taking it to the church to get the church warm before the service start. All of a sudden, the rev heard a long noise. He said (whispered), "Hey, deacon." Deacon said, "What's the matter, brother?" He said, "Did you hear that?" "Hear what?" "That strange noise I just hear." "No, I didn't hear nothing." He said, "Sound like a bear." He said, "Look, reverend, we is members of the church. Leaders of the flock. Prayer-giving men. Now if a bear come in this woods, the thing to do is to get down on your knees and pray that help be here and we be saved." He said, "Yeah, rev, but suppose help don't get here on time?" "Don't worry 'bout it. The Lord watches over all his sheeps." "All right."

So they kept working. All of a sudden rev looks up and he seen this great big grizzly bear coming through the woods. Rev dropped the wood, dropped the ax and he broke out. He ran about four or five of them old country miles. Them's long miles. And he sat down, just a-panting for breath. (pants)

After awhile, he looked up, saw a cloud of dust coming down the road. And he looked real good, there goes old deacon. He said, "Hold it, deac." He said, "Wait a minute." Deac said (panting), "What's the matter, son? Don't hold me now. I'm in a hurry." He said, "What's your trouble? I thought you told me that if a bear come you would get down and pray?"

He said, "Well, son, it was like this; I got down and said the shortest, quickest, fastest prayer came to my mind." He said, "Just what did you pray, rev?" "It was like this. I said to the great man up above:

> You delivered one man from the belly of the whale.
> Delivered three from the fiery furnace.
> That's what the good book say.
> Then a body declare,
> If you can't help me, Lord, please don't help that bear.

I kept on praying, brother, but there no help comes. Next best thing to do was to get on way from there." He said, "Yeah, but you didn't pray hard enough." He said, "Brother, I come to one declusion. Praying's all right at prayer meeting, but it ain't too good at bear meeting."

"Kid"

30. *THE PREACHER AND THE SINNERS*

This is one of the many stories here that could be classified under K 1961.1.2.1 (Parody sermon). For another reporting of this story, with the holdout a bootlegger, see TFSB, 24:110. Legman — This has various endings with far-less anti-preacher tone to them. In particular where the preacher excoriates "he-ing and she-ing," and all those sinners line up at the left; "he-ing and he-ing," also "she-ing and she-ing," until finally only one little boy is life, who quavers, "Reverend, how do you feel about me-ing and me-ing?"

One day preacher was sitting up in church and he looked down at the congregation. He said, "Brothers and sisters, we are all gathered here in this church, we are all gathered in this church today to pray. Be holy. Here there still is among us some sinners, hypocrites. Today, we gonna find the evil from the good. Pick out the good from the bad. The ones that's worthy of the flock, and the ones that ain't. Now I say, all you faggots get up and walk to the back of the room." All of the faggots got up and they walked to the back of the room. "Now I say all you bulldaggers, walk to the front of the room." All the bulldaggers, they got up and they walked to the front of the room. He said, "Now, I say, all you mother-fuckers, get over on the side of the hall." And all the motherfuckers got over on the side of the hall. He said, "Now all you no-good, you midnight ramblers, alcoholics, late players, out-stayers, wife-beaters, children deserters, get over on the other side of the room." So all them people got up and they walked to the other side of the room. He said, "Now all among you, these sinners is all around us. And there's not one man or woman or child in among us that is purified, and brother why are you sitting down on the front row?"

There was one little lonely brother sitting on the front row. He said, "Well, rev, you ain't called my name yet." He said, "Well, I said, all the bulldaggers in the back." He said, "I ain't none of them." "I said all you motherfuckers on the side." "I ain't none of them." "I said, all the midnight ramblers, the gamblers, the wife deserters and the wife-beaters get outside." He said, "I ain't none of them." "Then brother, what is your sin?" He said, "I'm a cock-sucker." "Come on up here with me, son."

"Kid"

31. *THE PREACHER BENDS DOWN*

This is once again K 1961.1.2.1 (Parody sermon). Dorson prints a text (NFTM), 170, and notes "This suggests Type 1831 'The Parson and Sexton at Mass' where two connivers communicate by chanting." Legman — Charlie Chaplin based many of his early comedy routines on well-known jokes of this kind (for instance the "swallowed whistle" of City Lights, *which is an expurgated version of a sat-upon cane ferule in a much older British joke). He clearly plays all sorts of cadenzas on the present story in his 1915 or 1916 comedy — which was very much resented — in which he is an ex- or escaped prisoner who has to pass himself off as the new minister. (In later theatrical pieces of this kind — for instance Maugham's*

Rain — *the minister has to be modified into an unspecified "reformer"* *with string necktie; also in burlesque stage anticlerical skits similar.)* *I have heard the present story given in the, essentially, more sacri-* *legious form, of a burlesque quotation from Scriptures, in which* *the ex-prisoner who has become a minister in the West, sees, to his* *horror, his former cellmate come into church just as he had to begin* *the sermon. He swallows and begins: "Brethren and sistren, I take* *my text tonight from the sixteenth chapter of Habbakuk, where it* *says — uh, uh — 'Thou who sees me, and thinks that you knows me,* *ixnay-ackencray ["nix cracks," say nothing, in pig latin], and I will* *split with you later'."*

This here preacher was in church doing his regular sermon. As you know, the regular ranting, up and down they go, kneeling down, standing up. Oh Lord this, and Oh Lord that. "My children, I want you to kneel down your head in prayer."

As everyone kneeled down their head in prayer, this cat's wallet fell on the ground. Preacher reached down and picked it up, and kept on preaching. "Well, Lord, Lord, if anyone saw me I'll split it with you later."

Freddie

32. GABRIEL BLOWS HIS HORN

This is Type 1785, Motif X 411 (Parson put to flight during his *sermon). This is a common story among American Negroes. See* *Dorson (NFTM), 169 (in notes lists two additional tales very close* *to this); Brewer (Brazos), 98-100; Fauset, 94 (Nova Scotia); JAF* *35:295; 41:552 (Phila.); Parsons (FLSI), 58.*

This preacher had a church strictly for ladies. Every night about six o'clock the congregation of ladies would come in. The preacher he would preach and preach, get home about nine o'clock. It got so it kept up so long the men in the town was getting mad about this.

So one day they went to church about 6 o'clock, the preacher was preaching. So the men in town they got together and they saw these two little boys. One of them had a bugle, and one was just running around playing. So he gave the boy that didn't have the bugle a match. He said, "Go play with these matches over there by the church." Boy said, "O.K." So he started playing with the match and set the church on fire. Church was just blazing. They told the other boy to walk through the woods and play the bugle. Church was just blazing. So the fire was coming up behind the preacher and he didn't see it. The ladies in the church started backing up heading for the door, just slowly back up. After a while all the people were out, the preacher was standing on the platform.

> When Gabriel blows we all shall go.
> When Gabriel blows we all shall go.

The preacher looked around and saw the fire, headed for the door and a beam fell and blocked it. He turned to go for the window and his coat got caught on a nail. Just then the little boy started blowing the bugle. Toot, toot, toot, toot. Preacher simply replied, "Oh, Mr. Gabriel, don't play that shit yet."

Freddie

33. PREACHER WALKS THE WATER

This is included in K 1970 (Sham miracles) and is close to K 1961.1.3 (Sham parson; the sawed pulpit). Brewer (Brazos), 46-47, prints a similar text.

33A.

This here reverend, he was preaching. "You know that Moses walked the water. So can I. What you think about that, deacon?" He hollered "Yeah," 'cause they was in cahoots.* But the deacon didn't like this preacher. He said, "Yeah, you can walk the water, brother." He said, "I tell you what I'ma do. Next Sunday, I'm gonna walk the water for you. I'm gonna smoke the water like Moses." Now everybody in church they wanted to see this. So he said, "Now look here, deac, early Sunday morning go out and put three boards out there. Tack 'em together, and I'll walk on the boards and it will look like I'm walking on the water." The deacon said, "O.K."

But instead of him putting three boards, he only put two boards. So the deacon came out there Sunday, the boards were nice and strong. He only tried out one, he figured the rest of them were the same way. So all the people coming 'round, he's already standing in the water. "Don't come no closer, 'less you all will knock the spirit off. I told you that Moses smoke the waters, didn't I?" Everybody looked and it looked like he standing on the water.

So he started walking out on his plank. He said, "Didn't Moses smoke the water?" The children hollered, "Yeah." He said, "I'm on the first one. Ain't that right, deac?" "That's right, preacher." He said, "I should be getting to the second one right now, shouldn't I?" "You're almost there." He said, "Well, pretty soon I'll be at the end of this journey." Deacon said, "Yes, you will." And by the time he said that, he had stepped off, he didn't step on the third board, but he fell down. He said, "Oh, Lord." Deacon looked at him and said, "What's the matter?" He said, "I wonder who moved that god damned board?"

Charley

33B.

There once was a preacher who used to make a yearly festival of walking on the water. He planned and he planned for this festival. But everybody never knew that the day before this festival this preacher would go down to the lake and put boards underneath the water, just a little lower, so the people couldn't see 'em.

So after the preacher went down there this day and put the boards under the water, these boys was down there and they wanted to go swimming. So one boy dived in and hit the board. He said, "I'll be damned, who put these boards under here?" They tore 'em down and took 'em out of the pool.

So the next day, the preacher said, "Yes, congregation, I'm gonna walk the water for you. God is surely with me, 'cause I'ma walk the water. Watch me walk the water." The preacher he walked out a little ways, the boys had left a couple of the boards there. Walked, walked, stepped off the end of the board and down the water he went. Came up gasping and struggling, hollering for help. Went down again. Each time he come up he hollered, "Oh, what motherfucker took these boards out of this water?"

Freddie

34. WHO BELIEVES?

This short anecdote is a vestige of Type 1826, Motif X 452 (Parson has no need to preach). For an Ozark text, see Randolph (Sticks), 129-31.

You know Father Divine. Well, he was holding this big meeting up in Yankee Stadium, or Shibe Park or Carnegie Hall and he had this big meeting. He was preaching and he said, "Who believes that I can walk the water?" Everyone shouted, "We do." "Who believes that I can walk the water?" "We do." So he just said, "Well, if you all believe it I don't have to do it."

Anonymous Informant

35. BAPTISM AND BELIEF

This could perhaps be included under Motif J 1260 (Repartee based on church or clergy). Dorson (NFTM) has a text of this on p. 173 from Michigan Negroes, and Brewer (Brazos), 54-56, has one from Texas Negroes.

You know Sunday service preachers have a baptizing. So the brother came down with his robe on, got down into the baptizing pit. Preacher put him down, grabbed him by the shoulder. He said, "Brother, I baptize you in the name, do you know?" He pushed him in the water and he held him down. Sister started talking to the preacher, he forgot he was holding the fellow. Pulled him up, he said, "Brother, I baptize you, do you know?" Pushed him down again. Guy was gasping for breath when he came up. Pulled him up. "Brother, do you know?" Pushed him down again. This time the guy could hardly get his breath, he was drinking water when he came up. Preacher said, "Brother, do you know?" Brother said, "I know god damn well you trying to drown me."

"Kid"

36. CURSING CURED

The next three stories are part of the large (but mainly unprinted) corpus of lore on how profanity can be eliminated from an offensive-tongued person's speech, and how it sometimes works. Legman — Mark Twain's story, on himself, about his wife trying to cure him of cursing by trying to outcurse him, appears to be a modified version of some story related to this, now lost. His "topper" line is rather good though (from memory): "My dear, you have all the words right, but you just don't know the tune." In another modified version the cursing is changed to "dialect accent," which is to be cured by an elocution teacher; the humor here rises from the attempted cure back-firing and a week later the teacher assures the "improving" (i.e., castratory) parents, "In a veek your liddle boy vil be spikking Henglish ez good like I'm spikking."

There once was a little boy that was continuously always cussing. So his mother and father was puzzled by him always cussing seeing that they was people that never used no foul language. So they asked the preacher to come over one night, give a suggestion how to stop the boy from cussing.

They had the preacher over for dinner. Preacher got there, everybody sat down at the table to eat. So the boy's mother went to say grace. Boy replied, "Damn, Ma, watcha doing?" So everybody started eating, so the boy wanted to season his food, so he called to the preacher, "Hey, bitch, pass the salt down here." Preacher didn't say nothing, just passed the salt.

So after they got finished eating, mother told the boy to go to bed. He put up a big squawk, but he went anyhow. The boy's mother asked the preacher what to do about the boy cussing. So the preacher told her, to late that night to take the boy out of his bed, don't awake him and take him to the woods. Dig a hole and put the boy in it. In the morning when he wake up, he'll never cuss again.

So that night they took the boy out into the woods, dug a deep hole and set the boy down in it. First thing, early the next morning the boy woke up. See himself laying in the hole with blankets wrapped around him, and first thing he replied, "Damn, it's Judgment Day and I'm the first motherfucker to arise."

Freddie

37. THE CURSER OUTCURSED

Legman — *There is a Negro protest story on this same situation-type, but I cannot retell it in rhyme, as I did not take it down many years ago when I heard it in Harlem. A Negro woman goes into a*

liquor store (thus dating it as mid-1930's?) and asks for some gin.
The clerk hoity-toities her and says "What kind of gin do you mean?
We got Gilbey's gin at $2 a fifth; White Rose gin at $1 a quart; and
plain ornery low-down nigger gin for 50¢." — "Yes," she answers,
"and there's three kinds of turd: there's mus-turd, horse-turd, and
you, you plain ornery low-down piece of dog-shit. Gimme the nigger
gin for fifty cents." This didn't exactly rhyme but it went with a hell
of a lilt to it. There is also a "racially-expurgated" white version of
this — much less situational, and more verbal, thus far weaker as
humor — about the "three kinds of tea: f-a-r-t, with the delicate airy
body; s-h-i-t with the heavy, heady odor; and c-u-n-t, the Tea of
Teas, at (some-price-or-another) a pound."

The use of "damn," etc., as intensives is the subject of an elegant
passage by John Brophy, in Brophy & Partridge's Songs and Slang
of the British Soldier *(London, 1930), pp. 15-19, concerning the word*
"fucking" — which should, actually, be spelled "fucken" as it is the
obsolete past particle (the modern "fucked-up") and not the present
participle, as is usually thought; which also explains why the ter-
minal "g" is invariably omitted: it does not belong there at all. The
commonest expurgation of this is "bloody," as in "The Great
Australian Adjective," of which my own interchangeable Army
version (with the last stanza omitted) is printed in Edgar Palmer's
(i.e., Erich Posselt's) G.I. Songs *(New York, 1944), pp. 207-208, and*
reprinted — with a pretended Korean War provenance — in Wm.
Wallrich's Air Force Airs *(New York, 1957), pp. 160-61.*

This man used to walk in this grocery store every day. So one day
he walked into the grocery store and said:

> I want some motherfucking meat
> For my motherfucking cat.
> Not too motherfucking lean,
> Not too motherfucking fat.
> I want it packed very neat in a bag.

Pop was tired of having this happening every day. Every day
when he wanted his meat for his cat. So the next day, Pop walking
down this street and he seen this boy shooting crap. "God damn,
I missed again." Pop looked down and looked at the boy. "That
motherfucker got a seven again. God damn it, baby, Momma needs
a new pair of shoes. Damn it, missed again. Motherfucking cocksucker." "Hey, son, you want a job?" "God damn right. How much
money I'ma make, Pop?" "I'll give you twenty dollars a week."

"Sure, what time you want me to come by? I'll be the fuck around three. God damn straight, I'll be there."

Next morning, early in the morning, little boy at the counter. So this stud walk in and said:

> I want some motherfucking meat
> For my motherfucking cat.
> Not too motherfucking lean,
> Not too motherfucking fat.
> Pack it very neat in a bag.

Boy looked up at him, grabbed his bag, and here's what he said:

> Here's the motherfucking meat
> For your motherfucking cat.
> Not too motherfucking lean,
> Not too motherfucking fat.
> Aim your feet at the motherfucking door.
> And don't come back no motherfucking more.

> *Petey*

38. *THE JUDGE REPLIES*

Legman — *Much like the cante-fable about the witness to a rape, reprimanded for using the word "fucking," who breaks into a rhyme about "His pants was down, his ass was bare/His you-know-what was you-know-where/His balls was dangling in mid-air/And if that wasn't fucking, then I wasn't there."*

This guy was standing on the corner, you know, he kept walking down the street. He said:

> My name is Fucking Pete,
> I walk the fucking street.
> I fuck all the whores
> That think they're so fucking neat.

So the police walked up to him, and said "What you say?" Said:

> My name is Fucking Pete,
> I walk the fucking street.
> I fuck all the bitches
> That think they're fucking neat.

Cop said, "I'ma take you in. Disorderly conduct, 'citing a riot, disturbing the peace, resisting arrest." "I ain't did nothing." "You're going in anyway."

So next morning he got up. Judge said, "What's the charge?" "Disorderly conduct, 'sturbing the peace, 'citing a riot." "Um, what's your name?"

> My name is Fucking Pete,
> I walk the fucking street.
> I fuck all these bitches
> Who think they're so fucking neat.

The judge said:

> Yeah, son. Well, I'm the fucking judge,
> Who's give you some fucking time.
> Here's fifteen years
> To get that fucking off your mind.

"Kid"

39. *ARGUMENT OF THE PARTS OF THE BODY*

Legman — *You have here a relic of an extremely ancient folktale — in fact a whole tale type. The family it belongs to is that of the argument in the* Arabian Nights *between the three sons, with the magic carpet, the all-seeing telescope (I mean crystal ball! — pardon my modernizing!), and the all-curing apple, who can't decide which of them is to get the princess cured by the combined powers of their three possessions. The specific argument between the parts of the body as to which "is more important" is very ancient indeed, and the rectum always wins, after the others pooh-pooh its claims (as I've heard this told in modern times myself!) when it says "Well, then, I'm gonna shut my mouth and not say another word." Whereupon all the other members of the body become deathly sick from constipation, and agree the rectum is the most important. Your own story begins this tale, but does not give it, as your ending has clearly nothing to do with being "most important," and is a pure complaint. That form, or subform, is at least as old as the mid-17th century, and I believe a rhymed form as a dream is given in one of the drolleries, with the testicles described as a hunter's dogs who stay by the side of the pond while he goes in swimming. There are also other forms of this complaint-tale, where the complaining is done by fleas or other insects (symbolizing the child in the womb — who also sometimes does the complaining) who describe the penis as an intruder or one-eyed giant of the Polyphemus sort in the Homeric legend. I myself would not hesitate to classify the Polyphemus story as a symbolic form of this same vagina-as-cavern tale, all the more so since the P. story includes and ends with what is the oldest re-corded joke in the world (where Ulysses tells the giant his name is "Nobody," so the giant later cannot explain who is hurting him), as pointed out by the Russian folklorist Afanasyev, in* Russian Secret Tales *in the 1860's. The element in your text, equating the rectum with an outhouse, also is found in a modern story about Henry Ford in heaven, who tells God that the creation of human beings was not well done because, in making Eve, "You put the exhaust too close to the intake."*

The parts of the body were all talking to themselves about which was the most important. Finally Peter rose up and spoke. He said, "I wear two stones tied around my neck. At night when I go to bed to take a little rest, I'm shoved in a dark hole, next door to a shit-house, and I stay till I puke. If I come out and stand up for my rights, I get shoved in again."

"Kid"

40. HIMSELF DISCOVERED

This tale, along with a number that immediately follow, is remi-niscent of Chaucer and Boccaccio in situation. As such it has much in common with many possible motifs: J 2136 (Numskull brings about own capture); J 582 (Foolishness of premature coming out of hiding); J 1805 (Other misunderstandings of words); X 111.7 (Mis-understood words lead to comic results). Baughman gives a motif (N 275.5.2 — subdivision of "Criminal confesses because he thinks himself accused") which nearest approximates the story. JAF, 32: 372, has two stories in which a similar misunderstanding of words leads to the unmasking of hidden lover.

Once there was a woman and man who were married, and the woman was a whore. Now the woman always cried broke when collectors came, so when the ice-man came and asked for pay, she said, "Come into my bedroom," and she gave him a piece of cock. So then the husband came home and said why does she have to fuck the collectors instead of paying. So she said, "All right, I won't do it again."

But as soon as her husband left, the colored insurance man came, so she told him, "I don't have any money but I can pay you with some cunt." So he accepted. Meanwhile the husband came home from work much earlier than usual, and knocked on the door. The woman said, "Hide. That's my husband." So he hid in the closet.

Her husband sat down and said, "You been messing around again, haven't you?" So he threw her down on the bed and started pulling the hairs on her cock. Meanwhile, remember the man is still in the closet. The husband gets down to two hairs, and they are hard to get out. So he starts cursing, "Come on out, you black bastards, damn it." The man in the closet starts shaking. The husband says again, "Come out of there, damn it, you black bastard." So the man comes running out of the closet with one shoe on and britches halfway up, running straight through the door.

Charley

41. *HIS EVENING KISS*

This anecdote is one of the most amusing elements of Type 1361, which we know best through Chaucer's version, "The Miller's Tale." For a full description of the tradition of the whole tale, see Bryan and Dempster, Sources and Analogues of the Canterbury Tales *(New York, 1941), pp. 106 ff. This one portion is Motif K 1225 (Lover given rump to kiss). See also J 1772.*

Now look here. This fellow was going home, this guy was blind, you know. So every night when this guy would go past he would stop by and kiss this little old girl. So this night her old man was there. So he comes knocking on the window, he says, "Who's outside that window?" He said, "Look ahere." She said, "That's the blind man lives down the street. He always stop by here every night and he always kiss me." "Put your ass out the window, let that motherfucker kiss your ass. I've been trying to fuck* him." So she puts her ass out the window, the old blind man hit her (kissing sound). So he said, "Honey, what's the matter?" She said, "Honey,

I'm sick." He said, "You sick?" She said, "Yes." "Let me kiss you
'gain." She puts her ass out the window, he smacks her one big
long one (long kissing sound). He said, "You ain't lying you sick,
honey. You jaws are swollen like you have the mumps and your
breath smells like shit."

"Kid"

42. COMING OR GOING

Remind me of the time I was sitting around this girl's house,
friend of mine's wife, and I was going to give her a little bit, you
know. Sitting up in her room. So all of a sudden I heard a door
open. I said, "who's that?" She said, "That's my husband." She said,
"Kiss my titties, I'm coming." I said, "Shit, you kiss my ass, I'm
going."

"Kid"

43. "GRANDMA, IT'S YOU!"

*The substitution theme is legion in anecdotes of this sort. The
Italian novelists of the late Renaissance made much of the theme.
The substitution of older woman for younger is, however, fairly
unusual. Thompson has a motif (K 1317.5 — Woman substitutes for
her daughter in the dark) but his reference to the Heptameron is
misleading and belongs elsewhere, and Rotunda (from whom
Thompson seems to have derived the motif) has a very different
accent to his description. Certainly this story fits somewhere in the
K1317 area (Lover's place usurped by another) and should probably
be around 1317.2.1 (Old woman as substitute for girl in man's bed)
but should be contrasted with this latter because in the stories
subsumed under it the woman is just a pawn of someone else, while
here she is the schemer.*

43A.

Now this is about a little old country boy. Yeah, this is about
a little country boy. Little country boy lived waaay out in the

woods. Man he lived so far back in the woods he had to pack a lunch to go to the mailbox. Now anyway, he was going with this little old country girl. Now she told him, "Now listen here, you come 'round here 'bout nine o'clock, I'll cut the lights out, put the window up, right after you whistle and you'll know that I'm all ready." He said, "All right." He said, "I be there." "All right."

So now her grandmother heard it. Grandmother, she was about sixty-eight, sixty-nine years old. She ain't had no joint* since Grandpop died 'bout twenty-five years ago. Well, she thinking to herself, "I'ma get some of this young peter." So just about ten minutes of nine, she said, "Daughter, you run down to the store, get me some snuff." She said, "But Grandma, store's almost thirty-five miles from here. Can I use the buggy?" "No, the horse is sick, you walk." "Grandma, I won't be back till 'bout four o'clock in the morning." "You go 'head." "All right."

So the little daughter thought she'd cut through the woods and catch up with Johnny, but Johnny duck 'round the other way. Johnny came in, looked up at the window and whistled (whistle). Grandma threw up the window, took off all her clothes and throwed herself in bed. Johnny jumped up in the window, throwed off his clothes and jumped dead on that old fashioned cock. And Johnny started to work and whirling, after awhile he said, "Damn." He come to life, looked down and saw (it) was Grandma. He said, "Grandma, it's you!" She said "Yes, son. It's me." He said, "Grandma, it stinks." She said, "Well, son, I'ma tell you, it's like this: it was just so god damn good. I'm too old to come, so I just went on ahead and shit."

"Kid"

43B.

Here go a little joke some fellow told me. There was this here man, an old lady and her grandaughter. They lived on this farm. This man was a hired man. He was the hired help, I mean. Well, anyway, the old woman, she hadn't been worked over in a long while. And this old lady, she said, "Well, shit, got to get me some." She said, "Ain't nobody within a hundred miles of here. Got to get me some dick from somewhere." Said, "Yeah, the hired help, I'll get him."

So she went down there to the hired help. She talked to him. She said, "Lookahere, Joe." Said, "You look up at my window tonight about nine o'clock, and when I put out the light, man, you can come up there and do a little style* there." "O.K., baby, I'll be there."

So that night, that old guy stand out there and he wait and wait. 'Bout nine-thirty, he seen the light go out. But he didn't know that Mom overheard the conversation, old grandmother heard the conversation, she was about seventy years old. So anyway, the light went out, old man snuck upstairs. Tip, tip, tip, up the damn steps he went, you know, the creaking floors, you know how those old farm houses, how they is. So he went on in there and opened the door. He said, "Is you ready?" She said, "Yeah." She said, "Come on in." So he come on in there and he start to working. And he still didn't know that Mom overheard the conversation and sent the little granddaughter all the way down the road to get a loaf of bread. So he was working there. After awhile, he started sniffing. "Damn," he said, "I smell — don't smell right." She said, "Ain't nothing, go 'head." So he just kep' on working. He was working out like a champ. Kep' on working. Kep' on working. So after awhile, he got finished, he got up. He said, "Damn, it sure do stink in here. Let me get the motherfucking out of here. Open up some windows. Open up some doors." "All right." So cut the light on, so god damn it, who be down there but grandma. Said, "Granny, what you doing down there?" She said, "Well, I overheard the conversation, son, and I just wanted a little bit of young dick and," she said, "so I just decided to take advantage of the situation." "Damn, Ma, what that I smell?" She said, "Boy, I couldn't come, so I just shitted."

Freddie

44. THE NIGHTLY RITUAL

This is basically the same story as above with a slightly different scene, technique, and punch-line.

This old guy, you know, he was sitting home, you know. He was coming home every night, certain time, all he did, he had a routine, he'd did it so long. His mother — mother-in-law, rather — father-in-law lived with him. And his wife. And every night he'd go to bed, his wife'd go to bed rather, and his mother-in-law and father-in-law, they'd go to bed, they lived under them. And you know, when he come home from work, 'bout two, three o'clock, he'd just get in bed, lay there for an hour or two. Then he'd get up and go on and work out. And his wife be hollering, "Oh, honey, you know I love you. You sweet thing, you. Ooh, you do it so good."

So his mother-in-law was lying there one night, said, "I'ma get me some of that young peter. First chance I get." So Thursday night come up, was a cabaret, so her husband had left for work early so she couldn't ask him. So mother-in-law said, "You go on, I'll watch the kids." So the father-in-law said, "Well, I'll take her to the cabaret, you know, so somebody be with her." She said, "Yeah, that be fine." She said, "Now I'll sneak upstairs while they're gone. I'll jump in bed."

She snuck upstairs, got undressed, got in bed, same side his wife lay on, you know. He came home from work that night, jumped in bed, you know. Routine. He didn't pay her no mind. He just crawled on over, got in bed. Layed there 'bout half an hour, got a little sleep. Rolled over, you know, started to work it out. He sweating and pushing, sweating and pushing. She wasn't saying nothing. He was wondering why his wife, you know usually she tells him how much she loves him and everything, tonight she quiet. It was windy that night, you know, getting ready to rain. The wind blowing real hard, summer night. And the front door was open. Ma, she wanted to say something so bad, she could scream. So all of a sudden the wind blew the door slammed. She thought it was her husband. So she jumped up, she said, "You dirty mother-fucker, you. Why you riding son-of-a-bitch. My own son-in-law, laying up on top of me like this here. Laying up here just a doing it to me. And knowing good and well that you're married to my daughter. Now look here, boy, you hit this thing one or two more time and get on down from here."

"Kid"

45. *THE HAIRY SCOREBOARD*

This is, as the informant points out, one of the standard "traveling salesman" stories, that series which, with the milkman jokes, gives greatest evidence of being the modern successor to the novelle.

This fellow was one of these traveling salesmen. That's what all these jokes are about. Traveling salesman riding along in the woods one night, that's when one of these storms come up. So he said, "I guess I'll stop in this little old shack here and see who's home." So he knocks on the door. Pop comes, says "Yeah." He says, "Pardon me, dad, my car broke down. I'd like to know could I spend the night here tonight?" "Sure. Look here now, you got a choice. You could sleep out the barn with my pet bear or you could sleep upstairs (with) me and my daughter." "I'd ruther sleep with you and your daughter." "All right. Dinner's at six and we going to bed at nine." "All right."

So he ate dinner, you know, talked to the daughter, got tight.* Nine o'clock he went to bed. Ten-thirty she rolled over and said, "How 'bout us getting a little piece?" He said, "I don't know. Suppose your father wake up?" "Don't worry about him. Pull a hair out of his ass, see is he woke." He reached over and pulled one — boinggg! "He's 'sleep." So they started working. Hour later she said, "Better stop, see is Dad woke." He pulled 'nother hair. Boinggg! So they worked 'nother fifteen, twenty minutes, she said, "Stop. See is Daddy woke." He pulled 'nother hair. Boing! So they fucked for four or five hours and every ten minutes they stopped, pulled a hair out of Dad's ass. At last, woke up. He reached over, said, "Wait a minute. Lemme tell y'all something. You paid your rent, you paid your board and mo'. Paid for your dinner, gave me twenty dollars extra. Now I don't mind you fucking my daughter, but be damned if I don't mind you 'bout using my ass for a scoreboard."

"Kid"

46. WASHDAY IN THE WOODS

The man who has had to do without seems of interest to the group, as is illustrated by the next two stories.

Now you 'magine yourself in the woods. This old lady out there washing clothes, and a fellow walking through the woods about two blocks away. There's a clear field now, and he can see everything. Now this old lady was washing wool, and she was bending over just rubbing in the bowl. Rubbing her old clothes in the bowl, down South, you know. This old guy come walking past. He just come out of jail doing seven and a half. He ain't had no kind of cock for I don't know when. Got blisters on his dick from jerking off so much. He looks through the woods and he spots the old lady rubbing down, he says, "Ummh, hmmh, the keast of that beast." Breaks down and charge through the woods where Ma is stroke down in the tub. He hit her. He hit her — zhagoop! She hollered, "UMMMMH, HMMMMH, Lord have mercy. Ummh. Son, I don't know your name. I can't see your face. Now get it, child, for you'll find me *every* Monday morning at the same old place."

"Kid"

47. GEORGE IS UPSTAIRS

This story is one that is very current in joke-telling sessions, Negro and otherwise. Since collecting this version, I have heard it a number of times, generally with the same details.

Now this here fellow, you know, he was in the Navy. He was in the Navy, you know. Stone sailor. He been out on the sea for 'bout a year. He ain't had nothing like a woman. So he came in 'bout four o'clock in the morning, got his pass, ran into city, come to this house he heard about. Knocked on the door, the guy said, "Yeah?" Said, "Look here, how's the chance of a man getting something did for me?" Said, "But, Dad, it's four o'clock in the morning and all the girls done split, man. But we got George upstairs." "I don't play that motherfucking shit." The guy leaves.

Next night he had KP so he had to stay a little late. Comes in late again. Knocked on the door. "Yeah?" "Look here," he said, "I just got in town, man, I got to have something done to me now. How's the chance in a fellow getting fixed up?" He said, "You keep coming late. The girls are gone, but we got George upstairs." " I don't play that motherfucking shit." Said, "You come 'round here tomorrow right, and I'll have you five girls, you can take your pick." "All right."

So next day they got to joking 'round, joking 'round, joking 'round 'bout two o'clock in the morning. He comes out of there ass shoving out like fire. Come by, said, "Look here, man, I hope you saved me a girl." "The girls, they waited till ten-thirty, they went

out and made some money. But we still got George upstairs."
"Man, I don't play that shit." He said, "Wait a minute, I got to get
something. How much is George?" "Three hundred dollars." "Three
hundred dollars? How is it three hundred dollars?" He said, "Well
see, lemme 'splain it to you. Now there's a hundred for George.
There's a hundred for me. And a hundred for Al." "Wait a minute.
Why Al got to get a hundred?" "Well, see, Al gotta help me hold
George, 'cause George don't play that shit neither."

"Kid"

48. THE WATCH

*Here is another tale about a signifying monkey whose guile is
defeated by a show of strength. One of the important counterparts
to the Marster-John type stories, and often told in conjunction with
them, is the "kind Marster" type, in which the faithful servant is
rewarded for his service and encounters the wide world for the first
time. A story which I heard often, but never recorded, concerned
just such a situation, but the servant worked out a way of tele-
graphing his master for more money until this practice is brought
to a halt through a humorous cryptic telegram.*

One day Sam's boss, Mr. Charlie, walked up him and said to old
sam. "Sam, you have been slaving for me ever seen you came out
of your mammy's cock. And since tomorrow is a special holiday and
all the niggers will be in town, because that is just about the only
time that you people, can come to town, unless us, white folks is
with you'll. I am going to let you wear my gold chain, and twenty
dollar gold piece to town and let those poor niggers gaze at my
Sam. So San, strached his head, and sweating all the same time,
said thank you Mr Charlie, boss man, and went on down to his
shack. When Sam got home and told his wife, what his boss had
give him to go to town with, she said that Sam was the richest
nigger in these parts of the south. So sam put on his suit that his
brother had sent him from up North, Sam had to hide the suit,
because his boss woundnt let him wear it, because he would have
taken it from him. When Sam hit the eadge of town, the poor
niggers, as his boss put it, started looking and running up to Sam
and ask, who did he kill, did he shoot his boss, are who did he rob,

and one said that Sam had better high tail it to the hills before they find out and get aposse started looking for him. Sam, Said hold on a minute, you poor niggers, I didn't rob, or kill anyone. My boss Mr. Charlie let me wear his gold chain and twenty dollar gold piece, to come to town and be a rich nigger, and show you poor niggers up. They all started to stcratch there heads, and talking to one another, saying that they wish they had a boss as good as Mr. Charlie was to Sam. Then Old Sam spotted something come-his way with something on a chain, and started to run when the crowd called him back, and told him that it was a monkey on a cahin, and that box that the music came out of was an Organ, and the man was a Organ Grinder. And the man tell hot numbers if you put something in the Monkeys cup. They told sam to go and see for himself, so he did. Sam went up the the Monkey, and said good morning Mr. Monkey, so the Monkey, looked at Sam, and said to him that he was the prettest nigger that he had seen all day, so Old Sam told the Monkey, how long he had been working for his boss man, and that his boss loved him, and let him wear his chain, and twenty dollar gold piece to town, for the holiday. So the Monkey looked Sam, over, and then asked., Sam where did he get the suit, so Sam told him that his brother had sent it to him from up North. So Old Sam reached in his pocket, and pulled out a dime, and Said, Mr. Monkey I want you to tell me a hot number, Mr. Monkey looked and Sam, and Said, hey nigger, I'll tell you what I will do, I will give you two hot numbers and show you a trick too. So Old Sam said okay, Mr. Monkey, so the monkey to him to let him hold the watch, so he took the watch off the chain, and let the monkey hold it, the monkey put the watch in his mouth, and swolloed it, which Sam did not know, so Sam, waited for a half an hour, and said Mr. Monkey, when are you going to tell me the numbers, and show me the trick, the monkey said, hold on nigger it takes time to do wonders like this, and more time for a nigger, and this is special for you. Sam waited, and asked again, the monkey, told Sam, "nigger you have to watch stuff like that, coming up to me and asking me for a hot, number with a dime, don't you know that me and my boss are City Slickers, and you a black nigger coming up to me, why the very idea. The reason I took you for the okey-dok, is because you was the sharpest nigger in town and after you told me that story I lead you in this hole, and he also told Old Sam, nigger, "That is the SHIT you have to WATCH",. So Old Sam, looked at him, and didn't say a word, but reached in his pocket and put out his switch blade, and grab the monkey by the neck, and put down his side of the story, he told the monkey, that he was old, was true, but he wasn't going to fall for that shit, "So that is the WATCH he had to SHIT" . . . .

From Manuscript

49. A PARTY

The following is basically the same story as the one explored in its relation to its Uncle Remus antecedent, in Chapter III. Here the ending is quite different, but the tone remains the same.

One day while bro lion and bro monkey was walking along in the jungle, they spyed a poster tacked on a tree, with a few of the home animals standing around in a bunch say- that they were, going, going where bro lion say to bro monkey, bro monkey shoke his head and said that he didn't know what was going on,. So they walked up to the tree, and and everyone of the animals that were standing there, move aside for bro, lion and bro monkey because bro lion was the king of the jungle, and bro monkey was his side kick, and every little thing that bro monkey would do the lion would take up for him, he was a nasty little son-of-a-bitch, he would fuck hi mother, if she was living, thought, bro, lizard,. The poster read, "To all the Brothers and the Sisters, of this jungle, you are invited to atend a party, given, by, Mr.&Mrs. Stip Tiger. and Etc. on the 12 day of the month. So the lion and the monkey said that they would go and turn it out, so the monkey agreed like he always did.

Came the night of the party, every brother, and every sisters, in the jungles were there, Bro, Deer, with his wife, Bro, Lizard, and his wife, Bro, Cheetah, and his wife, Etc. They had a band, and the place was decorated, they had all kinds of goodies, a bib cake, punch, whiskey, wine, woman, and song. Bro, monkey looked at bro, lion, and said that he was going to tear his little ass tonight, with all those whores, there and the others brothers wives, behind, all those drinks, and music, so the lion told him to go ahead and have a good time. Bro monkey started off by trying to pull Mrs Baboon, she was the prettiest bitch at the party, he stated dancing with her, on a slow record, and was trying to do the barrow house

with her, in others words the mooch,. He had to give that up because he was too short to grind with her, when he did let ther go
when the music stoped, his little prick had gotten hard, he didn't
give damm, he was so bold that he took it out and, said stop the
music, and cried out, to all the bitches in the house, and said look
what you can get for nothing, all the respectakle women in the
house scream, while all the whores in the house hollowed, "Daddy",
and ran over to him and made, bro, monky Cream, then at that
momeant bro, Tiger, came running through the crowd, and grab
the monkey by the collar and was going to throw him out, when
bro, lion said, no you are not, with his head all bad, and tight, and
told, bro, tiger, to put his buddy down and said the monkey was his
cut, and no mother- should put his hands on him, and to let the party
carry on. So the party started again, until, Mrs. Tiger, had heard a
noise from behind the couch, that said come on bitch and eat my
dick, she jumped up an got her husban, when they looked the
couch, there was bro, monkey laying there with two whores, one
was sucking his little, dick, and the other was kissing, him, Mr,
Tiger, said to leave him be, because he was scared of bro, lion.
The next little thing that the caught him doing, was pissing in the
punch bowl, so all they could do was to remove the punch, and bro
Tiger was taking the wine, away, because, all the whiskey had ran
out, as you know., bro lion shouted, for bro monkey to get, the
wine, bro staggered over to Mrs. Tiger, and took the wine, then
the guest had started to leave, when bro, lion, and bro monkey
went over to the dood and told evevyon that he had caught trying
to leave, to set there ass down in a corner, or fuck dance and be
marry, because this was, now his party, and bro, monkey agreed.
Bro lion had gotten so drunk that he said that he wanted to fuck,
he didn't a whore because that wasn't good enough for him. So he
looked at Mrs, Tiger, she was still young and good looking so he
grabed her and threw her down on the foot of the couch and
spread her legs and fell in, then someone told bro tigher that they
would all get them and gang them, so that they would stop all that
horse shit, and even throw them out, bro lion, said no, because he
would come back with his family, heard, gang, and not only fuck
his wife but wveryone wife, so they let him be, then, bro lion rolled
off and fell asleep, from the wine, Bro monkey walked up to Mr.
Tiger and asked him what kind of party it was, because the cake,
wasn't decorated, Mr. Tiger said that it was a birthday party, bro
monkey said that he worked in a bakery before and said that he
could decorated a cake, so he went over to the table, and pulled

up a chair a climb on the table and started to shit on the cake, so all the brothers, and sisters said that they were fed up with that shit, that bro lion, and bro monkey was puting down, so they grab monkey and told him that he was going to eat that shit, the monkey told them that he wasn't, and to go fuck, them selves, and then said that bro lion would get them and kick all there ass's when he got sober, by that time bro lion had woke up from all the noise that they were making, and he had to close one eye to see what every-one was doing, he heard them say, to Mr. Tiger, to make bro monkey eat that shit, so the monkey put up a fight, and broke away from them and ran over to bro lion, and told him that they were trying to make him eat some shit, that he had dropped on Mr. Tiger, birthday cake, and bro lion looked at him from one eye and told bro monkey, that he was too drunk to help him, bro monkey told him again that they were trying to make him eat some shit, bro lion looked at him again through one eye, and told bro, monkey that he heard, what the man said, "You are going, to eat that SHIT".

From Manuscript

50. A SLEEVE JOB

This is perhaps the most widely known story of the "Lady and the Tiger" type, often collected in less suggestive form as "The Purple Passion." It is in classic shaggy-dog form with the familiar letdown ending. Brunvand ("A Classification for Shaggy Dog Stories," JAF 76 (1963), p. 67) lists it as D 510.1 (misprinted 501.1), and lists only the twelve texts in the Indiana University Archives as his sources. Legman — This story is apparently first printed, as having been an original recitation by Henry Monnier, the French Mark Twain, under the title "La Diligence de Lyon" (The Lyons Stage-coach) in a letter giving several such jokes and recitations, signed "Marquis de C." in Jules Gay's bibliographical magazine Le Fantaisiste (San Remo, 1873), vol. I, pp. 176-185. As there given, the text is very long and precise as to its sexual details, but with a clear humorous intention throughout, and ends (p. 181) with the woman on her deathbed, while the "sucker," who has been searching for her, and the chimera of the "Diligence de Lyon," actually gets in with her so that she should show him how it is done with dying breath. "Mais, une crise se declare, elle retombe. . . . et expire, emportant son secret dans la tombe!!!!"

One day a nigger was standing on the corner, and up walked a white women, and said to him, did he want a sleeve job, the nigger rub his head, and reapeated, a sleeve job, and asked her what was a sleeve job, she said, to him, don't asked questions, just say yes, or no, the nigger rubbed his head again, and said yes mam, because she look so good to him and farther more, because she was white, and he didn't know what a sleeve job was and mainly, because he wanted to find out what it was, and he thought it was something good. So she gave him a address, and told him to be there a seven O'clock sharpe, and don't be late, and don't bring any company with him, because if he did he wouldn't get the sleeve job. So he told the white woman, yes man, and said that he wouldn't be late. He went on down the street, and met a buddy of his, named jack, he asked jack what was a sleeve job, Jack told him that he didn' know what it was, or is. He still had some time to kill before he had to be there to get his sleeve job, so he went in the bar, had a few drinks, and still he was wondering what a sleeve job could possibly be, so he asked the bartender what it was he said that he had never heard of it, so he left there and strooled on down the street and met old dirty slim. He called old dirty slim and asked him old dirty slim, was what you would, call a bushwacker, a nose diver, a canyon youdler, well in other words a cocksucker, or just say that he ate pussy. He was also a puck lover, and a whore mongler. in other words he was just plain dirtly Slim to everyone. So he asked Old dirtly Slim, and even Slim couldn't tell him. So he fucked around till it got close to seven. so he had money enough to hop a cab, so he got the cab and rode to the corner from whaere she had given the adress, so he got out of the cab a walked to the woman house, being very careful that no one would catch him going in. He went to the front door and rang the bell he heard a buzzer ring, he did had sense enough to know that it meant to turn the knob and enter, he went in looking all aroung with his hat in his hands twisting and ruffing his hat up, he heard a voice coming from the next room, saying to him to come in, where she was, when he went in to the other room, he saw abeautiful white woman laying on the couch, with white pinkish tits, with red nipples, and a firm white body, and one leg thrown up on the top of the couch, this spreading her legs, showing her pussy, with redish brown hairs running from the crack of her ass to her nable, and around her thighs, this made him start to sweat and also made his heart beat, and to think, and to know that he was going to endure her, to seduce her, and to be love by her, not just too be love by her, but just because she she was a white woman, and he had never experinced this sort of a thing, with a white woman, and mainly a sleeve job. She told him to come over to her and be scared because she lived there by herself and she had know husband, and they were alone. He went to her and all he could do was to stare a her taking pictures of her to remember her, and to remember the voilent moments that he would spend with. She said to him, did he still want the sleeve job, he answered he, and said yes man, so she told him to go up stairs to the bath room and take a shower, because he had to be very clean for a sleeve, and she told him that she always like the man to be clean when she was giving out a job. So the nigger went upstairs and was taking the shower, when he heard her call to him to hurry-up because she was on edge, and waiting for him, he said yes mam, and came running out of the bath room, and down the stairs steps, and he was breaking a record, until he hit that second step from the bottom, and fell down and broke his neck, and he never did find out what a "SLEEVE JOB", was.

"DO YOU KNOW WHAT A SLEEVE JOB IS"?

From Manuscript

51. *GOOD MANNERS*

This is one of the many stories which I have heard (the next story is also a variant) which concerns daughters reporting on sexual performance. The point of many of these stories often turns on the naivete of the girls and resultant comic sexual misunderstandings.

One time there was this woman, she had three daughters. Her daughters got big, about eighteen, mother sent them out to sell some pussy. So they all went out together. All got tricks* so they came home. They all went in different rooms. So they stayed in there 'bout fifteen minutes. The mother tip-toed upstairs, listened at each door. So one girl, her room she heard squeaking of the bed. So she tipped to the next room. She heard loud screaming. All right, she went to the next room. She ain't hear a motherfucking thing there. She was kind of curious. So she tipped back downstairs. When they all got finished they come back downstairs. So she asked the first daughter, she said, "Why was the bed squeaking so much?" She said, "Mama, he was doing it to me so good, that I had to move a lot." So she accepted that. Then she went to the next girl. She said, "What was all the screaming about?" Said, "Mama, that man was fucking so good." So she went to the next girl. She said, "What was happening in your room? I didn't hear nothing." She said, "Well, Mama, you always beat me about talking when I have a mouthful."

"Kid"

52. GOOD MORNING, THIS MORNING

For a similar code story, see 23. "The Reverend and the Deacon's Contest." This is one of the many stories (others follow immediately) overtly placing a Negro in contest with others (usually two others). Legman — This "code" story is also told of a woman whose twin daughters get married simultaneously, and who report to her in the morning how their respective husbands performed. The whorehouse version is evidently a more rational situation, and probably the original — the marriage form being then intended as more polite. (See remarks on last story.)

This woman had a whore house, you know. She had four girls that lived there. But the police was getting on them so bad that it was hot. Every time the police would come in they would trick with one of them, soon as they gave the girls money they would lock her up. The woman told them, she said, "Now girls, tonight is Friday night and everybody will be getting paid. Big Business. Now y'all ain't gonna see no money. When they first come there they gonna give me the money. Then you just count how many tricks you have. In the morning when you come down, every time you say 'morning' that means how many tricks you have." They said all right.

So one of the girls said, "I'm sick, I can't work tonight." "All right. I tell you what. Mary, Susie, y'all work." Three girls, one was a Puerto Rican girl, other was an Irish girl, other was a colored girl there.

So they went on that night and business was pretty fair. Next morning come downstairs. Puerto Rican girl come down, she said, "Nice morning, this morning." So she gave her enough for two tricks. This Irish girl come down, she said, "Good morning, this morning, how are you this morning?" Gave her money for three tricks. 'Bout two hours passed, then the colored girl come down. So everybody looked at her. They said, "How you doing?" She said, "Good morning, this morning. If every morning was like this morning, have a good morning every morning, wouldn't we?"

"Kid"

53. *IRISHMAN, JEW, COLORED MAN*

One of the most common esoteric-exoteric formulas is the story of the men of three different races, regions, or nationalities, who are vying against each other. Dorson has printed a number of Negro stories conforming to this mold. See (NFTM) 77; (NTPB) 89; WF, 13:96-97; see also Brewer (Brazos) 1, 88-89. A variation of this formula is having members of three groups attack a similar problem, but the humor lies not in who wins but in the different and characteristic ways the problem can be approached. The story as collected here is a vestige of the tradition of escaping the Devil's (or ogre's) clutches through cleverness. See K 210 (Devil cheated of his soul) and H 543 (Escape from Devil by answering his riddles).

These here three fellows, you know, they went down to Hell. Now the Devil looked on them and said, "Now Brothers, you have sinned. That's why you was sent to me. But I'ma give you a break. I'ma gonna let you go upstairs if any of you can be slick enough to do something that I can't find out how it was done."

So the Jew looked at him and said, "Well, now, I been down on earth, I done slicked everybody down there of all their money. Guess I can get past this old Devil here." He said, "Well, Devil, I tell you what you do. Give me a hundred dollars." The Devil gave the Jew a hundred dollars. The Jew went over to the colored guy and said, "How much money you got?" Colored fellow said, "I got 'bout four hundred dollars." He said, "I tell you what. I bet you can't tell me the president on the ten-dollar bill, quick." Colored guy said, "No, can't tell you that. What was we betting?" "We was betting four hundred dollars. Now give it here." So he went back to the Devil and said, "How'd I do that?" Devil said, "You cheated the man out of his money, that's how you did it." So he stayed in Hell.

Went over to the Irishman, he said, "You wanta do anything?" Irishman said, "Yeah." Irishman took a whole field of plain sand; Irishman planted, irrigated it, made grass grow. Asked the Devil, said, "How'd I do that?" Devil told him how it was done.

He got down to the little colored fellow sitting over in the corner, grinning to himself. "What you grinning for?" He said, "I'm just thinking. You done tricked the Jew, you done fooled the hell out of the Irishman, you gonna come over here now fucking with me. Now, I'ma tell you what I'ma gonna do for my gig. Want you to go find me a can. Get me a brace and a bit, and two cans of lima beans, and come back." So the Devil went and did what he told him. Came over and eat these two pots of lima beans, drilled four holes in the can. Sat on top and farted. He said, "Now Mr. Wise Guy, tell me which of them holes it came out of." The Devil said, "That one on the left." Said, "You're a lying motherfucker, that came out my asshole."

"Kid"

54. *CHINAMAN, JEW, NEGRO*

This is one of the most common (for the most part, unprinted) jokes in the esoteric-exoteric mold. Legman — *A version of this story, with the Jew given the triumph-line is printed in the original* Anecdota Americana *(1927), vol. I, page 314; and is quoted and discussed by G. Legman in "Rationale of the Dirty Joke," in* Neurotica *(New York, 1951), no. 9, "The Castration Complex," p. 56. In this form the story ends leaving the logical conclusion, with the Jew saying: "Me? I'm a nobody. I peddle lollypops."*

There was this Chinaman, a Jew, and a Negro. They was caught fucking the farmer's wife. So the farmer said, "Well, uh, Chink, how would you like to die?" So the Chinese said, "Er uh, well, my father, he was a swordsman, so I'd like you to chop my dick off." So he said, "O.K." So he asked the Jew, he said, "What was your father?" So he said, "My father owned a steel mill, so you have

to weld my dick off." So he got to the Negro. He said, "What about
you?" He said, "My father was a lollypop maker, so you have to
suck my dick off."

Charley

55. *THE DEVIL LETS THEM DREAM*

*There are a number of jokes that refer to the exoteric view of
the Negro (i.e., his traits as seen by outside groups). The most common of these jokes also collected among the Negro is where he
attempts to buy something from the Devil and to defer payment.
See Dorson (NFTM), p. 77. This comment on his supposed laziness
is the only reference to this attribute that I have found, and I was
surprised to find the story in this group, as its tone is frankly anti-
Negro. Legman — Your feeling about this story is clearly correct:
it is an anti-Negro story — in fact, anti-Jewish at the same time —
and it is surprising that it was collected from a Negro informant.
(Of course, dreaming one's way to riches is a fair enough dream.)
Negro stories and Jewish stories both show — in their authentic
forms — the most extreme difference from the usual dialect stories
told about these two peoples, which are almost always crude attacks,
though the persons retelling them imagine them to be humorous.
The present "laziness" story is also told about the Marseillais, in the
form of a prize for laziness, which the winner refuses to accept with
his hand, saying "Mind shoving it in my pocket, boss?" See a similar
story, obviously a "whopper," and not Negro in origin in Botkin
(TAA), p. 92. A closer analogue of your own story — and one which
perhaps explains what is really involved in this "laziness" — is about
two hoboes who find a packet of heroin, tossed out of a train window
during a raid. They each take a sniff and begin explaining to each
other what they are dreaming. One dreams he has a million dollars,
mountain of gold, etc. The other says, "Say, bo, if you got a million
bucks, willya give me half?" "Ah gwan," says the other, "dream up
yer own fuckin' mountain of gold!" This comes very close to the
punch-line of your text.*

One time there was a Jew, an Irishman, and a colored man. So
this man was going to give away a million dollars. So he wanted to
see who was the smartest of all. Whoever was the smartest he was

going to give him the million dollars. So he asked this Irishman, "What would you do if you went to sleep and dreamt that you had a million dollars and woke up and found that you had a million dollars?" The Irishman being a wise man he jumped up and said, "I guess I'd invest it. Get me a business of some sort, try to get me another million." So he said, "All right."

So he went to the Jew. So he asked the Jewish fellow, he said, "Uh, supposing you went to sleep, woke up, dreamt about a million dollars, woke up and found you had a million dollars? What would you do?" So the Jew jumps up all excited. He said, "I'd buy me a couple of meat markets, kosher markets, and so forth, try to get *me* another million."

So he came to this colored guy, he said, "Uh, if you went to bed and dreamt about a million dollars, woke up and had a million dollars, what would you do?" So the colored guy jumped up and said, "Shit, I'd go back to sleep and try to dream me up another million."

"Kid"

56. *THE DEVIL'S CHOICES*

The next two stories are really one, and come from the same informant who saw them as one with two different endings. They are both a variation on "Chinaman, Jew, Negro" without any trickery involved.

56A.

This guy went to hell and the Devil gave him his choice. He had these three rooms. He said, "Whatever room you go in, you'll have to stay for all eternity." So they went up to the first door, and he heard "Prrrrpp, prrrrpp, brack." Said, "Shit, I don't know what they're doing in there. I don't want to go in there." Second room, he heard a bed squeaking, moaning, and groaning. He said, "Shit, I know they fucking in there. I don't want to be fucking rest of my life." So this third room he didn't hear nothing, just "Ssshooo, splash, ssshooo, splash" (whispered). Said, "Shit, I wonder what's happening in there?" So he said, "Well, I'll go in the last one."

So the Devil took him up on a step-ladder, opened this trap-door, and kicked him in real fast. Here go another guy, standing up to his neck in shit, hollering, "Please don't wave, please don't wave."

Freddie

56B.

The Devil gave this guy three rooms to go into to stay for all eternity, but he gave him his choice. Well, the guy, listening at the doors, first door he heard this "Brrrrpp, brack." Second door he heard a bed, squeaking, moaning, and groaning. He said, "Shit, they probably fucking in there. I better let that slide. I don't want to do that for all eternity." So he goes to the third room and he hears "Ssshooo, splash, ssshooo, splash." So he said, "O.K., I'll take this one." So he goes in the last one and the Devil takes him up on the trapdoor and pushes him in, falls down in all this shit, starts swimming to stay on top. He sees this other person standing in the shit up to his neck, laughing his ass off. Cat said, "You up to shit in your neck and you're laughing. What's wrong with you?" He said, "You'd be laughing too if Joe was down on the bottom holding you up."

Freddie

57. *THE OLD WISE KING*

A further variation on the Devil's choices idea, here cast in a slightly different setting.

This here's about this old wise king, man. King Richard and all that shit. He told these guys, he said, "Lookahere." He caught these guys stealing, these three men. He said, "God damn it, next time I catch y'all son of bitches stealing, I'ma kill all you." So these motherfuckers say, "We ain't gonna steal no more. We ain't gonna steal no more." So they said, "Shit. That son of a bitch." So they went up the palace. They fucked the queen, man, they fucked the queen's maids, the chamber maids. They fucked every woman they could see. They all but fucked the king, but he got away a little bit.

221

Anyway, the king caught 'em. He said, "God damn it, I'ma kill y'all." He said, "But being as y'all don't do it so bad, I'ma . . . what I do to y'all, I'ma let y'all die 'cording to the way you want to die." So they said, "O.K."

"Man, I want to die," he said, "I want to *eat* myself to death." The king's all right, so the king said, "Put this motherfucker in a room there by hisself with nine guards and give him all the food he wants. Let him eat hisself to death." Asked this other guy, "What you wanto do?" Other guy said, "Well," said, "I want to cut paper dolls till I die." He figuring maybe he'll live a little longer than the rest of them. King have pity on them. Some shit he was talking about. He said, "All right. Put him in there with all the paper he can, and nine more guards to watch him to make sure he can't escape."

Got down to the last guy, he said, "All right, you, how do you want to die?" He said, "Well, king, old boy," said, "I want to fuck myself to death." King said, "All right," he said, "Put him in another room with a hundred women, and nine guards so this motherfucker won't escape." So they stayed in there.

So three months, king comes back to this motherfucker, to this place. So he said, "All right. Open this first door. What this guy doing?" Said, "This guy's eaten hisself to death." Said, "All right. Nine guards can come out, and go on back to your old duties." Said, "All right." So open the next door and this guy was in there, he had paper dolls all over the motherfucking wall, dead. Eyes looked like paper. So god damn it, he opened the door, he said, "What the fuck!" "Here's these women laying all in the corner fucked to death." The hundred women he put in there all fucked to death, guards standing over there, their ass all red, this motherfucker over there beating the meat. "Now ain't that some shit. Ain't that the most."

"Kid"

58. *THE COON IN THE BOX*

This is perhaps the most popular of the cycle of Negro stories, usually called "Marster-John" jokes. Joel Chandler Harris printed a story very similar to this in Uncle Remus and His Friends, *III*

("De Sparrer Kin Tell You"). It is a version of Type 1641, "Doctor Know-All," the pun in the early Grimm text being on "crab" (kreb). Motifs N 688 (What is in dish); K 1970 (Sham miracles); K 1956 (Sham wise man). Some printings of the tale in similar forms from Negro sources are: Dorson (NFTM), 51-3; Hurston, 111-12; JAF, 11:13; 32:370; 40:265-66; 41:542 (Phila.); Jones, 89-90 (1888); MWF, 8:130; Parsons (Cape Verde), pt. 1; 88; Southern Workman, Vol. 23, No. 12, p. 209; WF, 13:89. Randolph (Devil's), 135 gives a white Ozark text.

This here fellow was working on a farm. Colored fellow. One night they was sitting outside, boss said, "Sam, what's that over there behind that log?" "I can't see it, boss." He said, "Well, there's a rumor going 'round that you are psychic." He said, "Well, I gather that it's probably nothing but an old rabbit down there." So they went down and they took a peek and it was a rabbit. Said, "What's that behind the tree there?" Sam looked at the tree, "I can't see it, I guess it ain't nothing but an old squirrel. Maybe a black snake done got it." They look around there and a black snake had bit the squirrel.

White man looked and said, "If Sam is psychic, I'ma make some money off of that." So he said, "Sam, I'ma get all the people out here and next week we gonna get something, and you gonna tell us what it is."

So the white man went and bet up all his property, saying Sam could tell them anything they want. So the one guy, he betted him. He said, "I tell you what. I know thing you can't guess." So he went down got a steel box, then he caught a buzzard. They put the buzzard under the box.

So the white man said, "In the morning, Sam, you got to tell us what's in that box, or my land's up against it." Sam said, "All right, boss." But Sam knew he wasn't psychic, he was just guessing. He eased out of the house 'bout four o'clock in the morning, went and peep under the box. Then he went back to bed. That morning he woke up 'bout ten o'clock. Sam come on out. "What's in the box there, Sam?" Sam said, "Hmm, I don't know. Lord, let me see now. Size of the box, I guess you got a buzzard under there." "Sure is. Sure is psychic, ain't he?"

Guy said, "I'ma get you. Next week I'ma get you. Next week I'ma put something under that box, see if you guess it." "All right, captain." So that next Friday night, came out, put a coon under the box. Sam got up 'bout four o'clock, eased out of the house. The guy had two policemen sitting on the box. Sam couldn't see what was under that one. Sam went back in the house, back to bed. White man came 'round, said, "Sam, if you don't win in the morning, I'm broke. Out of business. I'm ruined. And if you don't say what's under that box tomorrow," he said, "you just one hung child." Now Sam was scared.

So morning came, they woke Sam up, 'bout ten o'clock. Sam came outside, he scratched his head, he looked at the box, looked at the people. Guy whispered to his friend, "He'll never guess there's a coon under there." Sam said, "Well, captain, you all finally got the old coon." So he went free just by saying that.

"Kid"

59. *DREAMING CONTEST*

Another Marster-John type story. As is usual in this kind of story, there is a duel of wits, with the Negro sometimes winning, sometimes losing. This kind of story developed into the much more overt protest tales that follow — such as the Negro, Chinaman, Jew jokes, and the ones about Harlem Negroes in the South. Dorson prints a text of this (NTPB), 95. He notes that Baughman lists Motif K 66 as "Dream Contests." See also PTFLS, 21:89-90. Dorson further notes that the joke is usually a contest between Indian and white man and refers to his article on the subject, SFQ, 10:122.

White fellows, they was sitting down at the club in the South. This only colored guy in there now. They let him 'cause he had millions. Land, property, homes, factories, cars. So he told these follows, "I bet you a thousand dollars you can't cheat him out of no money." Fellow said, "Shit, I cheat anybody I want out of some money. Give me two weeks." "All right."

Went over to the colored fellow, he said, "They tell me you're a gambling man." Said, "I'm a gambling man." He said, "Well, let's play a game called 'dream'." "How it go?" He said, "Whatever I dream, you got to make it come true." He said, "All right."

So at night, 'bout two o'clock, white man walked over, knocked on the door. He said, "Mr. John." "Yeah, what's the matter?" He said, "Last night I dreamt that you gave me your wife, your house, all your property." He said, "Well, I got to make it come true."

So the next morning, he had to move to hotel. Next night, the white man came to his apartment, he said, "John." "Yeah, what's the matter?" "You know I dreamt last night that you gave me all your money, your factory, all your stock, all your bonds, all of anything you got of any value." Colored fellow said, "I got to make it come true. This cat is getting slick. He's trying to break me. I got to think this over."

He went out to the woods, sat down on a log by the stream. He thought and he thought. It came to him. He broke out for town. Boy, he was running. He ran up to Mr. Charlie's door, nearly knocked down his door. Said, "Come on downstairs, man. Look here, I was sitting in the woods and I fell asleep. And I had a nightmare. I didn't have a dream. I had a nightmare. I dreamt you gave me all my money, all my land, all my belongings, all my stocks and bonds, all my valuables, everything you dreamt I gave you, you gave back to me. Then I turned around and dreamt you gave me everything you had, clothes and money, stocks and bonds, everything. Then I fell asleep and dreamt that we don't dream no god damn more."

"Kid"

60. WE GO BY WHAT YOU SEE

One day a man and a woman were fighting in the street. There was an old lady out there, she seen the man and the woman fighting. This woman, she was cutting her husband all up. So the old woman that seed the fight, she told the lady that lived next door that didn't see the fight, she said, "This woman was out there, cutting her husband like nobody's business." So the old lady said, "Yeah?" So the cops come and got the woman and the man. So they took 'em to court. So the old lady that didn't see the fight, she come to court. She was sitting down, so the Judge say, "Anybody in the courtroom see what happened?" So the old lady that didn't see what happened, she said, "Yeah." "Will you please take this witness stand?" She got up on the witness stand. Judge say, "What happened at the fight?" No, the judge say, "Did you see the fight?" Lady said, "No, I didn't see it but I heard about it." So the judge said, "Well, we don't go by what you hear, we go by what you see, up here. Will you please get down off the witness stand?" The old lady she went to get down off the witness stand, she had a shawl on. So the old lady, she farted. So the judge said, "Who done that?" The old lady said, "I did." "Give her ninety days in jail." She said, "For what, judge?" " 'Cause you farted." Old lady said, "Did you see it?" Judge said, "No." "Did you hear it?" Judge said, "Yeah." "Well, judge, you said you can't go by what you hear, you got to go by what you see."

"Kid"

61. *HE GETS WHAT HE ORDERS*

Belligerence takes the place of guile in the following stories concerning commerce between white and Negro. Though not mentioned, the protagonist is Negro, and the verbal "topper" a neat combination of world manipulation and courage.

Remind me of the time, this here guy was down South. He was from New York. He was the kind of guy, he didn't care about nothing from nobody. There were these two guys in front of him you know at this Mississippi store. Guy had stopped at the filling station. He said, "I want some cigarettes." "If you what?" "If you please, Mr. Charlie."

The guy in front of him said, "Could I have some hot-dogs please, sir." He said, "If you what?" "If you please, Mr. Charlie." He said, "all right."

Next guy walked up, he said, "Could I have a pound of hot sausage, please, sir." He said, "If you what?" "If you please, Mr. Charlie." He said, "All right."

So this here city slicker, you know, he didn't pay them no mind. He walked up to the counter, you know. He said, "Look here, throw me a pack of them Pall Malls right there, will you?" "If you what?" "If you got 'em, motherfucker, now what."

Charley

62. *HE GETS THE TANK FILLED*

Legman points out that this theme was used by the Marx Brothers in one of their early movies ("Out West"?) where one of the challengers says, "You see that fly out there?" making the other give up because of the great eyesight of the first man. I have heard this same story told in joke form many times.

This fellow, you know, came down South. And you know it was in this town, you know, it was prejudiced. He rolled in, had one of these big, long Cadillacs, one of these $400 suits thrown on, diamond rings. A colored fellow. When he ran on up, white fellow sitting down chewing tobacco. "Fill, the tank, will you, chief?" "You talking to me, boy?" "Yeah, I'm talking to you." "You know where you at, son?" "Yeah, I know where I'm at." He said, "Well, down here, you say 'mister' and you say it snappy, you hear." "Now I don't say 'mister' to nobody." He said, "You see that bush out there 'bout two hundred yards? Fly on top of it." He said, "I see it." So the old white fellow reached up and pulled the trigger, blew the fly clear off the bush. Didn't even touch the bush. He said, "That's what happens when you don't say 'mister,' boy."

He said, "Well, you trying to show off? You got a saucer on you?" "Yeah, I got a saucer." Throw it in the air." This old fellow throwed the saucer in the air, other fellow reach in the car, got an apple, throwed it in the air, took a straight razor, whipped it out, 'fore the apple hit the ground, peeled, cut the core out, sliced it up so thin that it land in the saucer, hit the ground, it was apple sauce. White fellow jumped up, and said, "What you want, sonny?" "Just regular."

"Kid"

63. *I DIDN'T DIE RIGHT*

This is built upon the basic structure of the ghost story of staying in the haunted house as a fear test (H 1411, E 281). It has an unusual ending for this type, however. It is seldom that one being tested wins with such bravado. Legman — Well-known "children's" story — that is to say, an adult's story told as of children, as with phoney Jewish and Negro "jokes" — is about the Lone Ranger in a desperate situation, tigers to one side, crocodiles on the others, angry Indian tribe coming at him up the hill, and Nazi dive-bombers coming down at him from above. . . . The enthralled listener is supposed to ask, "What happened?!" To which the mysterious, shaggy dog answer comes: "Don't fuck around with the Lone Ranger."

There was once a haunted house, where nobody would go in the house because it was haunted. So one day they put a reward up for anybody who could spend a night in the house. These three guys were willing to spend a night in the house. So they heard a voice howling out:

> I didn't die right.
> I didn't die right.

So he got up and he started to run. Ran out. Next guy went in, heard a voice:

> I didn't die right.
> I didn't die right.

He got up and ran out. Third man went in. He had his knife at his side. He heard a voice:

> I didn't die right.
> I didn't die right.

He simply replied, "Fuck with me and you will die right."

Freddie

64. TOO MUCH GRIEF

This is another common ghost story among American Negroes. For other texts, see Dorson (NTPB), 81; JAF, 40:270 (Ala.); SFQ, 18:130 (Ala.); Tidwell, 132 (from SFQ). It is a facet in the large group of stories about those who dress up a ghost in order to scare someone. The most common of these stories among American Negroes is the one in which Marster scares John for praying for death insistently. See Jones, 66-68, for an early reporting of this type story.

This lady and this man, their son just when he got to be twenty-one years old, he was in a gang fight and he got killed. So every night they prayed. "If I could only see Junior one more time. Please, Lord, let me see him one more time." They prayed loud. Two, three hours.

So the fellow that lived on the third floor, he couldn't ever sleep. "Now if I hear them praying tonight," he told his old lady, "I'ma put on a sheet. I'ma walk down there and stop all this. If they think they see their son, maybe, they'll stop all this noise." She said, "That's a good idea."

So that night 'bout eight o'clock they started praying. "Just let me see Junior one more time. Please let me see Junior." So about twelve o'clock he decided to put his sheet on. He walked down and knocked on the door. Tap, tap. She said, "Paw, did you hear that?" Dad said, "I didn't hear nothing. Keep on praying." Tap, tap. She said, "Paw, Junior's knocking." Said, "Ain't nobody come back from the dead, woman. That ain't Junior." So she said, "See who's at the door." So he said, "Maw. It's meeee." "That's Junior, Paw." "Don't you open that door, woman. Don't open that door." There he was, guy tied up, you know, with sheet over his head. Looked just like a ghost. Hallway was dark. She said, "Junior, you come back." He said, "Yes, Maw." She said, "Don't he look good, Paw?" He looked at him, he said, "Yes, you look good, son." He said, "You look good, son, now go on back." She said, "Go shake your father's hand, son." He said, "You look good, son, now go on back." Pop kept on backing up. Junior kept a-coming towards him. He said, "You look good, boy, now go on back." He kept a-walking. Pop kept backing up. He said, "You look good, son, now go on back, will you?" So he walked over and touched Pop on the shoulder. He said, "Dad." Pop said, "That's why your motherfucking ass is dead now. You're so god-damned hard-headed."

"Kid"

65. THE DRUNK DOES PUSHUPS

Jokes about drunks are legion. Many are to be heard among the Camingerly residents. Thompson leaves a whole section for stories about drunks, though he does not include many references within the section (X 800). I include here three representative stories, plus one of its close relatives, the "junkie" or "head" jokes, concerned with addicts. Both kinds are variations on the numskull or noodle pattern.

This here sailor, he got drunk. So he was going to the bar, there was 'nother sailor already in there. So the guy said, "Er uh, you can't get nothing to drink, 'cause you're drunk." He said, "No, I'm not drunk. I know what I'm doing. I can do some pushups, far as that's concerned." So the guy said, "O.K., lemme see you do twenty-five pushups." So here comes this other drunk sailor. "Give me a drink." "You can't have nothing to drink in here, you're too drunk." He said, "You think I'm drunk. Look at that guy. He don't even know his girl left him."

Charley

66. *THE DRUNK GOES AROUND TO THE SIDE DOOR*

Well you know how sailors is. Sailors, they get drunk all the time. Well, this here sailor, he went in the bar, er uh, guy said, "What would you like?" So he stayed in there and he got drunk. Tried to go to another bar. Guy put him out. So he went 'round the side door. Guy kicked him in the mouth and threw him out on his ass. Still wasn't satisfied. He go around the back and come in. Guy beat him up, threw him out again. Get up off the ground, brush his clothes off. Brush his hat off. Walked right back 'round the front and come back in. So the guy said, "Didn't I . . ." He said, "Hold it. God damn it, you don't own every bar in town now." (He thought he was going in different bars.)

Charley

67. *GOING FISHING*

Though this story is put in the form of a drunk joke, it really is one of the "madmen" cycle, a series of some antiquity, as Tom O Bedlam in King Lear *testifies.*

You know, these here fellows were out there walking New York. The fellow was up on a building, everybody was looking up in the air. "I say what's going on up there?" So the guy, you know, cop walked up to these three fellows on a ledge, you know. He said, "What y'all doing?" "All going crazy." They was high. Look here, boy, they was high. He said, "Officer, them two fellows, they is crazy." He said, "Now that guy sitting there throwing that wheel out like he's fishing, and that boy's sitting there with the net." He said, "They stone mad." He said, "Now officer, that one sitting on the roof, he think he's fishing. Now look at him. He's throwing the wheel out, he's winding it back. And the fellow with him, he's crazy, too. He got the net down there like he's catching a fish." So the officer said, "Well, you go out there and stop 'em." So the fellow said, "All right." " 'Cause you look like you're the only one sober." So the guy reached out and got two sticks and made like he was rowing and said, "I'm coming, captain."

"Kid"

68. *THE JUNKIE REFEREE*

Most "junkie" jokes, as with this one, make reference to the addict's inability to interpret actions realistically. (See 65. "The Drunk Does Pushups" above.)

Junkie's walking down the street. A car came up and hit a trailer-truck. Guy flew through the window, head was cut in half, his leg was broke, jaw was busted. Land in front of the junkie. Junkie looked down on him and said, "Safe."

"Kid"

69. *A REMEDY FOR SNAKEBITE*

Country origin is the basis for numskull decisions or observations in the next few stories. J 1919.5 (Genitals cut off through ignorance).

You know, this old cat was down on the farm. He went over to this guy, he said he seen this woman in this window, she putting a broomstick in herself. So he said, "Instead of doing that, you cut a hole in the floor and I'll get under there, and then me and you can do it together." She said, "All right." So he was doing that for a long time. One day this other cat he come, he say he want some. So he say to this guy, "I'll give you some tips on how to get some, see. Now, son, you go under there, you stick your thing up in there, woman come and lay on you, and you get what you want." All right, he did it. Did like that so Mom come in there, seen her throwing the lid on the floor. So she had a shotgun. She come from out in the yard 'cause she thought she heard something out there. She said, "Get up from that floor. Didn't I tell you about getting down there. Snakes could be down there." Girl is down there, scratching her face and everything, as if she was scared or something had bit her. So when she got up, Mom said, "Oh, my God, the snake done bit my daughter and is spitting his poison at me." She shot his head right off his shoulders.

"Kid"

70. SOME JAWS

J 1772.9 (One object thought to be another: excrement).

This guy was riding along with the train. He was riding and riding. He was looking for a bathroom. Couldn't find a bathroom. This guy thought, "Stick your ass out the window." Stuck his ass out the window, took a shit and two farmers are standing along the side of a road, hit one farmer in the face. Squash! He said, "Damn, those city slickers sure do chew some nasty smelling tobacco." The other one replied, "But did you see the jaws on that motherfucker?"

Petey

71. HE'S A POET

One day this country boy was in school, you know. Asked this boy something like this. He was standing up against the thing, he said:

> Right between them big beautiful clouds
> With the pass, you know, the pass allows.

He looked at him. He says:

> Right between them two big trees
> There is beauty, please.

So he looked at him, he said, "Here?" "Yeah."

So the guy went home to his girl friend. Said:

> Right between your big, beautiful eyes
> Is where your beauty lies.
> Right between them two big thighs
> Make my passion* rise.

Victor

72. *I WON'T DO IT!*

The immigrant numskull is an important figure in American folklore, but not among this group, perhaps because of the difficulty with dialects.

Now this guy was walking down the street, and he said, "I won't do it. I just won't do it." Cop said, "What's the matter, fellow?" "I just won't do it. I'm not going to do it. I just refuse to do it." Cop said, "You all right?" Said, "Yeah, I'm all right. I just won't do it." "Boy, I'ma take you in." He said, "Well, take me in." Took him down.

Next morning they got up in front of the judge. Judge said, "What's your problem?" Said, "I just ain't gonna do it, that's all. Just won't do it." Judge said, "You know you're in the courtroom now. Give you some time. Explain your problem to me." "I won't do it. Lock me up. Give me twenty years. I won't do it." He said, "What's the matter?" He said, "What's the matter?" He said, "Well, look — a-tirty-five-a years I come-a to dis country. I'se a good man, I get me a good job, and I make-a me a good business. I do everything a-right. But I won't do it." The judge said, "You won't do what?" He said, "I give-a my love to my wife, my heart to my children, I give my freedom to my country, and they got a nerve to put up a sign, 'Give your nuts to the squirrels.' I just won't do it."

"Kid"

73. *DOWN UNDER THE TREE*

You know this little girl, she lived in the country. She wasn't no little girl. 'Bout seventeen years old. Now her father and her uncle had a farm, but her uncle died and left three-fourths of the farm to her that when she was beturned seventeen she could do anything she wanted with it. Well, she was seventeen now. Now the farmer next door, he had a nice little young boy. He was nineteen. Very nice little boy. Little girl was stone in love with him, but he never said nothing to her. His father wanted the land of this little girl, but her father wouldn't sell it to him.

So the little boy was down by the lake one day. She called and she said, "Tommy." He said, "Yeah. What you want? Why you always bother me?" She said, "I just want you to talk to me." "I don't want to talk to you." She said, "Well, look. Will you come over and kiss me, please?" "No, I ain't gonna kiss you." "I'll give you $100." "All right, I'll kiss you and that's all." She said, "All right." He kissed her. She gave him $100 and he went on home.

Father said, "Where you been, son?" "I been down there playing. Little girl from across the road, she came over bothering me. Give me $100 just to kiss her." "All right."

Next day he goes down. She comes, says, "Tommy." "What you want now?" "Feel my titties, play with my stomach." "For what?" "I'll give you $500." "That's all I'ma do then." "All right." She paid him, he went on home. "What you do today, sonny?" "I was down there playing, little girl asked me to feel her titties, play with her stomach. She gave me $500. And I did it, so she gave me $500. But that's all I did." Father said, "Umm, you going down there tomorrow?" "Yes, sir." "All right."

So his father jumped up that morning, eased down to the woods, jumped up in a tree 'bout where they play at. So the little girl come down there playing. Tommy come down. She said, "Tommy, come over here." Took off her panties. "Do it to me?" "No." She said, "I'll give you $1,000." "All right. That's all I'ma do. Just gonna put it in." "All right." He put it in, got ready to get up. She said, "Tommy, don't get up now. Just move a little bit." "No, I ain't gonna move a little bit." Father up in the tree, he's looking down listening to all the conversation. She said, "You know that land your father's been wanting?" "Yeah, what about it?" She said, "If you move one more time I give it to you. You know that house your father's been wanting that's on my land?" "Yeah." "You move two more times and I add that in. You know that orange grove over there your father's been wanting?" "Yeah." "You move three more time and I throw that in." She said, "I got two million dollars. Now if you work real easy and take your time for 'bout an hour and a half, give that to you, too." Father said, "Go on, son, shake ass, son, shake ass."

"Kid"

74. A PARABLE

You know these two bulls were standing upon the field, you know, way up on the hill. Down in the valley was a whole lot of cows. Now the young bull looked at the old bull — you know, this old bull he had been in the bullfighting ring in his day and he was a very old bull — so the young bull he was spry, jumping around and healthy. All full of pep. He said, "Look here, old bull, let's run down in the valley and fuck a few of those cows." Old bull looked at him and said, "Son, if you take your time, we *walk* down, we might fuck 'em all."

"Kid"

75. THE OLD DOG AND THE YOUNG DOG

Another in parable form. Legman — *This story was told in the U. S. Army, almost as an item of indoctrination, during World War II, especially by the soldiers in Italy, and as then told represented their repugnance against the wholesale prostitution of the defeated Italians, as frighteningly recorded in Curzio Malaparte's* The Skin.

You know this young dog was standing there talking to the old dog. He said, "Young dog, you ain't been out in the world yet, is you?" Dog said, "No, sir." He said, "I'ma show you what life there is out here." He said, "All right." "Everything I do, you just come along behind me and do the same thing." "Yes, sir."

So the dogs they walked out and walked down the street and old dog got to a pole, smelt the pole, cocked the leg and he peed on it. So young dog cocked *his* leg and peed. So they walked along and old dog came to a car. He walked around the car, he looked at it, smelt the car, cocked his leg up and he peed on that. So the young dog, he walked up, smelt the car, cocked his leg and *he* peed on it. The old dog he walked down to the garbage can, looked over the side, got himself a bone and ate it. The young dog, he walked over to the garbage can, looked over the side, got himself a bone. So they walked on for maybe ten or fifteen minutes, they saw a she-dog. Old dog smelt her, kissed her, walked around, jumped up on her, knocked himself off a piece out. So the young dog he walked up to her, kissed her and he smelt her, jumped up on her, knocked *himself* a piece out.

So they went on down, you know, to the yard. Old dog said, "Well, son, how you like the world?" He said, "It's complicated." "What you mean?" He said, "Well, now, er uh, we went down, walked, came to a pole, smelt the pole, then we peed on it. Came to a car, we looked it over, smelt the car and peed on that. Then we walked down, seen girl, kissed her and even smelled her. Then we did it to her. That was all right. Even when we went to the garbage can, got something to eat. I guess it was all right. But what's the basis of being out in the world? I don't see no future in it." He said, "Well, son, take the advice of an old dog. Anything in this world that you can't smell, eat, kiss or fuck, piss on it."

"Kid"

76. MR. BUZZARD AND MR. RABBIT

This story has been a popular one at joke sessions for a number of years, though I have never seen a copy of it in print. It is a humorous complaint against the upward mobile. I think the names are prefaced by "Brother" because I had just asked the informant if he knew any of the Brother Rabbit stories. Legman — I have collected it with the rabbit having two friends: Mr. Buzzard, and also the turtle, who later becomes Mr. Tur-toole. Your text has also — except in the final line — lost the rhyming done on the names, in which the butler tells the returned rabbit, "Mr. Buz-zard is out in the yard" and"Mr. Tur-toole is in the swimming pool."

I have also collected toppers like this used in stories mocking pretentiousness. One in particular is of a woman in a beerjoint who wants to make an impression on a handsome man she sees at the bar and who tells the waiter, in a flutey voice, to bring her "an egg-whip cream, soft as a maiden's kiss, and ask that gem-man in the corner," and so forth; to which the man she is trying to impress counters by ordering "Waiter, gimme a tall beer, strong as a donkey's piss, with the foam farted off, and ask that damn whoor in the corner what's her charge."

Brother Rabbit was out on the job one day, you know, and he was spreading fertilizer 'round his garden. So Brother Buzzard came by, and he said, "Hey, Brother Rabbit." "Yeah, Brother Buzzard." "Whatcha doing?" "Spreading fertilizer." "Fertilizer, what's that?" "Nothing but horse, cow manure." "What it do?" "Makes the soil better. Makes the soil, grass, and crops grow." He said, "Look, I got a little small garden in the back of my house." He said, "How 'bout bringing me some of that over, Saturday night?" "I'll bring you a wagon load." "How much you charge me?" "I'll just charge you half price." Said, "All right."

So Brother Buzzard he went on home. Brother Rabbit got on up Saturday morning, load the wagon up, took it over to Brother Buzzard's house. Brother Buzzard, he'd got into a whole lot of money. He'd bought a big mansion. You know, he had a chauffeur, butler, and they was having a cocktail party that night. All these here rich animals from the forest were there, you know. So here comes the rabbit with his dungarees, full of shit, you know, hat broke down, rings the bell. Butler come to the door. Said, "I come to see Brother Buzzard." Said (haughtily), "I'm sorry, sir, but there is no Brother Buzzard here. Mr. Buzzard is the resident." He said, "Wait a minute, now. This is Brother Buzzard's house." "No, sir. Buzzard is the resident." He said, "Look now. Brother Buzzard tole me to bring him round a load of fertilizer. He told me to bring it today, right here. Now I know he lives here, 'cause I been here thousand times." Said, "I'm sorry sir, Mr. Buzzard live here."

By that time, all the confusion, all them rich animals come to the door. They looking. So the rabbits' getting mad. He said, "Tell Brother Buzzard I want to see him. I ain't gonna tell you no more." "Yes, sir, Mr. Buzzard live here." He said, "Well you go tell Mr. Buzzard that Mr. Rabbit is here with the shit."

Petey and Freddie
A Collaboration

77. TARZAN'S HOLLER

This modern etiological story is one of the many grotesques that have been floating around adolescent circles. The recent forms have conformed more closely to the sick-joke pattern.

You know practically everybody goes to the movies once or twice a night. Now I know everybody and them been to see

"Tarzan." Well you see, I'ma give you the deadline on Tarzan. See, everybody wondering where he get that big holler, you know that "Aaaaaaowaaah." Well, you see, I'ma tell you the true story 'bout that. Now see, when Tarzan was young, that's when he first found Jane. And him and Jane 'cided they was going to get married, 'cause they's in jungle by 'selves, and she went for him and he went for her. But see, in these days, he didn't wear no bathing suit like they got in the movies, see. He didn't wear a nair (?) of clothes.

So one day they was walking, and Jane 'cided she'd go one way and he'd go 'nother, you know, hunting food and stuff. So meantime, the hunters had been by that way and they had digged a big round hole. Deep. Catch this big ape. Well, they didn't catch the ape but they caught a gorilla. And, you know, how the wind blowing in the middle of the night, leaves had covered the hole back up. So Jane fell down in the hole. And when she fell down she started screaming when she saw this big gorilla. "Tarzan, Tarzan." Tarzan ran and he ran. He ran up on this here big high mountain. He looked down. He said, "Jane." He said, "Are you all right?" She said, "Yes, but there's an ape down here." Ape woke up and looked at her, said, "Ummh, hmmh." So he decided he was going to go on, knock, see what Tarzan'd been getting. So Tarzan said, "Well, you hold on, Jane. Me reach up and grab vine. Me swing down through hole, you grab vine, we swing out together." Jane said, "All right." So Tarzan jumped up off the cliff, took one of these here beautiful swan dives, about three or four hundred yards, and got hold of this here, when he went down he grabbed this vine. He was coming down beautifully. He swung down through the hole, and Jane reached for the vine and missed and grabbed his dick. Just when all that weight hit down on Tarzan's dick that's when he hollered "Aaaaaaowaaah!" Deep down in the jungle you hear the scream of the constipated ape. (Grunting, defecating noises.)

"Kid"

78. SHE CALLS HIS NAME

This is the first kind of joke a child learns and remembers, only in adolescent dress. The unfortunate-name story leading to amusing action, as here, or to embarrassing situation (Have you seen my Hynee?) was legion among at least my group of friends during grammar school. See Wolfenstein, Children's Humor, *64-65, for a discussion of the psychology of this joke.*

You hear about Johnny Fuck-a-little-faster? Once there was this boy named Johnny Fuck-a-little-faster. So his mother went out to the store. He had a box of cakes in the wagon. Little girl said, "Johnny. Can I have a ride in your wagon?" He said, "Yeah, you can have a ride in my wagon and a cookie, too, if you go home with me." She said, "For real?" He said, "Yeah." So he gave her some cookies and pulled her all around, that kind of thing. She got out. When he got her out, he opened the door and let her in the house. He said, "You want some more cookies?" He said, "I'll give you some more cookies if you'll pull down your panties." She said, "O.K." So she pulled off her pants, he gave her some more cookies and she ate them. She said, "Could I have some more cookies?" He said, "I'll give you some more cookies if you'll open your legs." "O.K." She opened her legs. So he got on there and he started, he started. Mother came in and said, "Fuck-faster!" That's what she was calling him. So he started fucking faster. So she said, "Fuck-faster!" So he started fucking faster. She said, "Fuck-faster, boy." He said, "I'm fucking as fast as I can, ma."

Charley

79. A RIDE IN HIS WAGON

Another one almost the same. This little boy, he was riding around in his car. Said, "Johnny, can I have a ride in your wagon?" He said, "No." He rode around the block again, came back, she said, "Johnny, can I have a ride in your wagon?" He said, "No!" So he rode around the block and come back again. She said, "Johnny, please can I have a ride in your wagon?" So he said, "If I give you a ride in my wagon, will you give me some?" She said, "Unh hunh." So he said, "O tay." So she rode around and she came back and they both rode to the alley. So he said, "I'll give you a penny too." So he gave her a penny and a cookie. She said, "O.K." She pulled her little panties down, and he said, "Oh, no. I don't want no — you ain't got no hair." She said, "What the hell do you want for two cents and a cookie?"

Charley

80. *THE MILKMAN COMETH*

The iceman is to the working man what Jody is to the soldier and convict. Consequently, he appears in many similar stories.

This little boy was tongue-tied. So he asked his ma, he said, "Mama, how tum my talk 'ike 'is here?" So she said, "Oh boy, I don't know." Said, "I don't know why you talk like that." So he asked his father. He said, "Daddy, how tum I tal' 'ike 'is here?" Father said, "Boy it's a mystery to me. I wonder myself." So the iceman came, and he said, "Mi'man, how tum I tal' 'ike 'is here?" Iceman said, "Get away f'om here, boy, I don't know how tum 'ou 'alk 'ike 'at."

Charley

81 - 97. *BOASTS, BRAGS, EXAGGERATIONS*

The next few pages will be made up of boasts and exaggerations. As such they all fit into Motif section X 1600. It is with the boast that we have the greatest connecting link with the proverb and other shorter verbal forms. It is impossible to draw the line where a boast is a tale and where it is a proverb, so I have included them all in this chapter. The first is obviously a story. After that they descend from conversational gambits to one-liners.

Concerning the one beginning "On top of that, I'm fast," Legman says — This precise story (and others more or less like it, on shaggy dog impossibilities) is told in the U. S. as of a "new" folk-character "Speedy Pete" the Mexican marvel of rapidity, who speaks in a soft, insinuating, comedy-Mexican dialect. Most of the same stories used to be told, as recently as the 1940's, in the 19th century framework of "heights," that is to say, as replies to the formula question "What is the height of speed?" and so forth. A German collector of similar "heights" is cited in The Limerick *(Paris, 1953), p. 427, note 917, dated 1892; and both polite and erotic collections of them were published in French in the 19th century.*

81.

I'll tell you about the coldest day. It was in '58, look ahere, it was colder than nine icebergs. I was standing on this corner, and I only had this short jacket on, and it was cold, and the wind was blowing about 215 miles an hour. And the snow was falling, sleet

was dropping, the rain was drizzling. Now you know it was cold.
I was standing up on Broad and Market. I was going to New York
that weekend of all weekends. The busses kept zooming by and
zooming by, zoom. I never seen the Greyhound bus. So all of a
sudden this big grey bus stopped. "Say, chief, you waiting for a
bus?" I said, "Yeah." He said, "Well, this is the Greyhound bus
stop." I said, "Well, there ain't no Greyhound bus here." He said,
"Well, this is a Greyhound bus, get on." I said, "No, it ain't." He
said, "Yes, it is." I said, "It's not." He said, "Why you say that?"
I said, "Well, the Greyhound is got a dog on the side of the bus."
It was cold. After awhile the window flew up and a dog put his
head out, said, "Shit, cold as it is out there, I better come in here."

"Kid"

82.

I used to be bad. I can remember a time I took a short stick and
beat a cat down so low that he had to reach up to tie his shoes.
That's no lie. I put my nose to a guy's face that weigh 240 pounds,
on a Wednesday and told him he better not move till Thursday
morning. But I don't know what he said. I hung up.

"Kid"

83.

I was fighting a guy in the ring and I swung at him with a
straight right and missed. And the wind was so strong that the
breeze gave his manager pneumonia and he died.

"Kid"

84.

On top of that I'm fast. Yeah, I'm fast. I'm so fast, a girl told me
one time, she said, "Kid, now if you can get some cock 'fore my
mother get back home, and she's coming 'round the corner now, you
can have it." So I said, "Lay down." She layed down, I pushed the
light switch, got undressed, jumped in bed, busted two nuts, got
dressed and got outside the room before that room got dark.

"Kid"

85.

I've seen it so hot that a man was driving his horse and carriage
by a field, and it was so hot the corn was popping, and the horses
dropped dead thinking it was snowing. (X 1633.1)

86.

I've seen it so hot that when hens layed, they came out hard-
boiled. (X 1633)

87.

I've seen it so cold that a nigger talked and it took him two weeks to thaw out the words. *(X 1623.2.1)*

88.

I've seen it so dark that I was in my room and I heard a knock on the door. You know who it was? A raindrop asking me for a match so he could see how to hit the ground.

89.

I've seen a man so fast that he was getting some water at the well and the bottom fell out the bucket and he went in the house and got another bucket and caught the water before it hit the ground. *(X 1740 and X 939.1* — Lie: person of remarkable speed.)*

90.

When I was young, I could run a rabbit down in a fast-footed race.

91.

I'm so broke, I couldn't buy a crippled crab a crutch if I had a forest of small trees.

92.

I'm so broke I couldn't buy a dick a derby, and that's a small fit.

93.

I'm so broke I couldn't buy a mosquito a wrestling jacket, and that's a small fit.

94.

My soles are so thin that if I stepped on a dime I could tell whether it's heads or tails.

95.

I'm so hungry my backbone is almost shaking hands with my stomach.

96.

I'm so hungry I could see a bow-legged biscuit walk a crooked mile. *(cf. the nursery rhyme beginning, "There was a crooked man . . .")*

97.

I'm so broke, if they were selling Philadelphia for a penny, I'd have to run, afraid they would sell it to the wrong person.

98. *THE BIG WATERMELON*

Some of the best of the boasts have become associated with the Texas jokes. This is one of that type. This might fit either Motif X 1411.1 (Lie: the great melon) or X 1420 (Lies about vegetables).

Fellow from Texas, he was telling how big Texas was. "In Texas, we got miles and miles and miles. Nothing but miles and miles and miles. Well, partner, I tell you, in Texas, when you get up in the morning, comb your hair, stick your comb down on the ground and you strike oil. Yes, suh."

So this Southern fellow said, "Well, has you all been up in New York?" "New York?" "Partner, New York is just the northeast side of Texas. That's all it is now." He said, "Gee whiz, wow, that's a big watermelon over there. Must be about fifteen feet in diameter. Must weigh a good bit. Ooh, it's a big watermelon." So the Southern fellow said, "You all talking about that cucumber laying there?"

"Kid"

99 - 100. *BRAND-NAME STORIES*

These final two pieces are not stories so much as routines; they give a story line but the object is to use as many brand names as possible. The first plays on names of alcoholic beverages; the second on cigarettes.

99.

This here little boy was coming out of the store one night. This cop picked him up. The cop told him, "Say, little boy, what's your name?" "Calvin." "What's your father's name?" "J. W." He said, "What's his last name?" "Dant." "What's your mother's name?" "Schenley Vacco." He said, "Where do you live at?" He said, "Well, I live all the way up in Valley Forge." He said, "Where about in Valley Forge?" "Around Four Roses." "Who's in that place with you?" "Must I tell?" He said, "Yeah! I asked you, didn't I?" "Tokay."

100.

Cavalier took a ride across the desert on a Camel, just 'cause he was in love with somebody called Fatima. Phillip was blasting off to Morris. Now Raleigh decided since he had made a Lucky Strike he was going down to Chesterfield's. He had a whole pocket full of Old Gold. And so, last but not least, he decided to go on a Holiday.

"Kid"

TOWARD THE DISCERNMENT OF OIKOTYPE

AS ARGUED IN THE INTRODUCTION, IF THE LORE OF ENOUGH AREAS OF the world were studied empirically from not only the cultural but also the structural and stylistic points of view, we could arrive at some sort of device which would allow us to look at a piece of lore and determine where it came from, from no other evidence than the internal clues provided by the piece itself. Furthermore, if we could develop our technique sufficiently, in this direction, we would be able to observe in a piece not only its present locus but also something of its past and perhaps even its place of origin. When one specific piece of lore of international currency has been locally isolated by means of this sort, we have called it a local or *oiko*-type of that piece.

But it is not really possible to isolate the oikotype of one piece without discerning those features which have made it characteristic of that specific locale or group. To say that a collected variant is an oikotype simply because it has been collected in one place a number of times and not in any other is not really enough. It is important both to isolate the oikotype and to know *why* it changed in that way at that place. In order to do so one must examine the folkloric conventions (or formulas, cliches, and commonplaces) and the cultural biases and imperatives operative in that area. Only in this way can we isolate all of the oikotypal forms of the group and only then can we begin to solve the riddle of the traditional process, oral transmission. By pursuit of this method we are enabled to see the relationships of the various oikotypes to be found among each group, and through such perceptions we would be able to predict place of collection, transmission or origin, at the same time as we are taking a look at the effect of the cultural biases of the group on folkloric forms.

But the problems of constructing a system of oikotypification of this sort are manifold. One's sampling of lore must be full enough, both in depth and breadth, that it can be said to be truly representative of that locale or group. The corpus of the sampling must also be large enough to see *all* of the traits which might affect the piece to make it truly "local."

The process of oikotyping is not the same as defining. We cannot attempt to say how one corpus of folklore stemming from one group differs from the lore of all other groups, which is what the process of definition would ask us to do. We can rather delimit those characteristics, substantive and structural, which recur, and trust that if our description is full enough, no other corpus will have exactly the same configuration of elements. Such description shares with defining a comparative approach.

But the comparing which occurs in this description is for the purposes of pointing to differences rather than similarities, such as we find in the comparative approach of those following the geographical-historical method. Instead of pointing to the schematic similarities of a series of pieces of lore, however, oikotyping calls for the isolation of the group's tropes, those elements toward which the creators and recreators of the group naturally (or culturally) are attracted. Such tropes may be strictly formal. Dundes[1] has recently pointed out an important trope of this sort in regard to the structural progression or movement in Lithuanian folktales, using Propp's[2] morphological techniques, and indicating that Propp was doing the same for the Russian *märchen* without knowing it. Such studies do a great deal to establish the necessity for structural analysis on the basis of a corpus of lore of one group. But as Dundes himself seems to realize, this type of formal analysis is only one of many devices useful in arriving at oikotypical constructs. There are other structural matters equally important, such as genre, convention, and many others. Equally important in oikotyping are matters of texture: diction, framing patterns, poetic models, type and frequency of repetitive devices, qualitative and quantitative use of key words, images, symbols, etc.

It would be impossible because of the geographical limitations of this study to establish the existence of New World or United States Negro oikotypes, or even those for the urban Negro, much as I am tempted to do so. It is my hope that future studies, both

1. Alan Dundes, "The Binary Structure of 'Unsuccessful Repetition' in Lithuanian Folktales," *Western Folklore*, XXI (1962), pp. 165-173.

2. Vladimir Propp, *The Morphology of the Folktale* (Bloomington, 1958).

by myself and by other investigators, will enable us to delimit and describe a set of tropisms which will show what is unique about the lore of the Negro in the New World, and how he has used the lore of other groups. It is in hopes of such study establishing just this criteria that the following resumé remarks are directed.

Most of the chapters of this book have been devoted to some extent to a description of the tropisms of the Camingerly group, ones which I feel are at least representative of the Northern urban Negro, if not of the contemporary Negro in the United States in general. Chapter II devotes itself in part to a discussion of the intimate relation of the "good talker" and his heroes through such devices as the "intrusive 'I'" and this is certainly a textural tropism as described above. The same chapter discusses another textural device similarly important in any discussion of tropisms, the strong reliance of these men on rhyme as a device of wit, both in everyday speech and in their narratives. Chapter III, in talking about the nature of the heroes of the group, not only points out the tropism toward the "hard man" hero and his values, but indicates the lack of any sort of satisfactory dramatic resolution in the hero narratives. This latter insight, if broadly observed, could be seen to be a binding structural convention. The lack of marriage or any sort of reintegration with society is, it is true, a convention *manqué* rather than a convention of itself, but it is a characteristic and, as such, must be regarded as a tropism. The fact that these hero stories both begin and end in midstream is, in itself, a structural consideration, and must be considered as fit material for our oikotypal discussion.

Chapter IV, as it describes one of the dominant forms in which the narratives were collected, the toast, is also descriptive of structural (direction of action) and textural (method of rhyming, framing devices, diction) tropisms. Subsequent investigations of this type of toast in other areas of the United States indicate that a full study of Negro tropisms and oikotypes would probably show that the toast is a characteristically Negro form. (That is, I have never collected a toast which is not demonstrably close to a Negro source. It is a form of expression which does not seem to have any firm tradition in contiguous groups. The same is true of other rhyming mechanisms of the Negro, such as the "dozens," but not as pronouncedly so.)

Finally, in Chapter V, it was pointed out that the interest in the cante-fable, observable in all other collections of New World Negro tales persists. However, the emphasis of the cante-fable was shown to have changed under the influence of modern forms of wit, specifically the joke. The use of the repeated song (or verse) for purposes of emotional increment is changed to one where the song becomes the *raison d' être* for the story, the witty or foolish changes effected at the end now providing the punch lines of these jokes. All of these devices, the insertion of the "intrusive 'I,'" the place of the "hard man" hero and his values, the almost compulsive use of rhyme, the importance of the toast form and technique and that of the (modified) cante-fable, all are elements which would have to be considered in any consideration of urban Negro oikotypes.

Up until now, I have only fleetingly used the most fitting device for the establishment of oikotypal forms, the comparative materials, the ways in which other groups have used the same or similar stories or forms. The headnotes to the stories do this, but only in passing. I have reserved most of such remarks until this time, noting however that this has never been my primary purpose because of the geographical limitations already alluded to. My remarks, consequently, will be tentative and exploratory, never categorical.

Let us look specifically at one story which was collected in Camingerly (27. "You Seen Willy?"):

> This little old preacher he was coming down the road one day. So he passed this here farm house. So he went over, "Er uh, say, er uh, do you have any rooms to put me up over night? I got my own food and everything. I just want a place to stay." She said, "Well, you go on down there to the shed house. Tell me it's a little haunted, but I guess you can make it over there." "Oahh. Well, could I borrow your frying pan, so I can fry my pork chops?" So she said, "Yeah."
>
> So the preacher went on over to the shed house, so long 'bout twelve o'clock he started reading his Bible under the candlelight. So here come this ghost. He said, "Er uh," tapped the preacher on the shoulder, he said, "You seen Willy?" He said, "No, I ain't seen Willy." So the ghost looked over, and went away rattling his chains and all. Came back 'bout five minutes later. He said, "You seen Willy?" So he said, "No, I ain't seen Willy." So *he* left.
>
> So here comes another ghost in. So he said, "Hey there, have you seen Willy?" Reverend said, "No, I ain't seen Willy." So he grabbed the frying pan, drink the hot grease, ate the pork chop, grabbed some of the hot coals to wipe his ass. The preacher looked up and said, "Well, god damn, you ain't Willy. Let me get the hell out of here."[3]

This is a common folk story throughout the United States, told in many ways, but always involving a repeated visit of a ghost or

3. Collected from Freddie.

ghostly voice or animal and its effect upon the person trying to stay in the haunted house. Dorson[4] says of this story: "Believed tales of haunted houses have generated this very popular folktale, an American oikotype of Type 326, 'The Youth Who Wanted to Learn What Fear Is'." By his citation of the number of American variants, Dorson indicates that the story's oikotypicality is probably determined by its provenance in this general form throughout the United States.

In looking into *The Types of the Folktale* of Thompson under Type 326 (p. 114 of the new edition) it becomes evident that the protagonist and the antagonist differ considerably in the Indo-European and the American variants. Also there is a contrast in the pieces and their outcomes. Type 326 concerns a boy who wants to learn what fear is so he goes through a series of frightful experiences searching for fear. One of these experiences is in a haunted house where a dead man's members fall, one after another, through a chimney, and ghost-like cats continually appear, but the boy doesn't learn what fear is until cold water is thrown on him in his sleep, or until eels are put down his back. Thus the story as collected in the Indo-European complex is in märchen form, and operates under the conventions of that form. As in such stories, we are concerned with the experience (of the young hero) as an element in the process of maturation, of confronting life. The incidents may be fairly humorous, but the humor is secondary to the growth experience.

The opposite is true of the American variants. Here the humor of the situation is paramount. The repetitions are for the purpose of building toward the humorous withdrawal. The protagonist is taught a lesson, to be sure, but it is one of prudence. We are never concerned with his age or lack of experience. He is a comic character, placed in an awkward position. There is no supernatural or logical reason why he must leave the house; only the conventions of the comic formula under which this joke functions demand it.

Just why this variation should be so typically American is impossible to say without a great deal of cultural inquiry, and even then I'm not convinced that an answer is possible because I am not sure that there is an "American culture." And without a culture exercising its biases and imperatives I don't believe we can talk in terms of oikotype. There are, however, two differences between the European and American variants which can be generalized into possible tropisms which might help us to eventually identify an oikotype. These are (1) the assumption of jocularity toward super-

---

4. *Negro Folktales in Michigan*, p. 220. He notes there a number of American texts. To this add Botkin (TAA), p. 222, from Alben W. Barkley, *That Reminds Me* (New York, 1954), p. 37; Dorson (NTPB), p. 78.

natural occurrences, perhaps because of our rationalistic bias, and (2) modification of stories to conform to the joke pattern, where interest (in this case, humor) is derived from uncomfortable situation and play of wit, especially in punch-line endings.

If the Camingerly group is representatively American, these are American tropisms. More important for our discussion is that they are tropisms for our group. This story is learned and remembered because it is in joke form and jokes are an important pattern in this group, and because they assume a jocular tone about spirits, a similarly important attribute of the stories of Camingerly. But these are not the only reasons for the persistence of this story in this neighborhood. The story is adaptable, and has been adapted, to the pattern of the unmanly (cowardly) preacher being exposed for what he is, a pattern observable in many of the other preacher stories collected here, and perhaps to be considered as an element of a tropism itself.

Another story collected in Philadelphia is very close to this one, but illustrates the effects of a further tropism, discussed at length in Chapter Three, the demonstration of manly deeds by "hard men."

> There was once a haunted house, where nobody would go in the house because it was haunted. So one day they put a reward up for anybody who could spend a night in the house. These three guys were willing to spend a night in the house. So they heard a voice howling out:
>
> > I didn't die right.
> > I didn't die right.
>
> So he got up and he started to run. Ran out. Next guy went in, heard a voice:
>
> > I didn't die right.
> > I didn't die right.
>
> He got up and ran out. Third man went in. He had his knife at his side. He heard a voice:
>
> > I didn't die right.
> > I didn't die right.
>
> He simply replied, "Fuck with me and you will die right."[5]

But in considerations of this sort, one must not just look for differences. It is as important to understand why a group learns and remembers a story as to consider why and how they change it. Let

5. Collected from "Kid."

us look at another story collected in South Philadelphia with some
of its relatives to investigate this idea further. Here, to begin with,
is a text as it is usually found in England and in most printings in
the United States.[6]

The Man That Stole the Parson's Sheep

There was once a man who used to steal a fat sheep
every Christmas. One Christmas he stole the parson's
sheep, and his son, a lad about twelve years old, went
about the village singing:

> My father's stolen the parson's sheep,
> And a merry Christmas we shall keep,
> We shall have both pudding and meat,
> But the moant say nought about it.

Now it happened one day that the parson himself heard
the boy singing these words, so he said, "My lad, you sing
very well; will you come to church next Sunday evening
and sing it there?"

"I've no clothes to go in," said the boy. But the parson
said, "If you will come to church as I ask you, I will buy
you clothes to go in." So the boy went to church the next
Sunday evening, dressed in the new clothes that the parson had given him.

When the service was over the parson said to the people,
"Stay, my breathren, I want you to hear what this boy has
to sing, it's gospel truth that he'll tell you," for he was hop-
ing that the boy would confess before all the people that
his father had stolen the sheep. But the boy got up and
sang:

> As I was in the field one day
> I saw the parson kiss a may; [maid]
> He gave me a shilling not to tell
> And these new clothes do fit me well.

And here it is as collected from two informants from Philadelphia:

A.

Now this here's about the reverend and the deacon.
Deacon said he had a bull. So the reverend's family was in

6. From Sidney Oldall Addy, *Household Tales* (London, 1895), p. 18.
This text is very close to the early American one printed by Botkin (TAA),
pp. 235-236, from Isaiah Thomas, Jr.'s *Almanack* for 1810. Johnson in *Folk
Culture of Saint Helena Island* (Chapel Hill, 1930), prints a Negro version
from the Sea Islands which is also very similar.

'dation. He had a whole lot of kids, reverend didn't have no money, buy nothing to eat, so he went and stole the deacon's bull. So he invited everybody 'round. He even invited deacon over. "Come over to my house Sunday, 'cause right after church we're gonna have all kind of beef." So the reverend said, "O.K."

So he came over and he sat down, and he, you know how they do in the country, kids eat first and then the grown-ups. So the reverend sit down, and he said, "This here sure some good food. Um, um, um. You know one thing, rev?" He said, "What's that, Brother Deacon?" He said, "You know somebody stole my bull." He said, "Um, ain't that something, people just going 'round taking other people's stuff." And all the same time he's the one that stole the bull.

So the kids was outside playing, so the reverend said, "I guess I'll go and sit out there in the back for a while, see the kids play." So at that time the kids had made up this here new game. Had each other by the hand going around the circle singing.

> Oh, Poppa stole the deacon's bull.
> All us children got a belly full.

So the deacon said, "Sing that song again. I'ma give you a nickel apiece if you sing that song again for me." So by them being kids and all, a whole nickel. You know a nickel's a whole lot of money to a kid. "Sing it again." So they start singing:

> Oh, Poppa stole the deacon's bull.
> All us children got a belly full.

So he said, "Thank you, kids. Now I want you all to come to church next Sunday, and I'ma give you all fifty cents apiece. I want you all to sing that same song in church. 'Cause that there song carries a message." So they said, "O.K."

So they ran and told their mother that they were going to sing in church. So their mother was glad to have the children sing in church. She didn't know what they was going to sing about.

So the deacon, he was going around to everybody's house, telling them, "Reverend Jones' kids gonna be in church, and they gonna sing a song, and it's carrying a message. And I want all you all to come down hear this here. The Lord sent them children to send this message.

I want you to come on down there and hear them." So he went on over to Sister Mary's house, told Sister Mary about it. Pretty soon he had gone to all the people in the community and the people had spread the word.

So finally that Sunday came. Children come to church, and they was clean. Well, by the time they got there, the church was so packed that so many people had to sit in the back of the church. So he told them, "Now when you go up there, I want you to sing loud so I can hear what you're singing, too." So they said, "Yes, sir, daddy, we gonna sing loud."

So the preacher, you know how the preacher do before he bring on gospel singers. He'd go to preaching, telling you this and that, so he building up the people to hear this song. He said, "Yeah, ladies and gentlemens, you don't know. Kids can bring a message. Yes sir, kids can sure bring a message." He said, "Now just listen to this here message that Reverend Jones' kids gonna bring to you. Now sing that song, children."

They got up there:

> Oh, poppa stole the Deacon's bull,
> All us children got a belly full.

So the reverend in the back couldn't hear them. So he said, "Sing up louder, here boy. Come on now, sing up louder so I can hear you." By that time the people down front are looking at him. So he wondered what they looking at him for. So they start singing:

> Oh, poppa stole the deacon's bull.
> All us children got a belly full.

He said, "Look boy, I want you to sing it louder now. You all sing that song so I can hear it." So they got to the top of their voices:

> Oh, poppa stole the deacon's bull,
> All us children got a belly full.

So the reverend look and said, "Oh yeah? Well, children

> When you told that you told your last,
> Now when I get home I'm gonna kick your ass."[7]

7. Collected from Charley.

B.

These little boys were walking through the town singing:

My father stole the preacher's bull, un hunh, un hunh.
My father stole the preacher's bull,
And me and my brother had a belly full, un hunh.

Some lady saw them. "Son, if you sing that song in church Sunday, I'll give you a dollar." "Sure, ma'am. I'll be there."

So next Sunday, the boys got up nice, bright and early, sitting in church. The congregation was gathering around and the lady told them to start singing. Jumped up, he said:

My father stole the preacher's bull, un hunh, un hunh.
My father stole the preacher's bull,
And me and my brother had a belly full, un hunh.

What he didn't know, his father had came to church. First time in his life that Sunday, his father was in church. Father was sitting way back in the corner of the church. So his father heard him, and stood up and he said:

You sung your first, you sung your last,
When you get home I'ma beat your ass, un hunh.[8]

The English and the Camingerly variants are remarkably similar, yet with some important differences. It is not too difficult to discern what tropes were at work causing this story to be learned and remembered. We have discussed the tendency of the Negro in general, and specifically the Camingerly man, to cast his stories in cante-fable form, and thus this cante-fable would naturally appeal to his aesthetic. Furthermore, the clever twist of the rhyme, found in the original, is consonant with that tendency in the Camingerly cante-fable. The repeated verse in the early version is already a structural factor in the humor of the piece, not merely textural. Just why the ending was changed is hard to ascertain, because in the earlier texts the preacher is placed in a compromised position, something which many of the other Camingerly narratives do, but which is eschewed here.

Another clear, formal tropism which has affected some of the narratives collected in Camingerly is the casting of contest into Negro-white terms, in the more traditional texts in the roles of Marster and John the slave. One portion of the international tale, "Dr. Know-All" fits (or has been fitted) into this particular pattern and thus has become the localized Negro form of the tale, here

8. Collected from Freddie.

called "The Coon in the Box" (58) and collected in similar form among Negroes throughout the United States. Here the pun on names ("Krebs" or "crab" in the German versions) is utilized to emphasize the Negro-white contest going on. ("You got this old coon at last")

This Marster-John pattern has persisted and proliferated, changing its tendency and strategy from a triumph of wits to a triumph of strength. The final story discussed here, "The Dream Contest," is a transitional story, between the older Marster-John type and the newer arrogant challenges. Here is the story as collected in Philadelphia (59. "Dreaming Contest"):

> White fellows, they was sitting down at the club in the South. This only colored guy in there now. They let him 'cause he had millions. Land, property, homes, factories, cars. So he told these fellows, "I bet you a thousand dollars you can't cheat him out of no money." Fellow said, "Shit, I cheat anybody I want out of some money. Give me two weeks." "All right."
>
> Went over to the colored fellow, he said, "They tell me you're a gambling man." Said, "I'm a gambling man." He said, "Well, let's play a game called 'dream'." "How it go?" He said, "Whatever I dream, you got to make it come true." He said, "All right."
>
> So at night, 'bout two o'clock, white man walked over, knocked on the door. He said, "Mr. John." "Yeah, what's the matter?" He said, "Last night I dreamt that you gave me your wife, your house, all your property." He said, "Well, I got to make it come true."
>
> So the next morning, he had to move to hotel. Next night, the white man came to his apartment, he said, "John." "Yeah, what's the matter?" "You know I dreamt last night that you gave me all your money, your factory, all your stock, all your bonds, all of anything you got of any value." Colored fellow said, "I got to make it come true. This cat is getting slick. He's trying to break me. I got to think this over."
>
> He went out to the woods, sat down on a log by the stream. He thought and thought. It came to him. He broke out for town. Boy, he was running. He ran up to Mr. Charlie's door, nearly knocked down his door. Said, "Come on downstairs, man. Look here, I was sitting in the woods and I fell asleep. And I had a nightmare. I didn't have a dream. I had a nightmare. I dreamt you gave me all my money, all my land, all my belongings, all my stocks and bonds, all my valuables, everything you dreamt I gave

you, you gave back to me. Then I turned around and
dreamt you gave me everything you had, clothes and
money, stocks and bonds, everything. Then I fell asleep
and dreamt that we don't dream no god damn more."[9]

The idea of a dream representing a controlled wish leading to
action is a common folkloric motif (K 444, to be exact). In the most
common story using this motif, three men have only one loaf of
bread and they agree to give it to the one who has the most
wonderful dream. One eats the bread while the others are asleep
and says that he has dreamt that he ate it. (Type 1626) The story
as we have it here from Philadelphia is at best a distant cousin.
The idea of the clever "dreamer" however unites the two and the
"dream bread" story may have provided the idea of casting the
present contest in dream form, if nothing else.

It is only by viewing the international relatives of this story that
we are able to see just how the story developed to its presently
perceivable form. The humor of this piece relies not only on the
triumph of wits of the Negro over the white man, but also on the
humorous situation which can arise when people start to give
things away because of an established protocol. In the case of this
version, the protocol is a badly worked out motivation for the
contest. The importance of the protocol itself is seen in some earlier
versions of the story. Here is a version from the beginning of the
19th century in the United States, but referring back to Colonial
times:

> Soon after Sir William Johnson had been appointed
> superintendent of Indian Affairs in America, he wrote to
> England for some suits of clothes richly laced. When they
> arrived, Hendrick, king of the Mohawk nation, was pres-
> ent and particularly admired them. In a few succeeding
> days, Hendrick called on Sir William and acquainted him
> that he had had a dream. On Sir William's inquiring what
> it was, he told him that he had given him one of those fine
> suits he had lately received. Sir William took the hint and
> immediately presented him with one of the richest suits.
> The Indian chief, highly pleased with the generosity of
> Sir William, retired. Some time after this, Sir William
> happening to be in company with Hendrick, told him that
> he had also had a dream. Hendrick being very solicitous
> to know what it was, Sir William informed him, that he
> had dreamed that he (Hendrick) had made him a present
> of a particular tract of land (the most valuable on the

9. Collected from "Kid."

Mohawk River, of about five thousand acres). Hendrick presented him with the land immediately, but not without making this shrewd remark: "Now, Sir William, I will never dream with you again, you dream too hard for me."[10]

In Protestant and mercantilistically oriented countries the whole idea of the give-away without any specific purpose is a natural butt for humor, especially where the method of giving away becomes a contest device. But the humor of the piece is not as intense, as well as not as "at home," as in countries where such largesse is much more the accepted norm of courtesy. Here are two versions of the same story collected recently by Dr. Americo Paredes in Mexico, which are much more humorous because of the Mexican attitude toward giving something away if it attracts someone's eye. The most recent of these concerns President Kennedy on one of his trips to Mexico:

> President Kennedy was greeted at the airport by Mexican President Lopez Mateos and as they were shaking hands, Jack in his most diplomatic way said, "What a beautiful watch you have." Lopez Mateos immediately gave Kennedy the watch, saying "You know, it is a custom in my country, when someone likes something and openly admires it, it is his." Later, at a state dinner in Jack's honor, the Mexican President leaned over to him and said, "You know, I admire Jackie." Quickly Jack replied, "Here take back your fucking watch."

The earlier version from Mexico has the same tendency and also illustrates much of the same gentle but sexually oriented anti-American feeling.

> An American was out on the range with a Mexican guide. He admires the Mexican's knife. The Mexican promptly gives it to him. Later, when the American is defecating, the Mexican says, "What beautiful white buttocks you have." The American promptly replied, "Here's your fucking knife."

10. Harold Thompson, *Body, Boots and Britches* (Philadelphia, 1940), p. 177, from *Funny Stories, or the American Jester* of 1804. Cf. Botkin (TAA), pp. 58-59, from *American Anecdotes, Original and Select* of 1830. Dorson (NTPB), p. 95, has a further Negro printing similar to the present one. He discusses the Indian story in an article, "Comic Indian Anecdoes," *Southern Folklore Quarterly*, X (1946), p. 122. Baughman lists these and others in his dissertation, a motif and tale-type index of English and North American tales, as K 77°, "Dream Contest."

A state of custom in many countries must be translated, and changed in the process when it goes to another where the custom does not persist. This is the direction I feel this story took. A natural social situation in Mexico (and many other Latin countries) has to be translated into dream terms in order to make any sense in our culture.

Each of these versions represents the effects of certain tropisms on what is basically the same story. In Mexico the story is cast in two patterns, both of them extremely common. The one, a confrontation of a Mexican and an American alone, often leads to an implication of sodomy, as it does here. The other, having men of importance placed in awkward positions for purposes of burlesque or satire, also modulates in the same direction, for the implications of sodomy or cuckoldry are equally humorous to the *machismo* (masculinity) oriented Mexican.

Similarly, the Sir William-Hendrick text is characteristic of the books of anecdotes of famous personages common and popular from the Restoration until the present day (though now libel laws have eliminated the printing of many of the legends which have floated around, and attached themselves to living notables, though in as recent a writer as Alexander Wolcott the same process has been extremely active). And the relationship of the crafty Indian and the white man, with the white man outwitting the Indian, was obviously affected by the values of the audience.

Most important to our considerations, though, are the application of this wide-spread story to the conventions of the Negro narratives. In the Philadelphia text, our interest is shifted somewhat from the protocol arrangement to the ingenuity of the Negro millionaire in resolving the ruinous conflict to his benefit. The story in this form, as a contest between the Negro and white man, is characteristic of Camingerly narratives, and probably of most Negro groups in the United States.

ON CERTAIN OBSCENITIES

ONE SUBJECT WHICH WAS SIDESTEPPED IN THE MAJOR BODY OF THIS study was the recurrence of obscenities in the lore of this group. The whole problem of the existence and use of obscenity is such a complex one that it would take a great deal more time and investigation with individual informants to even attempt to pursue the subject to some sort of hypothetical conclusion. Yet there are a few speculative generalizations which can be made that may cast light on the use of obscenity in this group.

The literature on the function of obscenity is sparse indeed. Even psychoanalytic writings which generally deal in matters of this sort yield only three works of any importance, and these, for the most part, deal with the subject from the point of view of the neurotic's use of obscene language. Prof. Freud treats the subject in passing in his *Jokes and Their Relation to the Unconscious*. Here he is primarily concerned with the psychological basis for expressions of wit, but his dicta that "By the utterance of the obscene words it compels the person who is assailed to imagine the part of the body or the procedure in question . . ."[1] provides the groundwork on which all subsequent remarks have been based. Obscenities subsequently are seen as aggressive tools, used to penetrate the defenses of the superego or the accepted and both to activate and, because of its generally approved nature when placed in joke form, to free guilt feelings in regard to bodily functions.

1. Tr. James Strachey (London, 1960), p. 98. Freud's assumption of the joke as expression of aggressive behavior is, of course, manifest here, and not inconsistent with the view put forth throughout the present work.

Sandor Ferenczi extends this idea considerably by pointing out that the triggered response of obscenity is one which reveals "the capacity of compelling the hearer to revive memory pictures in a regressive and hallucinatory way . . . the hearer himself . . . harbours in his store of memories a number of word-sound and writing images of erotic content that differ from word pictures in their increased tendency to regression."[2] He explains the difference between obscenities and other words by pointing out that "at a certain stage of development this concreteness, and with it probably a strong tendency to regression, applies still to all words"[3] because words have been associated with the attainment of gratification (through both power and the parental love-reward) and therefore are concrete representations of pleasure. When confronted with an anxiety situation, "what happens in the first primitive stage of mental development is that on the appearance of the wish the perception of the previously experienced gratification becomes regressively engaged and maintained in a hallucinatory way."[4] "It is the suppression of these sexual fantasies and actions, manifested in the weakened form of speech, that really connotes the beginning of the latency period proper, that period in which, 'the mental counter-forces against infantile sexuality, namely, disgust, shame, and morality, are formed,' and the child's interest is turned in the direction of social activity . . . the suppressed verbal material must, in consequence of the latency period (i.e., the deflection of attention), remain at this more primitive developmental stage, while the rest of the vocabulary gradually becomes, for the greater part, divested of its hallucinatory and motor character by progressive exercising and training, and is rendered through this economy suitable for higher thought activities."[5] The words are certainly not lost, but rather, under the onslaught of learning activities, they become less important. Then they reappear at puberty, "invested with the character of shamefulness,"[6] but retaining their former power to cause regression. The shame and the pleasure of regression cause a mixed reaction to the obscenity; whichever impulse dominates determines one's reaction to the word. In an important aside, he notes that "among uncultivated people, obscene words are perhaps more markedly invested with pleasure, and do not differ so essentially from the rest of the vocabulary. . . ."[7]

2. "On Obscene Words," in *Sex in Psychoanalysis*, tr. Ernest Jones (New York, 1956), p. 117.
3. "Obscene Words," p. 119.
4. "Obscene Words," p. 117.
5. "Obscene Words," pp. 122-23.
6. "Obscene Words," p. 127.
7. "Obscene Words," p. 130.

Edmund Bergler examines the nature of this "pleasure" considerably more than his predecessors:

> . . . the giving of words was originally an *oral proof of love*, just as the giving of the faeces is an anal expression of affection. Secondarily, as a result of a disappointment with the mother, a complete cessation of this giving may ensue. *Thirdly, the giving is reestablished after a negative pattern,* which in the form of obscene words serves as a means of heaping indignity upon her. In spite of this the old erotic desire worms its way in; these words are a magic gesture designed to show how the patient wants to be treated and also a voice of reproach against the mother for the kind of care she gave him: "See what you have made of me."[8]

Bergler accepts obscenity as an expression of regression, but shows how the pleasure which is involved is complicated by the mixed attitude directed toward the maternal image. Obscenity, he argues, is both a confession of love and a wish to be loved in its quality as a regressive tool and a simultaneous insult to the object of this love.

As has been pointed out consistently in this study, just such an ambivalent love-hate situation is at the very core of the lives of the Camingerly men, and is especially evident in their use of words. Words in general have retained their ability to produce pleasure regressively. Their use as tools of power in a conflict situation is something of an adaptation of the idea of words as gifts presented to mother (or mother-substitute). "See what I can give you" the Camingerly man seems to say in his power-use of words. But just as strongly, his obscene manner of expression is a blast against the mother-espoused vows of prohibition against such language. So his compulsive use of obscenities, like so many other elements of his expression, can be seen to be Janus-headed, attractive-rejective.

One obscenity is especially interesting in this regard, and that is the one most ubiquitous in this group, "motherfucker." This word is used in a number of ways. It appears constantly as an intensifier, "motherfucking." It is also used often as a noun. In both, context determines whether honorific or perjorative sense is intended, as either is possible. One of the best things which can be said of a man is that he is a "mean motherfucker" or a "tough motherfucker," but to call him just a "motherfucker" is to invite reprisal. Why such a word can find this variety of connotations and intentions is in-

8. "Obscene Words," *Psychoanalytic Quarterly*, V(1936), p. 236. The major facet of his argument concerns the oral nature of obscenity, based on his perception of the flatus in the anal stage and words in the oral.

herent in the ambivalent nature of obscenity itself, in its use as curse, expletive, epithet and intensifier. If one is trying to assume the mask of the rebel, the mother-defier, the anti-feminine, then to have it said that one is a "motherfucker" is honorific as it castigates the womanly and places both the speaker and the one to whom he refers in a position of power. Yet, one does owe emotional allegiance to one's own mother, therefore, to be accused of entering into such a defilement is to provide an insult. And this insult is especially strong because it activates at one and the same time a very strong taboo against incest and an equally strong oedipal wish. Thus, when the term is used in the very personal sense it activates strongly antagonistic and conflicting feelings that naturally will be answered with something else equally violent.

In a sense, the term is a telescoping of the whole process of playing the dozens. Because of its ambivalent capacities, the word can, at one and the same time, afford a release of mother-directed (oedipal) and mother-rejective forces. It also achieves a kind of semi-anonymous function simply because of its very wide and almost casual or ritualistic use. It serves as a constant reminder that the problem of relationship with women is something which has not been solved, while at the same time it helps to solve it temporarily.

This complex role for such an obscenity is, as the psychiatrists have pointed out, inherent in its existence, being as it is an offering (through a regressive use of words) and a rejection of the mother. Such terms as "fuck" and "shit" also emerge in both positive and negative contexts[9] and for very much the same reasons. Somehow, it is especially significant, however, that in this matrifocally-reared group with their violent attraction-rejection of mother-woman's world that the most frequent obscenity should be so obviously and overtly directed at mother.

9. C.f. Edward Sagarin, *The Anatomy of Dirty Words* (New York, 1962), especially chapters 7 and 23.

UNUSUAL TERMS AND EXPRESSIONS

Included in this section are those words and expressions which have been followed by an asterisk in the body of the work, and a few terms which were current in Camingerly of singular interest. I have made some effort to support my definitions from other sources, most notably the Dictionary of American Slang *by Harold Wentworth and Stuart Berg Flexner (New York, 1960). Peter Tamony and G. Legman have been especially helpful in the compiling of this glossary. As in the past, I shall refer to Legman's contributions by prefacing them with his name and a dash.*

Ball — Widely used in the sense of a dance, but used here in reference to an orgy. C.f. Wentworth and Flexner, 16. *Legman* — It does not refer to "dancing" but to sexual intercourse, especially in a secret orgiastic way, as in the similar song widely known in Scotland, "The *Ball* of Kirriemuir." These erotic "balls" are remnants of Witches' Sabbat — so called — sex cults in the late middle ages and were a paramount element in the "witch" persecutions in Scotland, and later in America. The word is plainly glossed only once, but very significantly, in Pepys' *Diary*, in the late 17th century, where he is invited to an orgiastic party held by a group who called themselves "The Ballers," apparently the group for whom Rochester's obscene play *Sodom* was written for naked presentation. . . . The first use of the word *in print* . . . is in Grose's *Classical Dictionary of the Vulgar Tongue* where he describes the same sort of dances and orgies under the term "Buff-Ball(ers)" the word *buff* meaning one's naked skin. The survival of this word, entirely underground, and (except for Grose) absolutely without the advantages of print, for three hundred years now is almost unparalled in philological history.

Bitch — Any woman. As used here, usually without usual pejorative connotations. Wentworth and Flexner, 39.

Blanshed — Knocked, ruined.

Boolhipper — Slick black leather coat, usually found, as here, with a belt in the back. Pronounced somewhere between boolhipper and boodlehipper or boodlipper.

Booty — As used here, an extension of "body," specifically the body of a woman. Oliver, p. 189 prints a blues verse in which the word is used in this way. On the other hand, "boot" has had a history of sexual connotation and may have affected the formation of this word. The term "Buckinger's Boot" meant the cunt in 18th century England, see Grose, *Classical Dictionary of the Vulgar Tongue*, 2nd ed., London, 1788. *Legman* — The reference to Grose here is interesting but does not cover the term itself, since that was a real *boot* (of a man without legs), where this is clearly as you say, an "extension" of *body*. Actually it is merely a variant pronunciation of it. . . .

Bulldagger — A lesbian. Variant pronunciation, bulldiker. *Legman* — The actual origin of *bulldagger* is simply a long series of mispronunciations and corruptions of the word *hermaphrodite*, extraordinary as that may seem at first sight. The series is even more extraordinary in that *all* the corruptions of the original word still co-exist simultaneously, namely: *harumphodite, morphodite, dike, dyker;* and *bull-dyker* or *bull-dagger* with the addition of the male "bull" element. Such very male-imitating lesbians are also called *diesel-dykes*.

Busted my nuts — Had an orgasm.

Camel-hair benny — In 18th century British slang, *Joseph* meant coat. C.f. *Genesis:* coat of many colors and Joseph's cloak left in the grasp of Potiphar's wife. Benjamin was, of course, Joseph's younger brother. In the early 19th century British slang, *Benjamin* or *Benny* came to mean a smaller or close fitting coat.

Cashmere — Any sweater.

Chickenshit — A corruption of *chicken feed,* i.e., insubstantial, small, insignificant, but in this case referring to a person rather than to the usual material things. The addition of *shit* as a suffix is wholly in line with other such additions to animal names, *bullshit, apeshit, horseshit,* etc. C.f. Wentworth and Flexner, 99.

Cock — Most commonly the female genitalia.

Cooling — Doing a *cool* thing, in other words, performing in complete control of oneself in the midst of a potentially explosive situation. Used much in jazz talk. Obvious derivation: *cool* as opposite of getting heated up, as in *cool as a cucumber* which is found as early as 1732 (Oxford, 109). Wentworth and Flexner, 121.

Cooncan — A corruption of the Mexican *Con Quien*, a card game in the rummy family.

Cotton — The hair on woman's pudendum.

Cue — Used here to mean *tip* in the sense of money given for services.

Crabs — Crab lice.

Crazy — Good, or highest good in jazz talk. See Wentworth and Flexner, 129.

Crazy Rim — Very good looking hat. May simply be descriptive of its good looks, with the addition of designation of the object by one of its parts for the whole (*rim* for *hat*).

Crut — Variant of *crud*, originally, dried semen which sticks to clothes, body, etc., after emission, but more generally referring to anything base. C.f. Wentworth and Flexner, 132, 133.

Cutting Man — Best friend. *Cut* has always been associated with contest of some sort. Cutting cards is a common way of sudden death gambling. Competition between jazz bands has been referred to as cutting. This expression may refer to the one you choose to do the cutting for you, thus someone you trust, thus a friend. Wentworth and Flexner, 136.

Dick — The penis. Perhaps a variant of *prick*. C.f. Wentworth and Flexner, 146.

Down — To place someone at a verbal disadvantage. Used both as a verb and adjective. You can *down* someone, or you can put someone *down*. Word may have sexual derivation, in that putting someone underneath you during the sexual act indicates that he is playing the female role, i.e., is by inference a homosexual. This parallels the use of the word *mount* which means to best someone physically or verbally, but which derives from the expression of animals having intercourse, the male *mounting* the female.

Fag — Male homosexual. Wentworth and Flexner, 176, point out that speculation has been that *fag* meaning homosexual came from *fag* meaning cigarette in that cigarettes were considered effeminate by pipe and cigar smokers pre-WWI. But *fag* has meant boy servant or schoolboy in England since before 1830 and the term probably derives ultimately from there. (*Fag* is for faggots or the sticks of wood the boys had to gather.)

Fix — In proper position, in pool slang.

Freak — A male homosexual. C.f. Wentworth and Flexner, 199.

Fuck — See *jive*.

Gat — A firearm, probably a corruption of "Gatling Gun." C.f. Wentworth and Flexner, 209.

Georgia Skin — A card game in the rummy family.

Gig — Job, situation. May have sexual origin as *gig* or *gigi* means vagina or rectum. A *gig* may have originally meant a sex date and expanded in meaning to a date of any kind, but usually a playing date for musicians. If sexual originally, much like many other jazz terms, see *jazz, jive.* Wentworth and Flexner, 214.

Goat-hair — Bootleg liquor.

Grinding — Sexual intercourse. Descriptive of movement during act. Wentworth and Flexner, 230. The movement used metaphorically in terms of striptease dance. This latter use is more common.

Herbs — Marijuana. Probably descriptive of common properties of feel, smell and texture.

Hoorah — Probably a corruption of "I roar" or "I rule."

Hung to — Very attached to, addicted.

Hustling — Making nervous signs at. Very different from common slang sense of the term.

Jazz — See *jive.*

Jibs — Teeth.

Jive — "A whole lot of talk." Originally and still used in the sense of *fuck* and *jazz,* i.e., the sexual act. All three have achieved similar changes, *jazz* being synonymous with *jive* in the realm of talk, *fuck* referring more to actions. Synonyms also, *shuck* and *shive.*

Joint — Male sex organs.

Lobstertails — Some sort of venereal disease, perhaps simply a bad case of crabs.

Main who' — Best girl friend.

Me and you — Short for "there's just me and you and we're going to fight."

Mount — See *down.*

Passion — When used in sense of "passion rising," a euphemism for the penis becoming erect.

Piece — Short for *piece of ass,* i.e., sexual intercourse or referring directly to the woman involved. C.f. Wentworth and Flexner, 388.

Pimp — Originally a procurer, but because of the style of this profession, now used among this group to refer to any "smart" person.

Punk — Young male companion of homosexual. Wentworth and Flexner, 411 (punk 4). More specialized than usual meaning of young, fresh person.

Rags — Clothes. Used in this sense since 1855. (DAE *rags*) Wentworth and Flexner, 416.

Raise — Stop, or "hold it." Shortening of the common order to "raise your hands" when pointing a gun at someone, with a more general application.

Rap — Conviction of a crime. Wentworth and Flexner, 419, print a possible derivation, the *rap* referring to the tap on the shoulder in a police line-up indicating the implication of the culprit.

Raunchy — Bad, especially over-loose, careless or inept. C.f. Wentworth and Flexner, 420.

Real down — Very good. Real is a synonym of very; *down* of *cool*, but only in this one expression. The usual meaning of *down* is quite different (see above, *down*).

Rockets — Bullets. Descriptive of shape and speed.

Roll — A double-breasted suit.

Sashay — Move (usually fast). May come from the dance step, which itself comes from the idea of courting. See Wentworth and Flexner, 443.

Satch — As yet undetermined type of jacket, perhaps designated by its use by Negro pitcher Satchel Paige or trumpeter Louis "Satchmo" Armstrong.

Shive — jive. See *jive* above.

Shuck — Fuck (mostly sound-alike), usually only in terms of talk and action rather than the sex act. Expression is usually "shuck and shive." See *jive* above.

Signify — To imply, goad, beg, boast by indirect verbal or gestural means. A language of implication. This use is quite broadened from that expressed by Wentworth and Flexner, 477, "to pretend to have knowledge; to pretend to be hip, especially when such pretentions cause one to trifle with an important matter."

Sissy — Young homosexual, or effeminate. Derives from *sister*. Wentworth and Flexner, 478.

Slick — One who is very adept. In this area can refer to any kind of endeavor. C.f. Wentworth and Flexner, 486-487.

Sound — "Playing the dozens." Word descriptive of activity. Wentworth and Flexner, 504, give a somewhat broader interpretation of the word.

Stake — A sum which is gambled. C.f. Wentworth and Flexner, 515.

Stingy brim — Small brimmed hat, often of the "pork pie" variety. Name is a euphonistic description of object.

Stomped — Corruption of *stamp,* grind under one's feet. Perhaps just a common Negro pronunciation. See Wentworth and Flexner, 522.

Stone — An adjective or adverb indicating a greater degree of whatever the noun or verb which it modifies originally meant. A "stone sailor" is a sailor who has all sailors' characteristics. May come from the expressions "stone cold," "stone dead," etc., which took actual attributes from stones as elements of description. "Stone blind" is an early extension that shows such a development of the word as used here.

Stud — Any male, especially one in the know. Obvious sexual origin. Wentworth and Flexner, 526.

Swith — Smell. (corruption of *sniff?*)

Tight — Good friends.

Tricks — Legman — The act of intercourse, itself, usually in the whorehouse phrase "to turn a trick."

Vine — A suit of clothing. Name perhaps descriptive of the "hang" of the clothes. Wentworth and Flexner, 565.

Whore — See *Main who'* above.

ig 'em — to assert your writes
to tell off

BIBLIOGRAPHY

Aarne, Antti, and Thompson, Stith. *The Types of the Folktale.* Helsinki, 1928. Revised and enlarged edition, 1961.

Abrahams, Roger D. *Negro Folklore From South Philadelphia,* dissertation, Department of English, University of Pennsylvania, 1962.

Adams, E. C. L. *Nigger to Nigger.* New York and London, 1928.

Addy, Sidney Oldall. *Household Tales With Other Traditional Remains.* London, 1895.

Baring-Gould, S. *A Book of Nursery Songs and Rhymes.* London, 1895.

Barker, W. H., and Sinclair, Cecilia. *West African Folk Tales.* London, 1907.

Beckwith, Martha Allen. *Jamaica Anansi Stories.* Memoirs of the American Folklore Society XVII, New York, 1924.

Beckwith, Martha Warren (coll., Roberts, Helen H.). *Jamaica Folk-Lore.* New York, 1928.

Botkin, B. A. (ed.). *Folksay, 1930,* Norman, Oklahoma.

Botkin, B. A. (ed.). *A Treasury of American Folklore.* New York, 1944.

Botkin, B. A. *A Treasury of Southern Folklore.* New York, 1949.

Botkin, B. A. *A Treasury of New England Folklore.* New York, 1947.

Bowman, James Cloyd. *John Henry, the Rambling Black Ulysses.* Chicago, 1942.

Brand, Oscar. *Bawdy Songs and Backroom Ballads.* New York, 1960.

Brewer, J. Mason. *Dog Ghosts.* Austin, 1958.

Brewer, J. Mason. *The Word on the Brazos.* Austin, 1952.

Brewster, Paul G. *Ballads and Songs of Indiana.* Bloomington, Indiana, 1940.

Brophy, John, and Partridge, Eric. *Songs and Slang of the British Soldier.* London, 1930.

Brown, Frank C. *The Frank C. Brown Collection of North Carolina Folklore* (ed., White, Newman Ivey), 5 Vols. Durham, North Carolina, 1952 and after.

Burke, Kenneth. *A Rhetoric of Motives.* New York, 1953.

Burne, Charlotte S. *Shropshire Folk-Lore.* London, 1884-86.

Burt, Olive W. *American Murder Ballads.* New York, 1958.

Cambiaire, Celestin Pierre. *East Tennessee and Western Virginia Mountain Ballads.* London, 1934.

Campbell, Joseph. *The Hero With a Thousand Faces.* New York, 1949.

Cassirer, Ernst. *Essay on Man.* New York, 1944.

Cazden, Norman (ed.). *A Book of Nonsense Songs.* New York, 1961.

California Folklore Quarterly. 1942-46.

Chambers, Robert. *Popular Rhymes of Scotland.* Edinburgh and London (New Edition, after 1859). n.d.

Chase, Richard. *American Folk Tales and Songs.* New York, 1956.

Clodd, Edward. *Tom Tit Tot: An Essay in Savage Philosophy in Folk Tale.* London, 1898.

Count Vicarion. *Book of Bawdy Ballads.* Paris, 1956.

Courlander, Harold, and Herzog, George. *The Cow-Tail Switch.* New York, 1947.

Creighton, Helen. *Folklore of Lunenburg County, Nova Scotia.* Canada Department of Resources and Development, Bulletin 117, Anthropological Series 29. Ottawa, 1950.

Davis, A., and Dollard, John. *Children of Bondage.* Washington, D. C., 1960.

de la Mare, Walter. *Come Hither.* New York, 1923.

Dollard, John. *Caste and Class in a Southern Town.* New York, 1937, 1949 (paperback reprint).

Douglas, Norman. *London Street Games.* London, 1931.

Dorson, Richard M. *American Folklore.* Chicago, 1959.

Dorson, Richard M. *Negro Folktales in Michigan.* Cambridge, Massachusetts, 1956.

Dorson, Richard M. *Negro Tales From Pine Bluff, Arkansas and Calvin, Michigan.* Bloomington, Indiana, 1958.

Elliott, Robert C. *The Power of Satire*. Princeton, 1960.

Erickson, Erik. *Childhood and Society*. New York, 1953.

Erickson, Erik. *Identity and the Life Cycle*. New York, 1960.

Fauset, Arthur Huff. *Folklore From Nova Scotia*. New York, 1931.

Finger, Charles J. *Frontier Ballads*. New York, 1927.

Folk-Lore. London, 1890-.

Folklore in Action, Essays in Honor of MacEdward Leach (ed. Beck, Horace). Philadelphia, 1962.

Folk-Lore Journal, 8 Vols. London, 1833-89.

Folk-Lore Record, 5 Vols. London, 1878-82.

Ford, Ira W. *Traditional Music of America*. New York, 1940.

Frazier, E. Franklin. *The Negro Family in the United States*. Chicago, 1939.

Freud, Sigmund. *Jokes and Their Relation to the Unconscious* (tr. James Strachey). London, 1960.

Freud, Sigmund. *Beyond the Pleasure Principle* (tr. James Strachey). London, 1950.

Friedman, Albert. *The Viking Book of Ballads*. New York, 1956.

Funk and Wagnalls Standard Dictionary of Folklore, Mythology and Legend (eds., Maria Leach and Jerome Fried). 2 Vols. New York, 1949, 1950.

Fuson, Harvey H. *Ballads of the Kentucky Highlands*. London, 1931.

Gardner, Emelyn Elizabeth. *Folklore From the Schoharie Hills, New York*. Ann Arbor, Michigan, 1937.

Gomme, Alice B. *The Traditional Games of England, Scotland, and Ireland*, 2 Vols. London, 1894-98.

Gordon, Robert W. *Folksongs of America*. National Service Bureau, New York, 1938.

Grotjahn, Martin. *Beyond Laughter*. New York, 1957.

Harris, Joel Chandler. *Nights With Uncle Remus*. New York, 1883.

Harris, Joel Chandler. *Plantation Pageants*. Westminster, 1899.

Harris, Joel Chandler. *Told by Uncle Remus*. New York, 1905.

Harris, Joel Chandler. *Uncle Remus and His Friends*. Boston and New York, 1892.

Hayemi, Phebean, and Gurrey, P. *Folktales and Fables*. London, 1953.

Henry, Mellinger E. *Folksongs From the Southern Highlands*. New York, 1938.

Henry, Mellinger E. *Songs Sung in the Southern Appalachians*. London, 1933.

Herskovits, Melville J., and Frances. *Dahomean Narrative*. Evanston, 1958.

Herskovits, Melville J. *The Myth of the Negro Past*. Boston, 1941, 1958 (paperback reprint).

Hinsie, Leland E., and Campbell, Roberts Jean. *Psychoanalytic Dictionary*. New York, 1958.

Hoosier Folklore. Bloomington, Indiana, 1942-50.

Hudson, Arthur Palmer. *Folksongs of Mississippi and Their Background*. Chapel Hill, North Carolina, 1936.

Hudson, Arthur Palmer. *Specimens of Mississippi Folk-Lore*. Mississippi Folklore Society. Ann Arbor, Michigan, 1928.

Hudson, Arthur Palmer, and Herzog, George. *Folk Tunes From Mississippi*. National Play Bureau, Federal Theatre Project, WPA. New York, 1937.

Hughes, Langston, and Bontemps, Arna. *The Book of Negro Folklore*. New York, 1958.

Huizinga, Johan. *Homo Ludens, a Study of the Play Element in Culture*. Boston, 1950, 1955 (paperback reprint).

Hurston, Zora Neale. *Mules and Men*. Philadelphia and London, 1935.

Hyatt, Harry Middleton. *Folk-Lore From Adams County, Illinois*. New York, 1935.

Jekyll, Walter. *Jamaican Song and Story*. Publications of the Folk-Lore Society IV. London, 1907.

Johnson, Charles S. *Growing Up in the Black Belt*. Washington, D. C., 1941.

Johnson, Charles S. *Shadow of the Plantation*. Chicago, 1934.

Johnson, Guy B. *Folk Culture on St. Helena Island, South Carolina*. Chapel Hill, North Carolina, 1930.

Jones, Charles C. *Negro Myths From the Georgia Coast*. Boston and New York, 1888.

Journal of American Folklore. Boston, New York, and Philadelphia, 1888-.

Jung, C. G. *Symbols of Transformation*. New York, 1956.

Kennedy, R. Emmet. *Black Cameos*. New York, 1924.

Kennedy, R. Emmet. *Mellows*. New York, 1925.

Kluckhohn, Clyde. *Mirror for Man*. New York, 1956 (Signet Edition).

Leach, MacEdward. *The Ballad Book*. New York, 1955.

Legman, G. *Love and Death*. New York, 1949.

Lomax, John and Alan. *American Ballads and Folk Songs*. New York, 1934.

Lomax, John and Alan. *Best Loved American Folk Songs*. (Folk-song: U. S. A.) New York, 1947.

Lomax, Alan. *Folksongs of North America.* New York, 1960.

Lomax, John and Alan. *Negro Folk Songs as Sung by Leadbelly.* New York, 1936.

Lomax, John and Alan. *Our Singing Country.* New York, 1949.

Lomax, Alan. *The Rainbow Sign.* New York, 1959.

Lord, Albert. *The Singer of Tales.* Cambridge, Massachusetts, 1960.

Nebraska Folklore Pamphlets. (Federal Writers Project) Lincoln, 1937.

Neely, Charles (coll.), and Spargo, John Webster (ed. and foreword). *Tales and Songs of Southern Illinois.* Menasha, Wisconsin, 1938.

Neumann, Erich. *The Origins and History of Consciousness.* New York, 1954.

New York Folklore Quarterly. Ithaca, 1945-.

New York Times Magazine

Odum, Howard W. *Rainbow 'Round My Shoulder.* n.d.

Odum, Howard W. *Wings on My Feet.* Indianapolis, 1929.

Odum, Howard W., and Johnson, Guy B. *The Negro and His Songs.* Chapel Hill and London, 1925.

Oliver, Paul. *Blues Fell This Morning.* London, 1960.

Opie, Iona and Peter. *The Lore and Language of School Children.* Oxford, 1959.

O Súilleabháin, Seán. *A Handbook of Irish Folklore.* Dublin, 1942.

Palmer, Edgar. *G. I. Songs.* New York, 1944.

Parrish, Lydia. *Slave Songs of the Georgia Sea Islands.* New York, 1942.

Parsons, Elsie Clews. *Folk-Lore of the Sea Islands, South Carolina.* Memoirs of the American Folklore Society XVI. Cambridge, Massachusetts, and New York, 1923.

Parsons, Elsie Clews. *Folklore From Cape Verde Islands,* 2 Vols. Memoirs of the American Folklore Society XV. New York, 1920.

Propp, Vladimir. *Morphology of the Folktale* (ed., Svatava Pirkova-Jacobson). Bloomington, 1958.

Publications of the Texas Folklore Society. Austin, 1916-.

Puckett, Newbell N. *Folk Beliefs of the Southern Negro.* Chapel Hill, 1926.

Radin, Paul. *The Trickster.* New York, 1956. (With essays by C. G. Jung and Karl Kerenyi.)

Randolph, Vance. *Ozark Folk Songs,* 4 Vols. Columbia, Missouri, 1946.

Randolph, Vance. *The Devil's Pretty Daughter.* New York, 1955.

Randolph, Vance. *Sticks in the Knapsack*. New York, 1958.

Randolph, Vance. *Who Blowed Up the Church House?* New York, 1952.

Rank, Otto. *The Myth of the Birth of the Hero*. New York, 1959.

Rattray, R. S. *Akan-Ashanti Folktales*. Oxford, 1930.

Roberts, Leonard. *South From Hell-fer-Sartin'*. Lexington, 1955.

Rohrer, John H. and Edmondson, Munro (eds.). *The Eighth Generation*. New York, 1960.

Sandburg, Carl. *The American Songbag*. New York, 1927.

Saxon, Lyle, Dreyer, Edward, and Tallant, Robert. *Gumbo Ya-Ya*. Boston and Cambridge, 1945.

Scarborough, Dorothy. *On the Trail of Negro Folk Songs*. Cambridge, 1925.

Scott, Charles T. *A Linguistic Study of Persian and Arabic Riddles: A Language-Centered Approach to Genre Definition*. University of Texas unpublished dissertation, June, 1963.

Simpson, G. E., and Yinger, Y. M. *Racial and Cultural Minorities*. New York, 1953.

Southern Workman and Hampton School Record, Vols. 20-23. Hampton, Virginia, 1904.

Stout, Earl J. *Folklore From Iowa*. New York, 1936.

Style in Language (ed. Thomas Sebeok). Boston and New York, 1960.

Sypher, Wylie (ed.). *Comedy*. New York, 1956.

Tennessee Folklore Society Bulletin. Maryville, 1936-.

Thompson, Stith. *The Folktale*. New York, 1951.

Thompson, Stith. *Motif-Index of Literature*. 6 Vols. Bloomington, Indiana, 1955-1958.

Thorp, N. Howard (Jack). *Songs of the Cowboys*. Boston and New York, 1921.

Tidwell, James N. *A Treasury of American Folk Humor*. New York, 1956.

Von Sydow, C. W. *Selected Papers on Folklore*. Copenhagen, 1948.

Wallrich, William. *Air Force Airs*. New York, 1957.

Wentworth, Harold, and Flexner, Stuart Berg. *Dictionary of American Slang*. New York, 1960.

Western Folklore. Los Angeles and Berkeley, 1946-.

Wheeler, Mary. *Steamboatin' Days*. Baton Rouge, 1944.

White, Newman I. *American Negro Folk-Songs*. Cambridge, Massachusetts, 1928.

Whitney, Annie Weston, and Bullock, Caroline Canfield. *Folklore From Maryland*. Memoirs of the American Folklore Society XVIII. New York, 1925.

Withers, Carl (comp.). *A Rocket in My Pocket*. New York, 1948.

Wolfenstein, Martha. *Children's Humor*. Glencoe, Illinois, 1954.

Wood, Ray. *The American Mother Goose*. New York, 1940.

Wood, Ray. *Fun in American Folk Rhymes*. Philadelphia and New York, 1952.

Wood, Ray. *Mother Goose in the Ozarks*. Raywood, Texas, 1938.

INDEX OF TALE TYPES AND MOTIFS

TALE TYPES REFERRED TO OR INCLUDED IN TEXT[1]

Type No.		*Page No.*
6	*Animal Captor Persuaded to Talk and Release Victim from his Mouth*	140
59*	*The Jackal as Trouble-Maker*	140
326	*The Youth Who Wanted to Learn What Fear Is*	187, 188, 249
1361	*The Flood*	202
1641	*Doctor Know-All*	223
1826	*The Parson has no Need to Preach*	196
1831	*The Parson and Sexton at Mass*	192
1833A	*"What Says David?" The Boy: "Pay Your Old Debt."*	186

MOTIFS REFERRED TO OR INCLUDED IN TEXT[2]

Motif No.		*Page No.*
A2433.3.19	*Why monkey lives in tree*	139

1. Tale type numbers are from Antti Aarne and Stith Thompson, *The Types of the Folktale* (Helsinki, 1961).

2. Motif numbers are from Stith Thompson, *Motif-Index of Folk-Literature* (Copenhagen and Bloomington, Indiana, 1955-1958), 6 volumes.

Motif No.		Page No.
E281	*Ghosts haunt house*	187, 188, 227
E292	*Ghosts frighten people (deliberately)*	188
H543	*Escape from devil by answering his riddles*	217
H1411	*Fear test: staying in haunted house*	187, 188, 227
J582	*Foolishness of premature coming out of hiding*	201
J1260	*Repartee based on church or clergy*	196
J1262.5	*Parishioner hears preacher say that alms are returned "100 to 1"*	183
J1262.5.1	*Whoever gives alms in God's name will receive tenfold: preacher's wife gives sweetmeats away*	181
J1264	*Repartee concerning clerical incontinence*	184
J1269.1	*The parson's share and the sexton's*	184
J1495	*Person runs from actual or supposed ghost*	188
J1495.2	*When Caleb comes*	187
J1772	*One object thought to be another*	202
J1772.9	*Excrements thought to be meat and therefore eaten*	232
J1805	*Other misunderstandings of words*	201
J1919.5	*Genitals cut off through ignorance*	231
J2136	*Numskull brings about his own capture*	201
K210	*Devil cheated of his promised soul*	217
K561.1	*Animal captor persuaded to talk and release victim from his mouth*	140
K1225	*Lover given rump to kiss*	202
K1317	*Lover's place in bed usurped by another*	203
K1956	*Sham wise man*	223
K1961.1.2.1	*Parody Sermon*	185, 191, 192
K1961.1.3	*Sham parson: the sawed pulpit*	194
K1970	*Sham miracles*	194, 223
K2131.2	*Envious jackal makes lion suspicious of his friend the bull*	140
N275.5.2	*Criminal confesses because he thinks himself accused*	201
N688	*What is in the dish: "Poor Crab"*	223

Motif No.		*Page No.*
Q21.1	*Old woman gives her only cow believing she would receive a hundred in return from God*	183
X111.7	*Misunderstood words lead to comic results*	201
X410	*Jokes on parsons*	181
X435	*The boy applies the sermon*	181
X435.1	*"What says David?" — Boy: "Pay your old debts"*	186
X452	*The parson has no need to preach*	196
X800	*Humor based on drunkenness*	229
X939.1*	*Lie: person of remarkable speed*	242
X1411.1	*Lie: the great melon*	243
X1420	*Lies about vegetables*	243
X1623.2.1	*Lie: frozen words thaw out in the spring*	242
X1633	*Lie: effect of heat on animals*	241
X1633.1	*Lie: weather so hot that corn pops in fields, animals freeze to death thinking it has snowed*	241
X1740	*Absurd disregard of natural laws*	242

INDEX OF SUBJECTS, TITLES AND PERSONS

Addy, Sidney Oldall, 251

agonism, (see dialectic; contest)

anthropological approach, 5

Argument of the Parts of the Body, 200-201

Arthur, 31, 96, 117-118, 132-134, 146-147, 147-149, 158-159, 168-169

badman hero, 66, 69-70, 77-83, 105, 117, 124, (see also *The Big Man, The Great MacDaddy, Jesse James, Squad Twenty-Two, Stackolee*)

balanced line, 101-102, 103

Baptism and Belief, 196

Barbecue Bob, 139

Baughman, Ernest W., 179, 201, 224, 257

Bear Meeting and Prayer Meeting, 190-191

Beckwith, Martha Warren, 175-177

Belden, Henry M., and A. P. Hudson, 113

Berdie, R. F., 55n

Big Maceo (Merriweather), 139, 140

The Big Man, 161-162

The Big Watermelon, 243

blackface shows, 106-107

boasts or brags, 36, 46, 47-48, 60, 100, 240-243

Bobby, 30, 31, 36, 94, 122-123

Bontemps, Arna, (see Langston Hughes)

Boots, 97, 185

Botkin, Ben A., 124, 127, 179, 187, 190, 219, 249, 251

Brand-Name Stories, 243-244

Br'er Rabbit, 73, 74-77, 137, 211, 236

Brophy, John, and Eric Partridge, 198

Brown, Oscar, Jr., 139

Brown, Sterling, 24n

bully, 123-128

Brewer, J. Mason, 179, 193, 194, 196, 217

Burke, Kenneth, 8n, 13

Burt, Olive W., 127n

caesura, 101

Camingerly, explanation of name, 19

Campbell, Joseph, 65
Campbell, Robert Jean, (see Leland E. Hinsie)
Carolina Slim, 112
Cassirer, Ernst, 6n
casual utterance, 91-92
catch, 48-49
Charley, 30, 37, 94, 95-96, 121-122, 134-136, 144-145, 151-156, 157-158, 159-160, 165-166, 167-168, 180-181, 181-182, 183, 194-195, 201-202, 218-219, 226, 229-230, 238-240, 253
Chickering, Geraldine Jencks, (see Emelyn Elizabeth Gardner)
child-raising, 28-29
cigarette brands, 244
Chinaman, Jew, Negro, 218-219
Clarke, Kenneth and Mary, 175
Clayton, Paul, 127n
cliché, 104, 106
collecting technique, 20
Coming or Going, 177, 203
conflict, 6-8
Constance, 27
contest element, 35, 41-63
contest hero, 69
The Coon in the Box, 178, 222-223, 255
culture, 5-8
The Curser Outcursed, 177, 197-199
Cursing Cured, 196-197

Davis, A. and John Dollard, 56n
Davis, Arthur Kyle, 190
The Devil Lets them Dream, 219-220
The Devil's Choices, 220-221
dialectic, 5-8, 13, 42-43
La Diligence de Lyon, 213
division of sexes, 29, 31-32, 32-36, 80
Doctor Know-All, 222-254
Dodds, Johnny, 127n

Dollard, John, 49n, 50n, 55-56 (see also A. Davis)
Don Juanism, 33n
Dorson, Richard M., 66n, 67n, 92-93, 99, 109, 124-125, 129, 138, 178, 179, 186, 187, 188, 190, 192, 193, 196, 217, 223, 224, 228, 249, 257
Down Under the Tree, 233-235
dozens, (see *playing the dozens*)
dramatic analysis, 8
Dreaming Contest, 224-225, 255-258
dress, importance of, 33n, 38, 77
Dreyer, Edward, (see Lyle Saxon)
The Drunk Does Pushups, 229-230
The Drunk Goes Around to the Side Door, 230
Dundes, Alan, 246

Edmondson, Munroe, (see John H. Rohrer)
ego identity, male, 31-36, 43-44, 65
ego psychology, 15
THE ELEMENT OF VERBAL CONTEST, 41-63
The Elfin Knight, 158
Elliott, Robert C., 56n, 58n, 59
Elton, William, 55n
employment opportunities, 21, 30
English, Logan, 127n
epic, analysis of toast as, 101-105
Erickson, Erik, 15n, 42-43
esoteric-exoteric formula, 217-219
Eugenia, 24, 25-26
Eula, 24, 25-26

Faier, Billy, 113n
faggots, 33n, 168-170, 265, 266, 267 (see also homosexuality)
family, child raising in, 21-24; explanation of Negro f. system, 22-24n; importance of grandmother in, 24, 24n; importance

of mother in, 21-24; maternity, 21, 23n, 24, 27; matrifocality, 23-24; middle-class f. system, 27; place of males in, 31-33
The Farmer's Curst Wife, 117
Father, Son, and Holy Ghost houses, 19
Fauset, Arthur Huff, 109, 179, 186, 193
Ferenczi, Sandor, 260
fictive playground, 7-8, 15, 60-63, 66
Finger, Charles, 127n
folklore, as play, 41-42, 59-63; comparative method, 9-12; eclectic discipline, 4, 16; form and function, 9; function, 8, 9; in culture, 5-8; linguistic approach toward, 13-14, 91-92; literary approach toward, 12-14; narrative, 4; psychological approach toward, 14-15
folk narrative, 4
Ford, Ira W., 190
formulas, 103
Frazier, E. Franklin, 22-24n
The Freak's Ball, 33n, 168-170
Freddie, 97, 163-164, 171, 182-183, 184-185, 185-186, 187-189, 189-190, 192-194, 195, 196-197, 204-205, 220-221, 228, 236-237, 254
Fresh Off the Farm, 172-173
Freud, Sigmund, 65, 259
Fuller, Jesse, 127n

Gabriel Blows His Horn, 193-194
Galoob, Debra, 99, 111, 129, 139
gang life and values, 31, 33-35, 65
Gardner, Emelyn Elizabeth and Geraldine Jencks Chickering, 116
George Is Upstairs, 208-209
Gladys, 24
Going Fishing, 230
Goldstein, Kenneth S., 111, 138

Golightly, C. L., and I. Sheffler, 55n
Good Manners, 215-216
Good Morning, This Morning, 216-217
good talker, 59-62
Gordon, Robert W., 127n
Gould, Jay, 111
Grandma, It's You!, 203-205
grandmother, importance of in Negro family life, 24, 24n
The Great MacDaddy, 69, 162-163
Griffin, William, 49n
Grose, Francis, 263, 264
Grotjahn, Martin, 73n
Gunfight at O.K. Corral, 166-167
Guthrie, Woody, 127n

The Hairy Scoreboard, 206-207
Halpert, Herbert, 176-177
Hambone, 37
hard man, 74, 77, 80, 105
Harris, Joel Chandler, 66, 74-76, 222
Harry, 97, 156-157
He Gets the Tank Filled, 226-227
He Gets What He Orders, 226
Henry, Mellinger E., 116
THE HEROES, 65-86
heroes, badman, 66, 69-70, 77-83; relationship between narrator and h., 65-66; their values and actions, 36-37, 65; trickster, 66-69, 70-77
Herskovits, Melville (and Frances), 14-15, 15n, 21n, 22n, 68
He's a Poet, 232-233
Himself Discovered, 201-202
Hinsie, Leland E. and Robert Jean Campbell, 72-81
His Prayer Is Unheeded, 184-185
homosexuality, 29, 33n, 168-170, 265, 266, 267
Houston, Cisco, 127n
Hudson, A. P., (see Henry M. Belden)

Hughes, Langston and Arna Bontemps, 99, 111, 124, 129, 138
Huizinga, Johann, 58n
Hurston, Zora Neale, 190, 223
Hurt, John, 127n
Hutchinson, Frank, 127n

ideolect, 90, 93
I Didn't Die Right, 227-228
I Just Learned to Dance, 172
I'm Hauling Sand, 188-190
improvisation, 102-103
insults, 59-60
INTRODUCTION, 3-16
Intrusive "I", 61-65, 110
Irishman, Jew, Colored Man, 217-218
isochronic verse, 100
I Won't Do It!, 233

Jackson, Bruce, 139, 158
Jakobson, Roman, 92-93
Javester, 97
Jesse James, 35, 69, 101, 104, 163-165
Joanna, 26-28
Jody the Grinder, 170-171
John Henry, 80n
Johnson, Charles S., 21n, 22n, 27n, 49n, 56n
Johnson, Guy B., 251, (see also Howard W. Odum)
Johnson, Lonnie, and Spencer Williams, 139
THE JOKES, 175-244
joking relationship, 55n
Jones, Charles C., 190, 223, 228
Jordan, Luke, 113
Josie, 28
The Judge Replies, 177, 199-200
Jung, C. G., 65-67, 68, 69
The Junkie Referee, 231
Just Looking for a Job, 167-168

Kahn, Ed, 138
Kerenyi, Karl, 67n

Kid, 36, 37, 59, 74, 76, 94-95, 116, 119-121, 130-132, 141-144, 147, 149-151, 159, 161-162, 162-163, 164-165, 166-167, 168-169, 170-171, 181, 184, 186-187, 188-189, 190-192, 196, 199-201, 202-204, 205-209, 215-218, 219-220, 221-226, 227, 228-229, 230-232, 233-236, 237-238, 240-241, 243-244, 250, 255-256
Klapp, Orrin E., 67, 69
Kluckhohn, Clyde, 5, 8, 9

Leach, MacEdward, 125
Leadbelly, 114, 115
Legman, G., 1, 29n, 33n, 47n, 62, 89, 108n, 111n, 184, 185, 187, 191, 192, 196-197, 199, 200-201, 213-214, 216, 218, 226, 227, 235, 236, 240, 263, 264, 268
lesbianism, 29, 264
Lewis, Furry, 127n
local form, (see oikotype)
Lone Ranger, 227
Lord, Albert, 100, 102n
Lomax, Alan, 125, 126, 127, 170
Lomax, John A. and Alan, 114, 115, 125, 126, 128
love-hate ambivalence, 33n, 34-36, 51, 62-63, 85-86, 259-262

Mama, 29n
The Man that Stole the Parson's Sheep, 251-254
manuscript, 169-170, 172-173, 209-215
Margaret, 26
marriage, attitude toward, 26-27
Marster-John stories, 67, 68, 137, 179, 209, 222, 224, 228
Marx Brothers, 226
masochistic personality type, 29n, 31, 32-33, 72-73, 85
matrifocal family, 29, 31-35, 72
McCormick, Mack, 139

McCurdy, Ed, 127n
mean, 37, 78
THE MEN, 30-39
men, attitude toward masculinity, 31-39, 41-43, 46-48; attitude toward words, 44-63; employment opportunities, 30; gang life and values, 31, 33-35; in matrifocal system, 31-35; masochistic type of m., 29n, 31, 32-33, 72-73, 85; mobility of, 30-31; personality formation, 31-39, 41-43; rejection of women and feminine, 32-36, 80; transition from boys to m., 31-39
The Milkman Cometh, 240
Mr. Buzzard and Mr. Rabbit, 236-237
The Monkey and the Baboon, 77, 129, 136-147
The Monkey and the Lion, 54-55, 70-72, 136-140
Monnier, Henry, 213
mother, importance of, 21-24; rejection of, 32-36, 57-59, 261-262
motherfucking, 261-262

narrator, importance of, 59-63, 64-65
Negro family (see family)
Negro gangs (see gang life and values)
Negro migration, 23-24n
THE NEIGHBORHOOD, 19-39
neighborhood, delineation, 19; description, 19-20
Neumann, Erich, 65
The Nightly Ritual, 205-206
noncasual utterance, 91-92

obscene words, 105-106, 259-262
Odum, Howard W., 113n, 126
Odum, Howard W., and Guy B. Johnson, 61n, 124, 125

oikotype, 10-12, 245-258
The Old Dog and the Young Dog, 235-236
The Old Pooh-Pooh, 171
The Old Wise King, 221-222
Oliver, Paul, 24n, 33n, 49n, 50n, 58n, 104n
ON A METHOD OF FOLKLORE ANALYSIS, 3-16
ON CERTAIN OBSCENITIES, 259-262
Open Them Doors, 177, 185-186
Oster, Harry, 126

Palmer, Edgar, 198
A Parable, 235
Paredes, Americo, 257
Parson, Elsie Clews, 179, 186, 190, 193, 223
Partridge, Eric, (see John Brophy)
A Party, 211-213
Perkins, A. E., 114
permissiveness, 59
Petey, 26, 97, 197-199, 232, 236-237
playing the dozens, 34, 49-59; function, 57-59; origin of name, 49-50n; recordings, 50n; rhymes, 51-52; rules, 52-53, 59; scholarship on, 55-56; and *signifying,* 54-55
play element, 41-42 (see also contest element)
poetic technique, 103-105
pool hall talk, 47-48, 52
Porgy and Bess, 124
Powdermaker, Hortense, 56n
The Preacher and the Sinners, 33n, 191-192
The Preacher and His Song, 177, 181-182
The Preacher and the Farm Woman, 183
The Preacher and the Pickles, 177, 180-181
preacher as man of words, 62

The Preacher Bends Down, 192-193
The Preacher Is Caught, 181
The Preacher Is Lost, 182-183
preacher stories, 180-197
Preacher Walks the Water, 194-195
printing, influence of, 5
Propp, Vladimir, 246
Puckett, Newbell Niles, 46n, 49n
The Purple Passion, 213

Rainey, Ma, 127n
Randolph, Vance, 180, 196, 223
Rank, Otto, 65
Reich, Wilhelm, 72n
A Remedy for Snakebite, 231-232
The Reverend and the Deacon's Contest, 184
rhetoric and dialectic, 8-9
rhyme, importance of, 44-49, 52-53, 56-57, (see also *playing the dozens, toasts*)
A Ride in His Wagon, 239
Ring Dang Doo, 171
Roberts, Leonard, 180
Robinson, *Sugar Ray,* 37, 38, 112
Rohrer, John H., and Munroe Edmondson, 15n, 33, 34, 43, 56n

sadism, 78, 80, 85, (see also badman hero; *mean*)
sado-masochism, 82n, 85
Sagarin, Edward, 262
Sandburg, Carl, 113
Saxon, Lyle, Edward Dreyer and Robert Tallant, 112
Scarborough, Dorothy, 125
Schoolteacher Lulu and Crabeye Pete, 165
Scott, Charles T., 90n, 91n
See you later, alligator, 45
sex, attitudes toward, 26-29, 31-32, 33n, 35-37
shaggy dog story, 213-215

She Calls His Name, 238-239
Sheffler, I., (see C. L. Golightly)
Shine, 111-123 (see *The Titanic*)
The Signifying Monkey, 35, 38, 38n, 83, 136-157, 211-213
signifying, 54, 54n, 70, 72, 267
Simpson, G. E., and Y. M. Yinger, 137
Sissy, 27
A Sleeve Job, 213-215
Smiley, Portia, 108
Smith, M. G., 22n
Smith, W. V., 116
Some Jaws, 232
sounding, (see *playing the dozens*)
Spaeth, Sigmund, 127n
Speedy Pete, 240
Spencer, Onah, 124
Sperling, Samuel, 55n, 56n
Squad Twenty-Two, 103, 157-158
Stackolee, 35, 69, 78-83, 85, 103, 104, 107, 110, 123-136
Strachey, James, 259
style, narrative, of group, 92-93; of individuals, 93-97; problem of definition, 90-91; use of verbs in s., 93-94
STYLE AND PERFORMANCE, 89-97
synthesis, (see dialectic)
Sypher, Wylie, 85

Tallant, Robert, (see Lyle Saxon)
Tamony, Peter, 49n, 58n, 263
Tarzan's Holler, 237-238
taunt, 48
THE TELLERS, 17-86
THE TEXTS, 87-244
themes, 103-104
Thompson, Harold, 256
Thompson, Stith, 180, 277n
Thorp, N. Howard, 129
Tidwell, James, 190, 228
The Titanic, 83-84, 105, 107, 111-123
THE TOAST, 99-174

toasts, belief in, 110; as epic, 101-105; framing pattern, 99; function as entertainment, 110; improvisation in, 102-103; source of practice, 106-109; stress pattern, 99; structure, 100-110; themes and formulas, 103-104
Too Much Grief, 228-229
tough, 38
TOWARD THE DISCERNMENT OF OIKOTYPE, 245-258
The Travelling Coon, 113-114
trickster, 66-69, 70-77, 83, 84, 105, 137
Twelfth Street, 19

Uncle Remus, 66, 211, 222
Uncle Tom type, 29n, 32-33, 68, 72
UNUSUAL TERMS AND EXPRESSIONS, 263-268

verbal contest, 41-63, 65
verb tenses, 93-94
Victor, 30, 97, 232-233
Voegelin, C. F., 91n
Von Sydow, C. W., 11-12

W.P.A., 113
Wallrich, William, 198
Walsh, Doc, 113
Washday in the Woods, 177, 207-208

The Watch, 209-211
We Go By What We See, 225-226
Wentworth, Harold and Stuart Berg Flexner, 263-268
What Did John Say?, 186-187
Wheeler, Mary, 104n, 126-127, 128
Whiskey brands, 244
White, Newman Ivey, 49n, 113n, 114n, 115, 190
Who Believes?, 196
Wilgus, D. K., 129, 138
Williams, Spencer, (see Lonnie Johnson)
Witter, Henry, 113
Wittke, Carl, 106-107
Wolfenstein, Martha, 53n, 239
THE WOMEN, 21-30
women, and maternity, 21, 23n, 27; attitude toward marriage, 22, 26-27; attitude toward men, 28-30; financial independence of, 21-22, 24; opportunities for employment of, 21; personality, development of, 24-26; rejection of, by men, 32-36, 80
Woodretta, 28
Woody, 26, 28
woofing (see *playing the dozens*)
words and power, 44-45, 63
words and sexuality, 46-49, 58-63

Yinger, Y. M., (see G. E. Simpson)
You Seen Willy?, 187-188

DEEP DOWN IN THE JUNGLE . . .

has been printed in the linotype face Caledonia.

Design and typography by Kim Taylor
Drawings by Philip Trussell

1 9 6 4